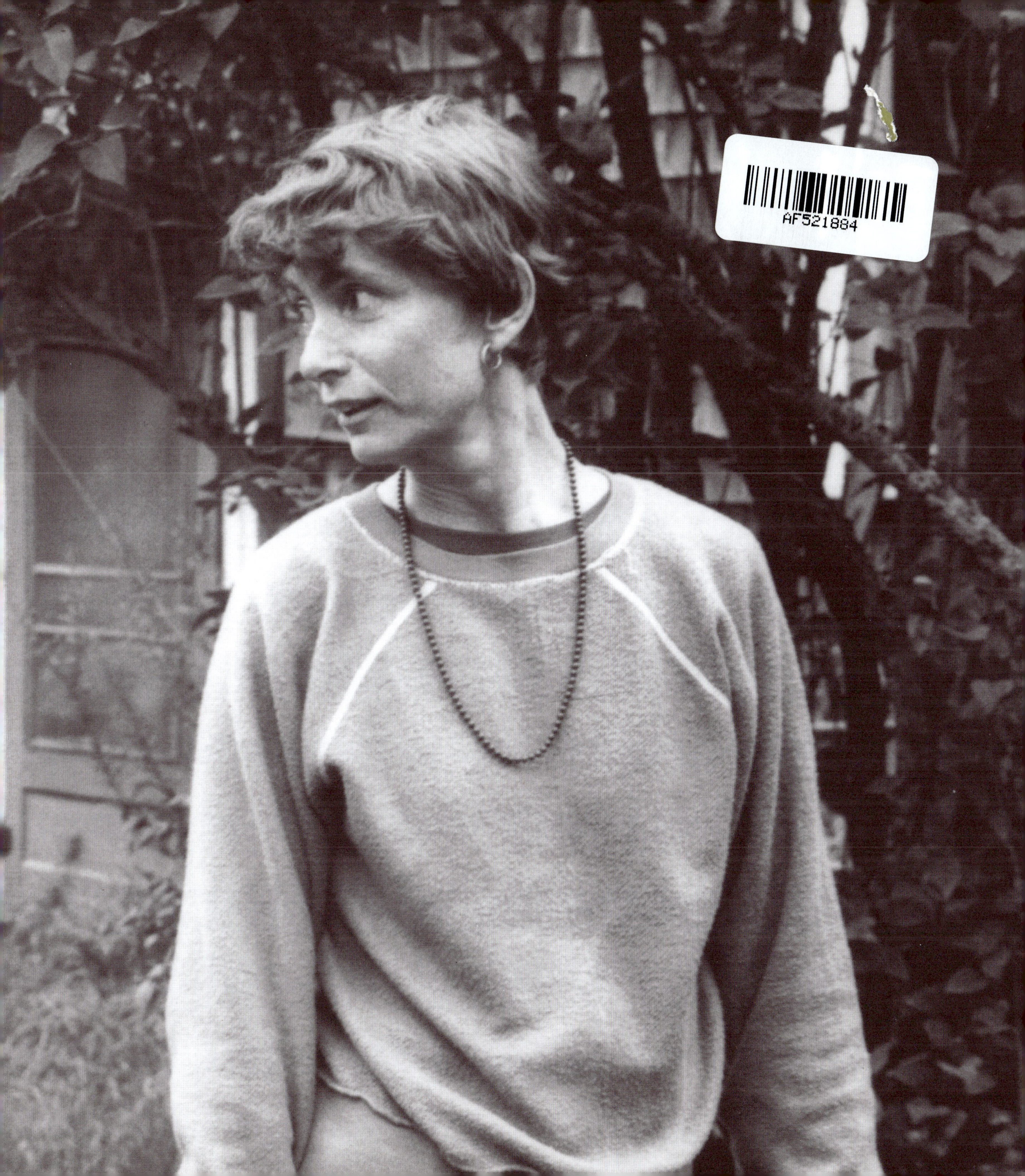

PICTURING NEW YORK:

THE ART OF YVONNE JACQUETTE
AND RUDY BURCKHARDT

Picturing New York

THE ART OF YVONNE JACQUETTE AND RUDY BURCKHARDT

ANDREA HENDERSON FAHNESTOCK
VINCENT KATZ

INTRODUCTION BY BILL BERKSON

MUSEUM OF THE CITY OF NEW YORK
BUNKER HILL PUBLISHING

www.bunkerhillpublishing.com

First published in 2008 by
Bunker Hill Publishing Inc.
285 River Road
Piermont, New Hampshire 03779
USA

10 9 8 7 6 5 4 3 2 1

Library of Congress Control Number
20077938536

ISBN 9781593730659

DESIGN
HvADesign
Henk van Assen, Amanda Bowers

Printed in China by Jade Productions

FRONT COVER LEFT
Rudy Burckhardt
Flatiron Building I (detail), c. 1975
Gelatin silver print [see plate 70]

FRONT COVER RIGHT
Yvonne Jacquette
Chrysler Building Composite at Dusk II (detail), 1997
Oil on linen [see plate 20]

BACK COVER LEFT
Yvonne Jacquette
George Washington Bridge at Night II (detail), 1988
Oil on canvas [see plate 12]

BACK COVER RIGHT
Rudy Burckhardt
Subway, 1947
Gelatin silver print [see plate 54]

ENDSHEETS
Yvonne Jacquette and Rudy Burckhardt in Searsmont, Maine, 1984
Photograph by Vincent Katz

TABLE OF CONTENTS

Yvonne Jacquette and Rudy Burckhardt
in Searsmont, Maine, 1984
Photograph by Vincent Katz

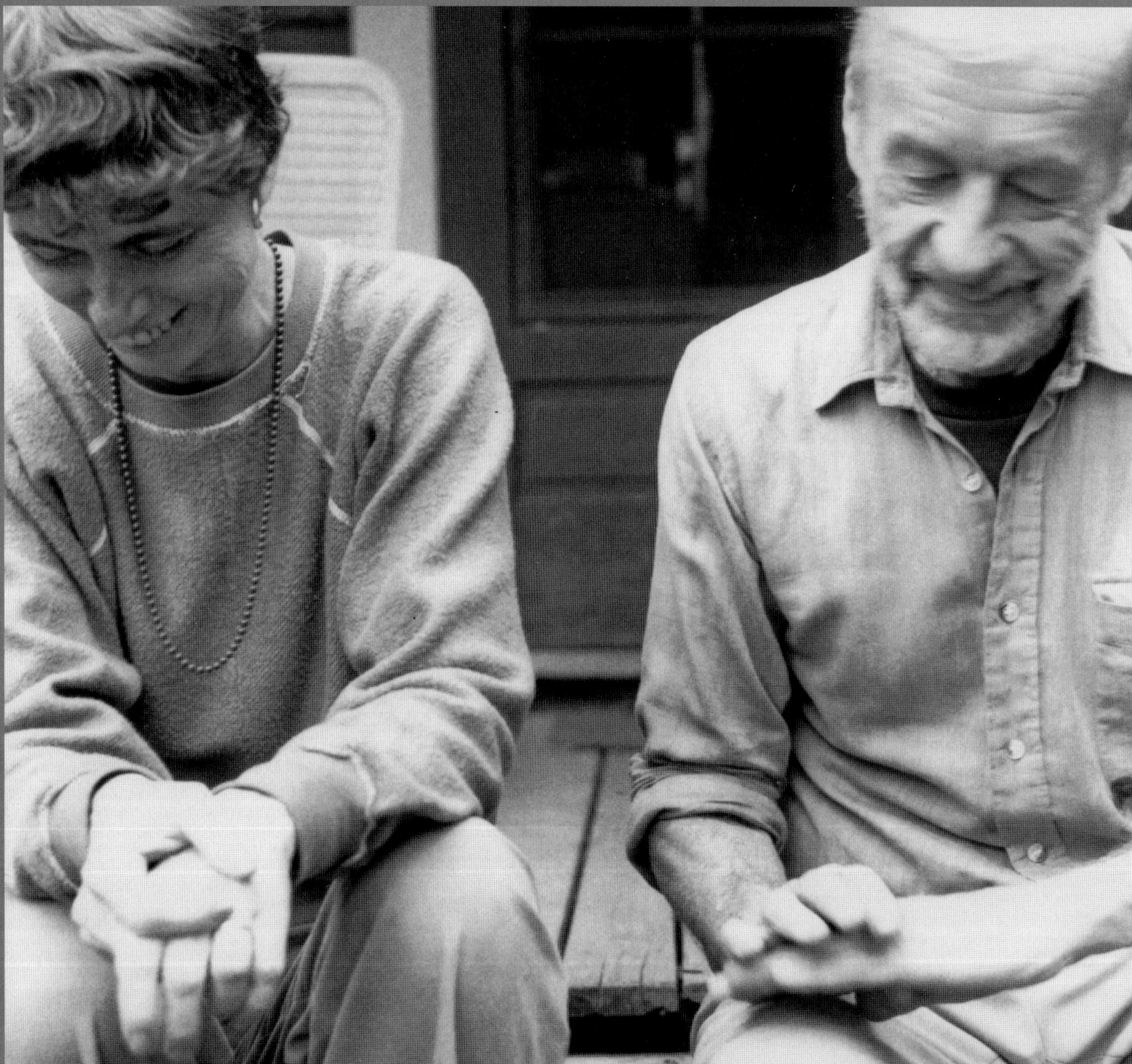

FOREWORD

The Museum of the City of New York is delighted to present concurrent exhibitions of the New York paintings and pastels of Yvonne Jacquette, one of America's most distinguished contemporary artists, and the New York photographs of her late husband Rudy Burckhardt, a photographer, filmmaker, and painter whose unconventional art has spawned a large and devoted underground following. Though the work of Jacquette and Burckhardt has been much exhibited, published, and celebrated over the last sixty years, this will be the first opportunity to examine together the New York images of both artists.

To coincide with the exhibitions at the Museum, this publication explores the place this artistic couple held in the New York art world from the late 1930s to the present. Yvonne Jacquette (b. 1934) and Rudy Burckhardt (1914–1999) were creative and personal partners for nearly forty years, from the time of their meeting in 1961 until Burckhardt's death. Although they traveled broadly for artistic subject matter, they were based in New York City—Burckhardt arrived here in 1935 and Jacquette twenty years later—spending most of their careers in Chelsea, where Jacquette's studio still is. They sometimes collaborated, usually on films, but mostly each pursued separate work. Despite this independence, their approaches to representing the city share visual and philosophical parallels that are explored in the exhibitions and in three essays.

In the introductory essay "Two for Manhattan," art critic and poet Bill Berkson reflects on the overlap of art and life for Jacquette and Burckhardt, both longtime friends of his, and considers their creative partnership against the backdrop of New York's art world, particularly the scene in Chelsea. In "Under New York Skies: Nocturnes by Yvonne Jacquette," Andrea Henderson Fahnestock, Curator of Paintings & Sculpture at the Museum of the City of New York, looks at Yvonne Jacquette's brilliant paintings and pastels of New York at night. The aesthetic possibilities offered by the nocturne inform the discussion of Jacquette's aerial images of the city. Her work is considered as part of the long tradition of New York imagery, in which the city and its transformations have been alternately celebrated and vilified by artists. In the final essay, "Street Dance: The New York Photographs Of Rudy Burckhardt," guest curator Vincent Katz examines Burckhardt's position in the history of photographers of New York. In particular, he places Burckhardt's images of the city in the context of the work of other photographers of New York, including Alfred Stieglitz, Edward Steichen, Berenice Abbott, Walker Evans, Helen Levitt, Garry Winogrand, and Robert Frank. Finally, Katz compares and contrasts Burckhardt's use of New York City as a backdrop and subject in his photographs and films.

I am grateful to the many people who have made possible the exhibitions and book. First, to Yvonne Jacquette, who graciously shared her work and her thoughts with the Museum of the City of New York. The exhibitions were conceived by Andrea Henderson Fahnestock, Curator of Paintings & Sculpture, and Bob Shamis, former Curator of Prints & Photographs, and the project was organized by Ms. Fahnestock. Guest curator Vincent Katz shared his expertise on Burckhardt's work in both the exhibition and in his thoughtful essay here, and Bill Berkson brought perspective and insight to the work of the artists and their times, and we are thrilled to have had the chance to collaborate with both of them.

Deputy Director and Chief Curator Sarah M. Henry kept the project on track and gave careful editorial guidance. Others on the staff contributing to the success of the project were: Barbara Livenstein, Vice President for Communications; Giacomo Mirabella, Chief Registrar, with assistants Abby Lepold and Shelley Wilson; Autumn Nyiri and Susan Gail Johnson in the Curatorial department; and Kassy Wilson and Eddie José Bartolomei in the Exhibitions department.

We are fortunate to have worked with an excellent team on the project: Stephen Saitas brought his elegant style to the design of the exhibitions; Henk van Assen gave us a beautiful book design in record time; and Ib and Carole Bellew of Bunker Hill Publishing brought the book to fruition.

We are extremely grateful to the public and private lenders who agreed to part with their treasures; without the paintings, pastels, and photographs there could be no exhibitions. At Yvonne Jacquette's gallery, DC Moore, the help of Bridget Moore and Heidi Lange was given freely and frequently, as it was at Tibor de Nagy, Rudy Burckhardt's gallery, by Andrew Arnot, Eric Brown, and Meghan Jewett.

Greatest thanks go to the supporters of this ambitious project. Lead funding for the exhibitions and publication comes from the Robert Lehman Foundation and The Kaplen Foundation, with additional support provided by The Judith Rothschild Foundation. This is the first project funded here by the Robert Lehman Foundation, and we welcome them heartily to the Museum of the City of New York family and thank Michael M. Thomas for his shepherding. The exhibitions and publication are part of the ongoing series "Picturing New York," begun by The Kaplen Foundation in 2004, and we are thankful to Lex Kaplen for his continuing support.

Susan Henshaw Jones
President and Director

Yvonne Jacquette and
Rudy Burckhardt, 1997
Photograph by Peggy McKenna

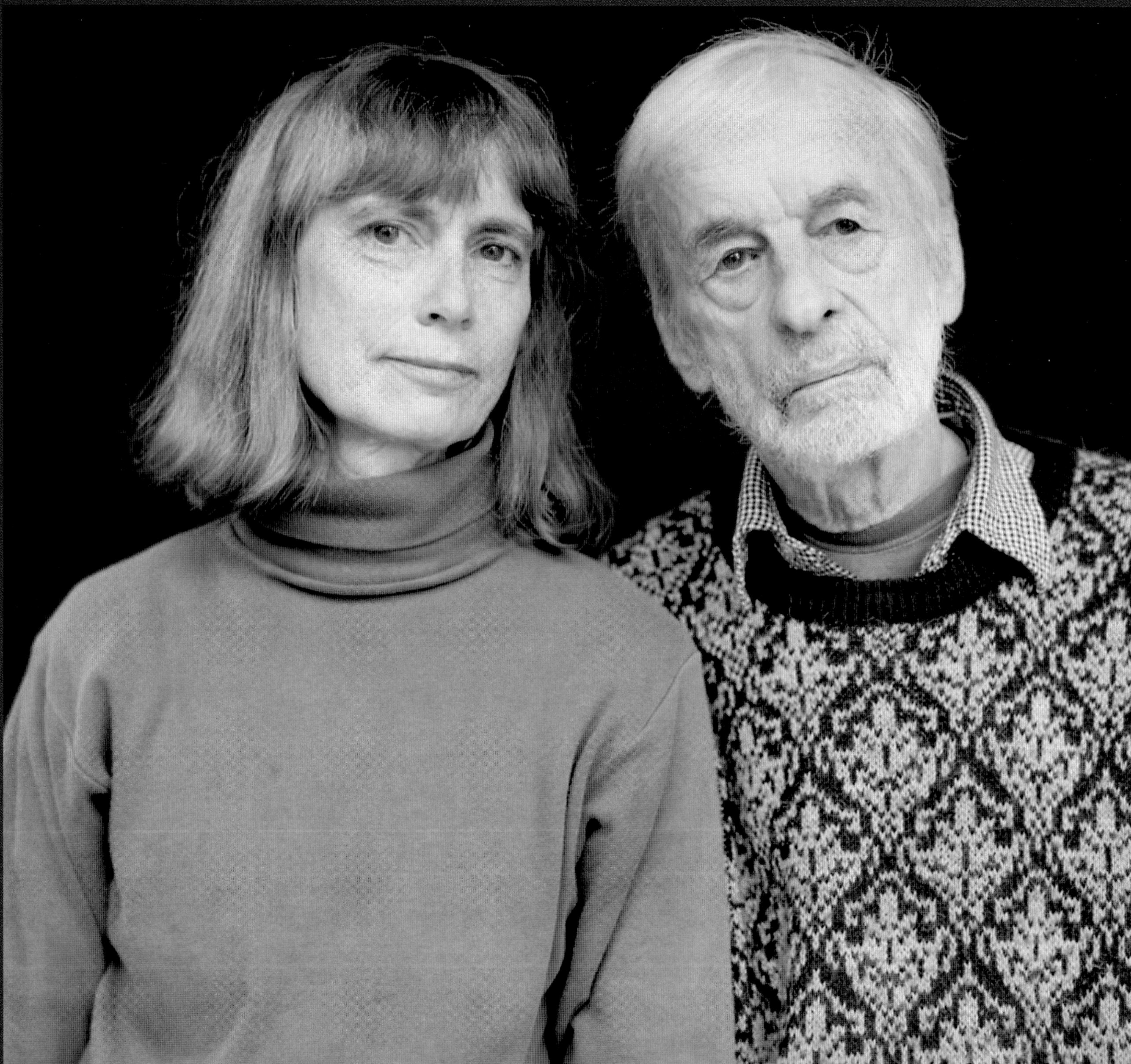

Two for Manhattan

BILL BERKSON

We were happy to be in a city the beauty of which was unknown, uncozy and not small scale.
—Edwin Denby, "The Thirties"[1]

Art to me is like walking down the street with someone and saying "Don't you love that building?" (Too.)
—Joe Brainard[2]

No one, not even anyone born there, becomes a New Yorker instantaneously. Nor is it uncommon for those who arrive from elsewhere to become more deeply identified with the city than locals who merely learn their local idioms as if by rote. The alert interloper from elsewhere can have the dual advantage of first-impression amazement that such a city exists and a growing confidence that its ways can be negotiable as one likes. Presumably, anyone who comes to live in New York—sometimes referred to by even its cheeriest citizens as "our Unfair City"—does so with some purpose in mind, professional, metaphysical, or other. In the 1940s, when I was a child, New York was the place to be, even if then I was oblivious to the qualities that made it so. Both my parents had fled their backgrounds for success in their fields, both of which—journalism and fashion—they soon found to be centered in Manhattan. My mother liked to say of her teen years in Crawfordsville, Indiana, that all she could think of was "how to leave, to get to New York." For myself, at 19, after nearly four years away at school and college, it dawned on me that everything I was interested in in the way of poetry and the other arts was happening, so to speak, in my own backyard. Most newcomers to art and literature, even those growing up in New York, find it hard to believe that the exciting activity of their time is where they have been all along, unless the media says so or their elders are immediately involved with it in some way. Admittedly, my sense of "backyard" needed significant extending: I had grown up on the Upper East Side, and what was happening then was largely below midtown, not much of it publicized, the majority due already to older artists like Rudy Burckhardt and a little later to contemporaries or near-contemporaries like Yvonne Jacquette.

A native New Yorker's appreciation of the big city can be simultaneously reinforced and jolted by the keenness and enthusiasm of someone else's freshly or long-term acclimated view. Behind the registering of such views is the recognition that New York has become someone's objective measure of what a great city can be. In Burckhardt's films, photographs, and paintings and Jacquette's paintings I discover by turns the metropolis of my youth and another place yet to be seen, or perhaps never to be seen in quite the same way except by going to look again at their images. The images tell of urban life in city-dwellers' terms—battered but unbowed, ever watchful for how all of it fits, and, when given enough breathing space, suitably enraptured. Jacquette portrays her adopted hometown as a luminous mix of clarity, refraction, and delicious vertigo, her realism augmented by what she calls "philosophical viewpoints."[3] Burckhardt shows what other photographers and filmmakers always seem to miss: the variable intensities of air and light in the streets, how high and/or heavy the sky appears between buildings, the tempos and spatial intricacies, the ever-irrational disjunctions of scale, the bluntness and hilarity of crowds. Jacquette recalls how first seeing Burckhardt's pictures returned her to her original ambition to become "a portraitist of American cities."[4]

One thing Rudy and I discovered about each other, we both had a literal mind, and it's not to be disparaged.
—Yvonne Jacquette[5]

Rudy Burckhardt was born in 1914 in Basel, Switzerland, came to New York in 1935, and died in 1999 by his own volition. He made his first film on location in the city in 1936 and began making street photographs two years later; his portraits of people in the subways and earliest top-floor views of Astor Place and the Flatiron Building were coincident with his first marriage, to the painter and writer Edith

1
Alex Katz
The Cocktail Party, 1965
Oil on canvas
72 x 96 inches
Collection of Paul J. Schupf

Pictured from left to right: Sheyla Lima, Frank Lima, Yvonne Jacquette, Joe Fiore, Ada Katz, Donald Droll, Bill Berkson, Betty Spiegel, Al Held, Rudy Burckhardt, and Edwin Denby.

Schloss, in 1947, when he was 33. Over the years, his photography and films made him celebrated among his artist and writer peers but of such low visibility to the general public that in 1980 John Ashbery famously pronounced him "unsung for so long he is practically a subterranean monument."[6] I first met Burckhardt in 1961, the same year he met Jacquette. Alex and Ada Katz brought me to a film show at his 21st Street loft; the show consisted of his latest movie *Millions in Business as Usual* and an older one call *Eastside Summer* with a soundtrack by Mozart and Thelonious Monk, shown to an open-night audience of maybe twenty people, including Frank O'Hara, Red Grooms and Mimi Gross, Alex and Ada, Edwin Denby and me.

Burckhardt was 20 years older than Jacquette, who was 27 when they first met, introduced at a party at Nell Blaine's by Kenneth Koch. In a recent conversation, Jacquette recalled the circumstances:

> I had already seen a photograph of Rudy's of the Depression in one of those booklets that Mrs. Poindexter had put out, *The 30's*—with a picture by Rudy with a barbershop pole. Then, within a day or two, I saw a painting of Rudy's of Deer Isle, an aerial view looking down on all these pine trees and then the water. I thought, That's the same person—wow, that's quite interesting. Then I thought, oh Burckhardt, I can remember that. Those two things. Then I met him at the Nell Blaine party. Then I was going off to a life-drawing class on Eighth Street, an open class that anybody could go to. He started showing up there, which had nothing to do with me. We started going out for coffee afterwards. So I got to know him a bit for a while before sort of any of the sparks happened. The sparks happened in a couple of months.[7]

Precipitously, not long after, as Burckhardt would later recall: "I turned 50, got divorced, married Yvonne Jacquette from Pittsburgh, Pa., Thomas was born—all this within one month in 1964."[8]

When Burckhardt first came to New York it was partly to escape the confines of his tidy Swiss surroundings and partly because his new, older friend the poet Edwin Denby was going and urged him to join him there. Living at first together, then separately, in commercially zoned lofts on West 21st Street, Burckhardt and Denby became archetypal cosmopolitans in a milieu where, as Denby wrote, "everybody drank coffee and nobody had shows."[9] In 1955, Jacquette, having veered away from her Catholic girlhood in Pittsburgh and Stamford,

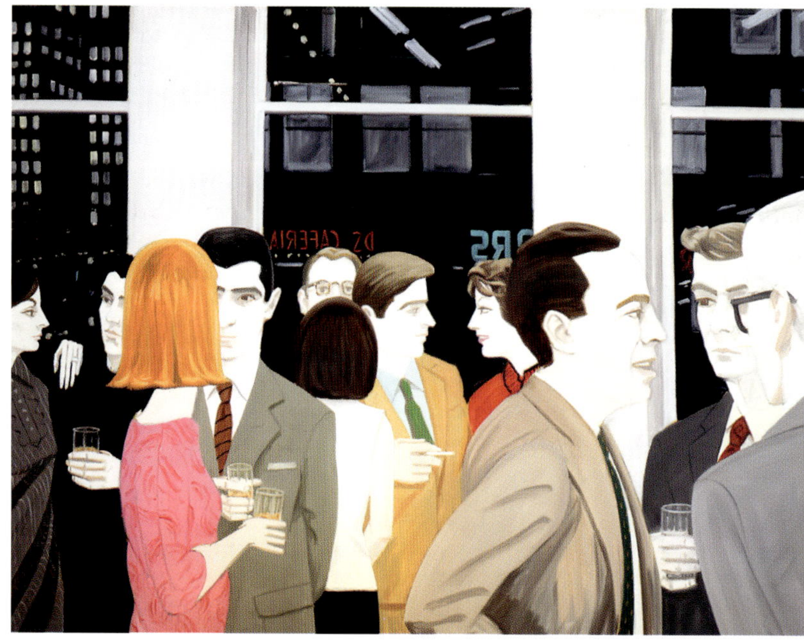

Connecticut, left off studying at the Rhode Island School of Design and rather prophetically took a loft on nearby West 25th Street. By then, the urban economy had become more hospitable to young artists; not that the prospects were struggle-free—few women had shows, and adventurous art, whether abstract or representational, when exhibited, was still taken to be a bothersome cinder in the public eye—but at least there were eager new galleries and a museum or two friendly to fresh art and the arrivals of young artists who saw New York, as Jacquette did, as the proper site for exploration.

The part of Chelsea in the West 20s first inhabited in the 1930s by Burckhardt, Denby, and their friends Willem and Elaine de Kooning and later by younger artists like Alex Katz and eventually Jacquette was, and mostly remains, a district, properly, of warehouses, wholesale clothing businesses, and taxi garages. (Katz settled on West 28th Street in 1953; Jacquette still lives and works in the 29th Street loft she and Burckhardt moved to in 1975.) Pretty much left unchanged to this day, it is a neighborhood, if at all, only surreptitiously, and not an artistic center by anyone's design; neither the genteel Chelsea of "high-quality" 19th-century row houses nor the more recent, avaricious one of big-time fine-art showrooms—both discrete micro-cultures which, anyway, sit further west. The ambience of the immediate cultural neighborhood of the mid-60s when Burckhardt and Jacquette got together is registered—indeed substantially glorified—in Katz's big

2
Rudy Burckhardt and Yvonne Jacquette
Night Fantasies, 1991
16mm film still
Dancer Henry Shepard before vintage prints of modern New York

painting *The Cocktail Party*, 1965 [figure 1], in which the couple occupy separate stage-front positions, each to one side of the center, surrounded by painter and poet friends, most of whom lived within walking distance of one another. Probably because of the fluorescent lighting and the set of large windows against which Katz's figure groups mix and mingle, the site has been mistaken for an art gallery but was really the Katzes' live-work space at 182 Fifth Avenue, bordering on 23rd Street and across from the Flatiron Building and Madison Square Park.

The assumption that art is a form of social behavior seems radical or obscure only if you have forgotten that people are the ones who do it, with the general idea that there will be others who respond. Vincent Katz has remarked that, in the 1930s, Burckhardt's "experience of the art world was largely the experience of seeing friends."[10] Hovering over what might be called the Chelsea Ethos, exemplified early on by Burckhardt's and de Kooning's images and Denby's poetry, is the reverberation of an attitude expressed in indigenous mandarin that everything, including an artist's criticality, is in the work: if it is interesting, one's immediate audience, friends included, will approve; if then it has a wider interest, a larger audience will seek it out. Well into the 60s, to be "underground" as an artist implied an Uptown-Downtown divide, not just between the sleeker galleries on 57th Street and above and the 10th Street artist-run spaces, but also between conceptions of what art and an artist's life should be. (Uptown, for one thing, tended to be haughtily at war with popular culture; Downtown enjoyed being, as Franz Kline liked to say, part of the noise.) Denby's remark in his memoir of the 30s that "Tchelitchev was the uptown master then" is clarified by his seeing something in Picasso's "steady wide light [that] reminded me of the light in the streets and lofts we lived in."[11]

The film collaboration that was quite equal between us was Night Fantasies. *I had the idea, when this new piano piece of Elliott Carter's was recorded. We went out filming together, and I could take [Rudy] to all the places in New York that I had spent time drawing at night. Then he conceived of some shots for the Maine landscape, and I would drive the car slowly while he sat on top, shooting. We discussed the editing together although he did the actual cuts. We never fought about it.*
—Yvonne Jacquette[12]

Night Fantasies, the movie Burckhardt and Jacquette made in 1991, stands as a fair portrait of their New York life in common, with its extensions in world travel and their summer home in Searsmont, Maine. Assuming Paul Jacobs' recording of Carter's keyboard piece as both soundtrack and ground plan, the two artists took the opportunity to work together hands-on; at least half the footage was shot in Manhattan, some in Maine, and the remainder in Hong Kong, a location chosen expressly for the project, as well as for Jacquette to draw new motifs for her paintings. Both filmmakers make cameo appearances—he twice in the context of girlie posters and sex parlors (a bit of characteristic self-mockery in his old age), she in a life-drawing session and in two odd, potentially *noir*-ish shots of her changing clothes before a window.

Individual shots in this nocturnal cinematic fugue have "the wholeness so that the eye can take it in at once more quickly" that Burckhardt's and Jacquette's works separately seek to maintain.[13] Connecting various glimpses of buildings, streets, and weather, and sometimes imbedded in them, are several sequences of dance or dancelike movements: figure skating, yoga, tai chi, a striptease, and a masterful soft-shoe solo superimposed on an old print that resembles some of Jacquette's grand Manhattan overviews, which in turn redoubles the on-site views she shot for a sequence earlier in the film. Even snowflakes and votive candles on a pond seem to partake of this supernal choreography. Carter's music, with the exception of two early pieces written around 1940 for George Balanchine, has not been much associated with dance in any idiom, but it is with the sense that dance perennially carries of a sort of spillway of impermanence that the music and film images conjoin.

Carter himself describes the musical structure of *Night Fantasies* as one "of continuously changing moods, suggesting the fleeting thoughts and feelings that pass through the mind during a period of wakefulness at night."[14] The movie Burckhardt and Jacquette made is not so

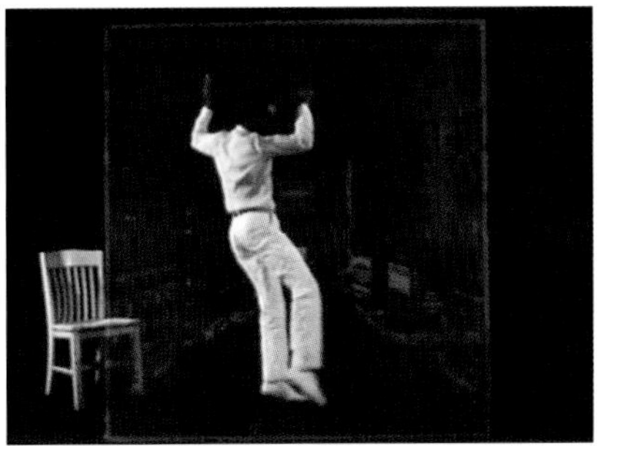

3
Yvonne Jacquette
Chelsea Composite II, 1995
Oil on canvas
80 x 59 inches
The Samuel P. Harn Museum of Art,
University of Florida, Museum purchase,
gift of Mary Ann P. Cofrin

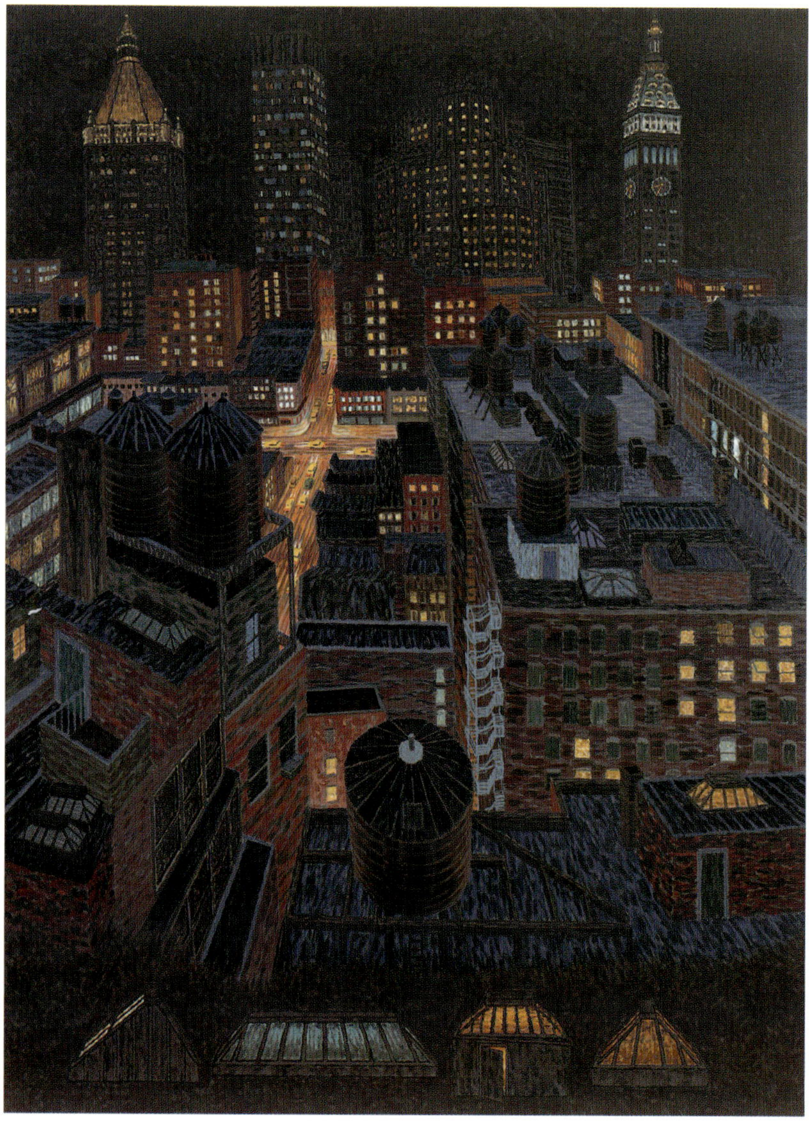

moody. The cutting, which is faster than the shifts between Carter's pulsating episodes, cumulatively builds to a pitch of high, extended urban lyric—a lyricism strikingly more lyrical than in most of Burckhardt's or Jacquette's individual works. The exaltation is of two sensibilities in unison, singing a melody evoked in the course of combined effort.

Rudy has come into the room and wants to film Yvonne painting a little. She agrees to paint a lower portion of the panel instead of the upper, so he can film her.
—Vincent Katz [15]

The essence of collaborative life—the art part, anyway—may lie in just such mild adjustments as Katz recorded, along with various inevitable (and salutary) personal contrasts. Unlike Burckhardt's, much of Jacquette's work depends on visual memory, and her perceptual interconnections tend toward the ecological where his are more plainly intuitive. Burckhardt's irony finds its counterpart in Jacquette's readiness to accept the absurd elements her viewpoints often offer up. Part of the charm of Burckhardt's paintings (the least known but no less considerably pleasurable part of his output) is due to the undisguised doggedness of their execution—a labor-intensiveness he enjoyed in contrast to "too quick" photography.[16] Although his old painting teacher Amedée Ozenfant once warned him, "Watch out for the tight corridors that don't mean anything," Burckhardt's meticulousness in all forms stayed at the mercy of his detail-oriented photographer's eye.[17]

Burckhardt once described his philosophy as "distinctly pessimistic, existential, negative thinking. . ."[18]—which either did or didn't help when, with Jacquette, he took up serious Tibetan Buddhist practice in the 1980s. (To Jacquette he claimed he was only a "partial Buddhist."[19]) Neither appears to have been in a hurry to make a mark in the art world: Burckhardt hardly ever showed his work commercially until the late 40s; Jacquette took almost ten years after leaving RISD to arrive at a consistent way of working and even then, waited another ten for her first one-person show. Jacquette is more particular about craft and presentation than Burckhardt was. When in the 1990s I asked a museum curator about her interest in Burckhardt's photographs, she told me, "Oh, I love Rudy's work, but you can't get good prints." Jacquette's work was informed early on by experiences in technical drafting and textile design. The closest Burckhardt ever came to commercial art was his standing as the photo-documentarian par excellence of art and artists for *ARTnews* and the galleries, starting in the 1950s, for nearly 30 years. Both operate in the area where what Jacquette calls "a contemplative kind of time" meets the unanticipated vitality of moment.[20] The results in each case could serve widely as models of artistic sociability in the way an image transmits rather than forces an instance of acute seeing and understanding. What the viewer gets are reliable accounts of the city these two have lived in at its best. New York never looks better than when looked at in its most elusive particulars and contingencies, with no preconceptions but the right kind of care.

4
Rudy Burckhardt
Times Square at Dusk, c. 1947
Gelatin silver print
Courtesy the Estate of Rudy Burckhardt and Tibor de Nagy Gallery, New York

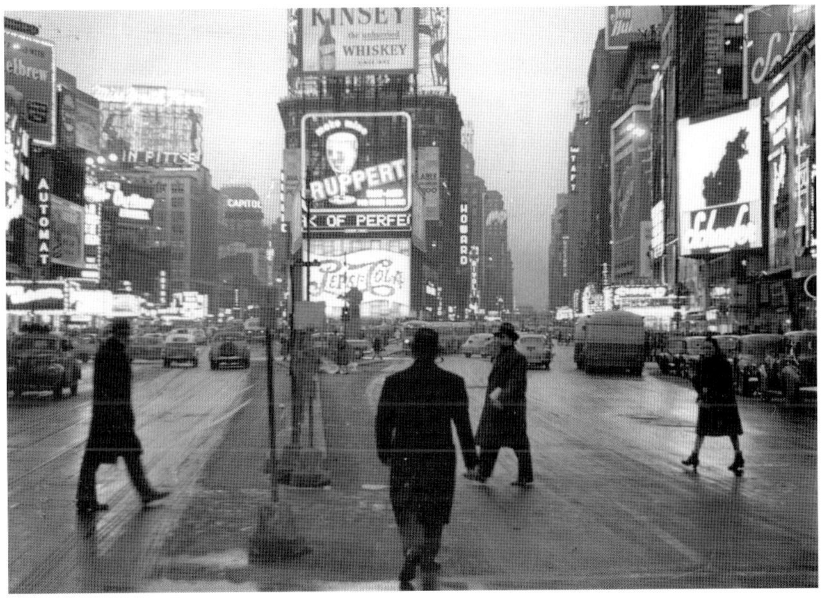

1
Edwin Denby, "The Thirties," in Robert Cornfield, ed., *Dance Writings and Poetry* (New Haven and London: Yale University Press, 1998): 2.

2
Joe Brainard, "Selections from 'Self-Portrait: 1971'," *New Work* (Los Angeles: Black Sparrow Press, 1973): 12.

3
Barbara Shikler, Interview with Yvonne Jacquette, New York, June–October, 1989. Archives of American Art Oral History Project, unpublished transcript, 80.

4
Arts & Minds #62: Yvonne Jacquette, videotape. Producer: Ken Russell, 31 January 2002.

5
Shikler, 239.

6
John Ashbery, "The Reluctant Polymath," *New York*, 28 January 1980, 64.

7
Yvonne Jacquette, conversation with the author, 28 May 2007.

8
Rudy Burckhardt, *Mobile Homes* (Calais, VT: Z Press, 1979), 34.

9
Denby, 5.

10
Philip Lopate with Vincent Katz, *Rudy Burckhardt* (New York: Harry N. Abrams, Inc., 2004), 47.

11
Denby, 5.

12
Yvonne Jacquette, in conversation with the author, 28 May 2007.

13
Yvonne Jacquette, in conversation with the author, 1988.

14
Elliott Carter, preface to the score of *Night Fantasies*. New York: Associated Music Publishers, 1982.

15
Vincent Katz, "A Day in the Life of Two Artists: The Art of Yvonne Jacquette and Rudy Burckhardt," *Milk Magazine*, no. 3 (December 2001): no page numbers.

16
Rudy Burckhardt and Simon Pettet, *Talking Pictures: The Photography of Rudy Burckhardt* (Cambridge, MA: Zoland Books, 1994), 24.

17
Yvonne Jacquette, in conversation with the author, 28 May 2007.

18
Burckhardt, *Mobile Homes*, 28.

19
Yvonne Jacquette, written response to the author's queries, 22 May 2007.

20
Yvonne Jacquette, slide lecture, San Francisco Art Institute, 19 November 1997.

Yvonne Jacquette in her Maine studio,
working on *Metropolitan Triptych II*, 2007
Photograph by Kristin Cammermeyer

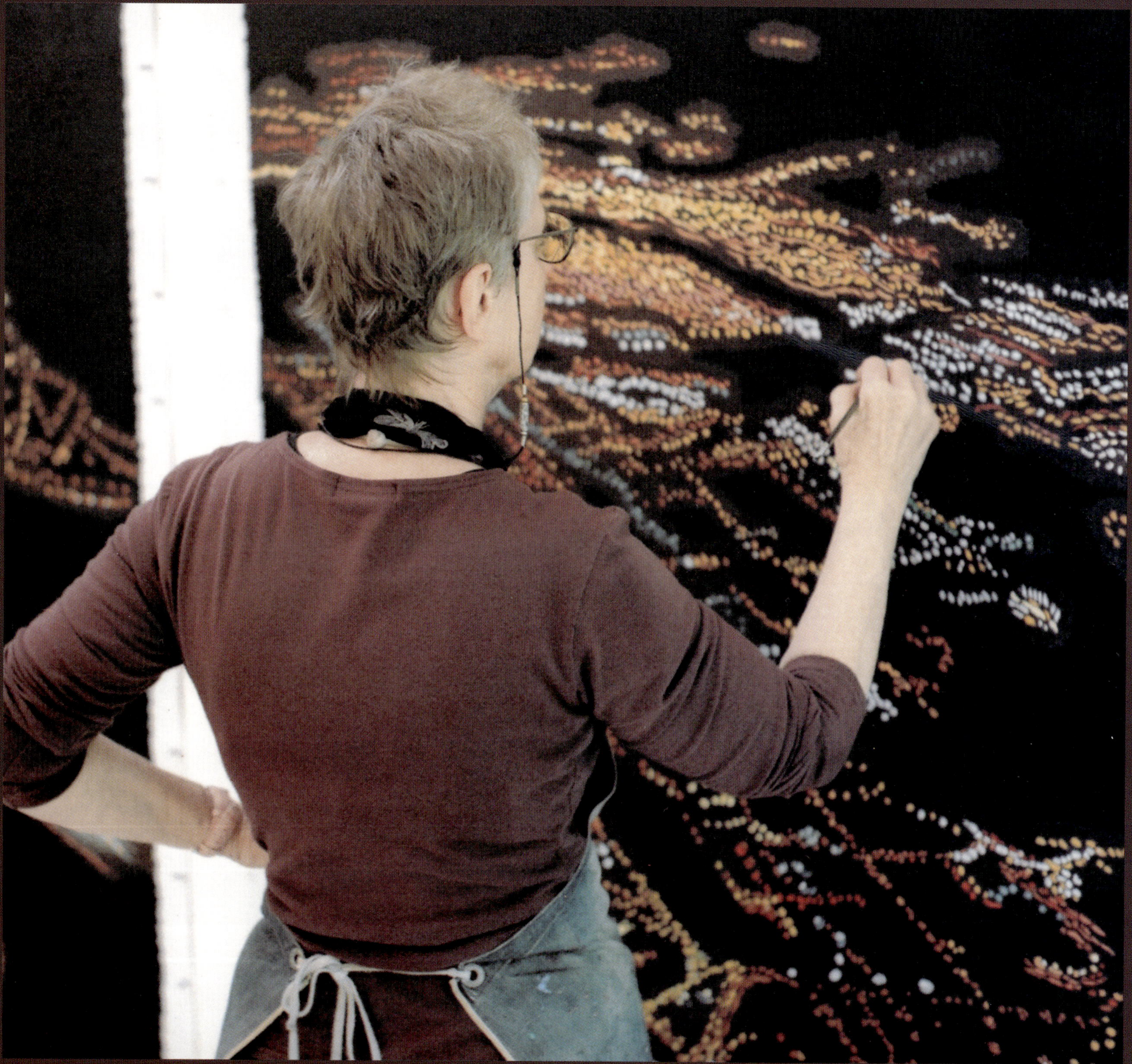

Under New York Skies

NOCTURNES BY YVONNE JACQUETTE

ANDREA HENDERSON FAHNESTOCK

For 30 years, Yvonne Jacquette has been making nocturnal paintings and pastels from aerial vantage points of such cities as San Francisco, Chicago, Washington, Tokyo, and Hong Kong—along with bird's-eye views of Maine and Midwestern farmland—but her images of New York at night are deservedly the most celebrated. She has described herself as a portraitist of American cities, and none has been more frequently or more affectionately depicted than New York.

Her paintings of New York are striking for their bold, angled compositions, surface richness, and the powerful presence of their grand scale [plates 6, 19, and 22]. Their radiance, and the festive, celebratory sense they exude, derives in part from the patterning of light and color against the dark night skies and in part from the intentionally tremulous touch of the artist. Despite their often panoramic sweep, they retain an intimacy: Jacquette's work is not realism of the detached, cool, mechanistic sort, but a warmer, more engaged interpretation of the city around her. The complex views, distinguished by their wit, convey the pleasure of observation, allowing the artist to share her sense of visual delight in the cityscape with the viewer.

If her paintings are broad in scope, her working method is specific; the pastel studies for the large paintings, as well as the documentary photographs she takes, are filled with detailed visual information about the city. Much selection and compression is required of the artist to represent even a small shard of the sculptural city on the flat plane of a painting. In this journey from three dimensions to two, Jacquette has her playful way with perspective and topography, compositing scenes that would not be visible from any one vantage point. Her approach, then, is hybrid in nature: the paintings are part precisely observed reality and part invention—imaginary vistas, created of authentic architectural elements seen from different positions.

From the time of the emergence of the New York skyline view as a genre, images of the city's tallest buildings embodied the very

American notions of progress and promise, opportunity and aspiration, and Jacquette's work is no exception. The diversity of design and lack of planning that she captures speak to the firmly democratic nature of this city: the unconforming structures, singular and egocentric, reflect New York's culture of staunch individualism. Divergent architectural styles happily keep company in her paintings, enriching the character of the view and revealing layers of the city's history. In 1925 Fitzgerald wrote that the Manhattan skyline held the "wild promise of all the mystery and the beauty in the world."[1] More than 80 years later, Jacquette's paintings tell us she shares his sense of wonder about New York.

THE CITY, THE AERIAL, AND THE NOCTURNE: THE LONG VIEW

New York has been alternately romanticized and demonized since artists began to paint the city in earnest near the end of the 19th century. It has been depicted by some as energized and glamorous and by others as dangerous and troubled, a breeding ground for alienation and loneliness among its people. The portrayal has varied by generation. Impressionist painters like Childe Hassam and William Merritt Chase idealized New York; by concentrating on park scenes, their images seem more pastoral than truly urban. The grittier vision of such Ash Can artists as John Sloan and George Bellows, who focused on Greenwich Village, unveiled the unpleasantness of city life that had been ignored by their predecessors. Following the great building boom of the teens, 20s, and early 30s, artists like Georgia O'Keeffe, Charles Sheeler, and Louis Lozowick turned their attention to architecture, producing sleek, Precisionist works that glorified the modern. After the end of mid-century abstraction, when recognizable urban images had fallen from favor, the Photorealists of the late 60s and early 70s took as their subject more mundane elements of the cityscape, rendered with sharp focus that emulated photography.

Elements of all of this work have informed Jacquette's vision of New York, but perhaps none more than Precisionism, which she acknowledges as a source. The Precisionist artists' search for "architectonic structure underlying the chaos of reality" resonates with Jacquette.[2] Their response to New York went hand in hand with the development of the modern city. New feats of engineering and the explosive building boom of the early 20th century completely remade the skyline, and the pace made it seem as if the city grew almost daily. Artists recorded—and for the most part celebrated—the changes around them, venerating the skyscraper as the symbol of all that was new and progressive. Images of the skyscraper "succeeded in giving New York City a unique, global identity," which endures into the present.[3]

New York is the crossroads of commerce and culture, of fantasy and reality, where possibility hangs in the night air. In 1912, even before the city's most remarkable skyscrapers were built, poet Ezra Pound understood the singular allure of nocturnal New York:

> No urban nights are like the nights there. I have looked down across the city from high windows. It is then that the great buildings lose reality and take on their magical powers. They are immaterial; that is to say one sees but the lighted windows . . . . Squares after squares of flame, set and cut into the aether. Here is our poetry, for we have pulled down the stars to our will.[4]

Pound's words were prophetic, for they describe perfectly the enchantment of Jacquette's paintings.

The nighttime view of Manhattan dazzles, both from the sheer density of light and the spectacularly ornamented finials of its iconic skyscrapers. Built before anyone worried over architectural context, these "cathedrals of commerce" are not shy about calling attention to themselves. Their flamboyant, floodlit spires were designed to advertise the companies headquartered below, among them Paramount Pictures [plate 27], Chrysler [plate 20], and the New York and Metropolitan Life Insurance companies [plate 18]. Like generations of painters and photographers before her, Jacquette is "interested in different styles of architecture and how light illuminates these landmark buildings."[5] Operatic in scope, sometimes comic in detail, Jacquette's paintings embrace the theatricality and exuberance of the radiant buildings.

It is sometimes said that the city reinvents itself after dark. Splendid in its sparkling jewelry of colored lights, the commonplace—or unsightly—is transformed into something of beauty at night. And beauty, a much-maligned concept in art today, does not offend Jacquette, nor does she feel diminished by recognition of the decorative and the beautiful in her work.[6] She makes us all spectators at the nightly light show that is New York. The blazing skyline gives Jacquette rich material, however it sometimes makes her wonder "why so much electricity is being wasted," and to improve the pattern on a building's façade in her paintings, she confesses to turning lights on or off.[7]

New York is the ultimate megawatt city. The durable image of New York at night—dominated by towers shining like beacons—was established by modernist artists seeking to express enthusiastic approval of everything novel and advanced. New York at night embodied the "apotheosis of electricity" in 1939 to writer Odette Keun (known mostly today as having been H.G. Wells's mistress).[8] The construct of the nocturnal city was, in a sense, "galvanized into being by the divinity of electricity."[9] During the decades when skyscrapers were created and first the subject of art, discussions of the buildings and their illumination were often couched in such religious terminology; when skyscrapers were new and strange, the language "reflected an effort to further legitimize the tall building," and by extension the whole idea of the modern city.[10]

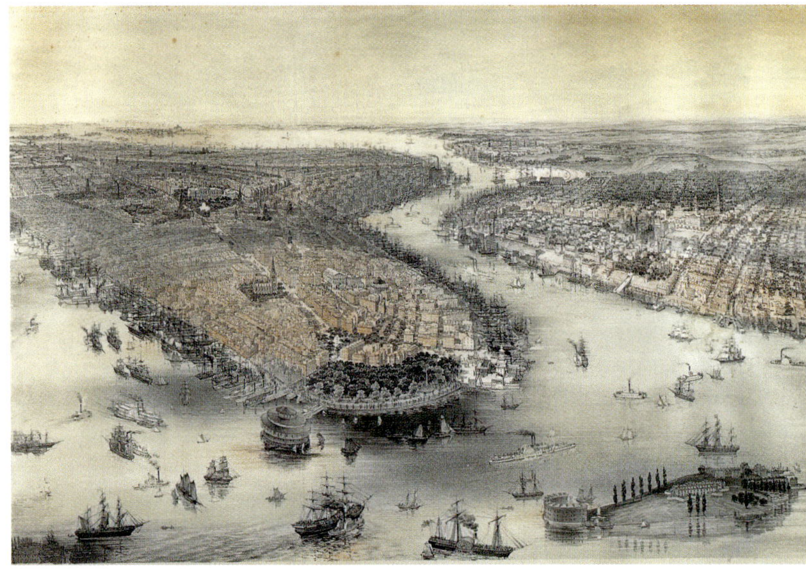

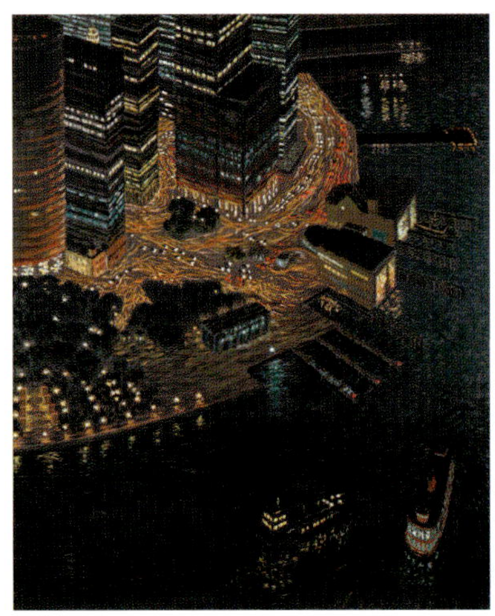

1 TOP
John Bachmann (1814–1896)
Bird's Eye View of New York and Brooklyn, 1850
Colored lithograph
21 ½ x 31 inches
Museum of the City of New York,
Gift of Miss Anna M. Bogart, 37.12.3

1A LEFT
Yvonne Jacquette
Manhattan Nocturne: Late Evening Traffic II, 1988
[see plate 13]

Long before Jacquette and her 20th-century American forebears examined either the aerial or the nocturne, these genres were developed on other shores. Today aerial views are commonplace, but in their earliest manifestations they were a source of wonderment: how did an artist draw what only birds could see? Besides simple curiosity about the omniscient viewpoint, aerial images carry a sensory charge from the risk of a dizzying plunge, one alluded to in such early artistic representations as Brueghel's *The Fall of Icarus* of 1558. The myth is a cautionary tale for all—don't venture too high—but despite the natural acrophobic in us all (or perhaps because of it), viewers and artists alike have long been intrigued by the airborne view.

Precedents for the compositional type of the aerial are centuries old. In the earliest panoramic maps, the view was sometimes recorded from a nearby hilltop, but just as often it was a fiction of the artist's invention, appearing to show from overhead what was visible from the ground. In paintings and prints, the panorama is rooted in the 16th- to 18th-century *vedute* traditions of Flemish, Dutch, and Italian city and landscape paintings; large in format, detailed in style, and vast in scope. As technology allowed man to reach new heights—first in hot-air balloons (1783) and later in airplanes (1903)—the aerial view became an observable phenomenon. These developments meant that artists finally could have a true bird's-eye view rather than work from imagination. Aviation offered a view unlike any other, giving way only to the global perspective from space.

In America, the earliest forms of urban aerial representation were the illustrated map and the bird's-eye prospect [figures 1 and 2], based on 16th-century European models. In mid 19th-century New York, these overviews helped residents understand the staggering growth around them. The market for such images was enormous, keeping artists, engravers, and publishers busy delineating the city. From a fabricated vantage point over New York harbor, John Bachmann's lithograph looks northeast toward Manhattan, making clear the extraordinary compaction of the city by 1850. This density was experienced by inhabitants at ground level, but incomprehensible in its totality except from above. The Hill/Papprill view, drawn from the steeple of St. Paul's Chapel on Broadway, looks over the crowded streets of lower Manhattan toward Brooklyn in the distance. Seen from closer range and from an insider's perspective, this view would have been more familiar to residents, with individual buildings and their signage clearly recorded. The high vantage point helped make comprehensible the most closely packed New York district, then as now.

When Jacquette began working from airplanes in the early 1970s, extreme aerial views were part of the zeitgeist: in 1972, the crew of *Apollo 17* took the first fully illuminated earth photograph, the so-called Blue Marble, among the most widely seen images in existence.[11] Twenty-five years later, we are still amazed by the view, now accessible to anyone with a computer and Google Earth technology, allowing users to zoom in on points around the globe.

The first painted nocturnes appeared in Western art beginning in the 14th century, reaching a crescendo in the 16th and 17th centuries. These early night paintings were typically of religious subjects, images of the *Nativity*, or the *Annunciation to the Shepherds*, or more ominously, the *Descent into Hell*. Artists penetrated the darkness with such devices as candles, torches, fire, and moonlight—or shafts of divine illumination with no logical source. Night generally had allegorical or devotional significance, with light connoting the miraculous. Then, as now, the night brought a sense of heightened experience.

The nocturne flourished in 18th-century Romantic art, with secular, or semi-secular, subject matter and a preoccupation with the poetic mystery of the night. Beginning in the later decades of the 19th century, artistic interest shifted to the urban night, its scenery and entertainments. Sometimes picturesque, sometimes licentious, images of cities and their inhabitants attracted increasing artistic attention. Most influential was James Abbott McNeill Whistler; his paintings of London at night set in motion a fascination with the aesthetic possi-

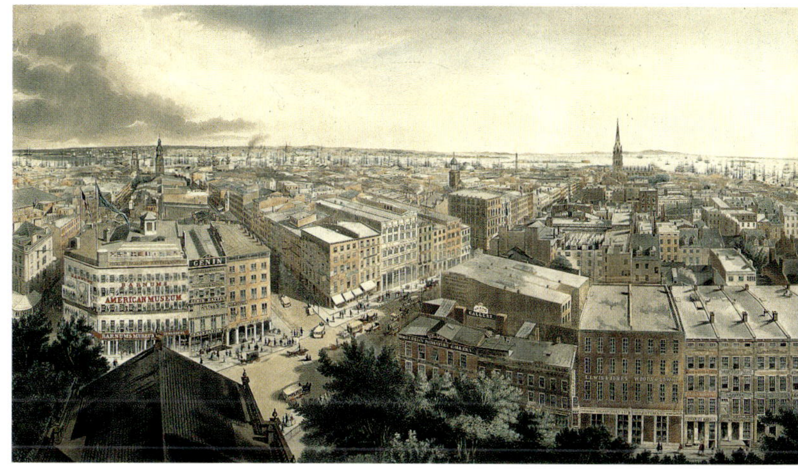

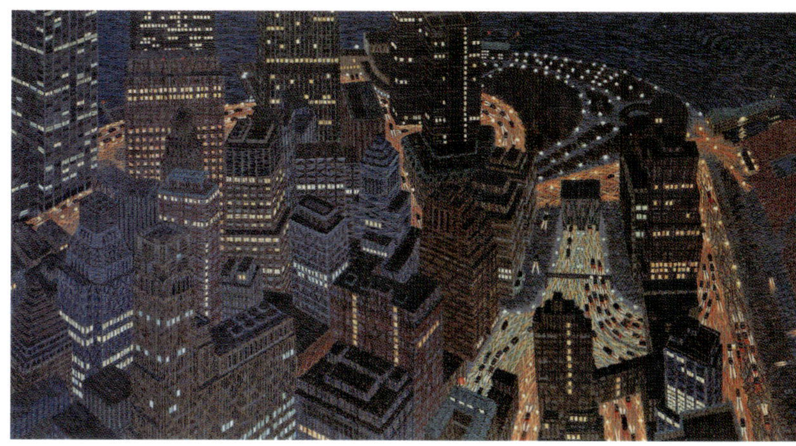

2 TOP
Henry Papprill (1817–1896), after watercolor by John William Hill (1812–1879)
New York from the Steeple of St. Paul's Chapel: Looking East, South, and West, 1849
Hand-colored aquatint
21 ½ x 36 inches
Museum of the City of New York, The J. Clarence Davies Collection, 29.100.2373

2A BOTTOM
Yvonne Jacquette
Lower Tip of Manhattan II, 1981–82
[see plate 5]

bilities of nighttime imagery, with the modern city as subject. *Nocturne in Black and Gold: The Falling Rocket* of 1875 [figure 3], the most infamous of Whistler's radical nocturnes, was shocking in its day for the abstracted approach to its token subject matter—a fireworks display in a London public garden. The poetic, atmospheric painting, which is little more than a shower of sparks against the night sky, outraged contemporary critics but proved of lasting importance to the generation of painters and art photographers that followed.[12] Manhattan's twinkling skyline echoes the appearance of fireworks, but unlike the evanescence of the real things, which dissolve and fade from sight, the spangles of light are on permanent display in Jacquette's controlled pyrotechnics.

In America, painters born near the end of the 19th century like George Bellows, William Glackens, Joseph Stella, and Edward Hopper, and photographers like Edward Steichen and Alfred Stieglitz, cemented the modernist construct of the New York nocturne. In the early 20th century, the aerial and nocturne views married over New York's skies in some of the most celebrated modernist works: John Sloan's views over Greenwich Village [figure 4], Georgia O'Keeffe's iconic depictions of New York skyscrapers [figure 5], and paintings and prints by artists associated with the Precisionist movement like Ellison Hoover [figure 6], Anton Schutz [figure 7], and Walter Tittle [figure 8].

Overlooking the jumbled streets of Greenwich Village from the roof of his studio, Sloan concentrates on the life of the neighborhood, as cars and pedestrians move on the wet pavement, and the elevated train snakes through the streets carrying commuters. But in contrast to the darkened roofscape of the unprepossessing foreground, in the upper right the financial district glistens like a beckoning utopia, the emblematic Woolworth Building (the city's tallest structure at the time Sloan painted) prominent above the rest. One of the earliest scenes to illustrate the city's evolution from its low-rise past to heights of the future, Sloan's painting captures the transition of artistic attention from the street to the sky.

In O'Keeffe's *New York, Night* of 1929, the pagoda-crowned Beverly Hotel is pictured from the high-rise apartment she shared with her husband Stieglitz in the neighboring Shelton Hotel. The painting is a clear ancestor of Jacquette's explorations of New York architecture at night, and Jacquette acknowledges the influence of O'Keeffe in her work.[13] Light from the windows, the crown, and the Lexington Avenue traffic

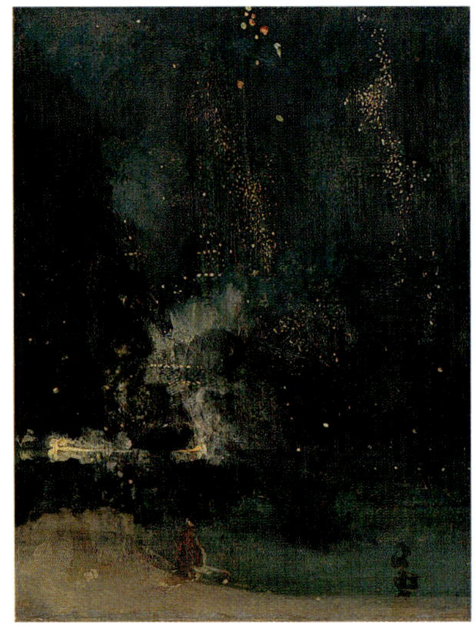

3 ABOVE LEFT
James Abbott McNeill Whistler (1834–1903)
Nocturne in Black and Gold: The Falling Rocket, 1875
Oil on panel
23 ¾ x 18 ⅜ inches
The Detroit Institute of Arts,
Gift of Dexter M. Ferry, Jr., Photograph
© 1988 The Detroit Institute of Arts

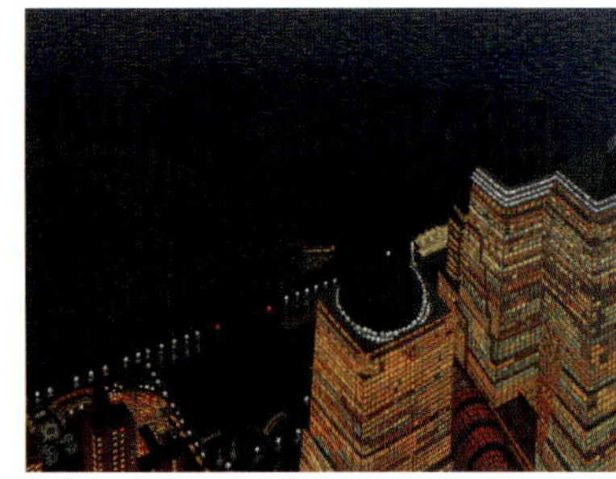

3A ABOVE RIGHT
Yvonne Jacquette
South and West Views from World Trade Center II (detail), 1996
[see plate 19]

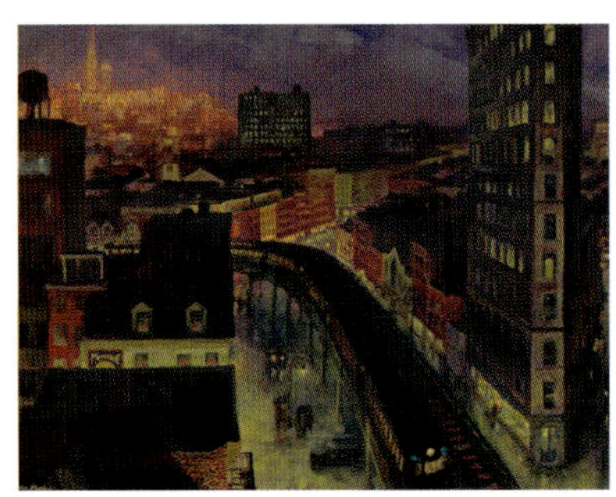

4 ABOVE LEFT
John Sloan (1871–1951)
The City from Greenwich Village, 1922
Oil on canvas
26 x 33 ¾ inches
National Gallery of Art, Gift of Helen Farr Sloan, 1970.1.1, Image courtesy of the Board of Trustees, National Gallery of Art, Washington

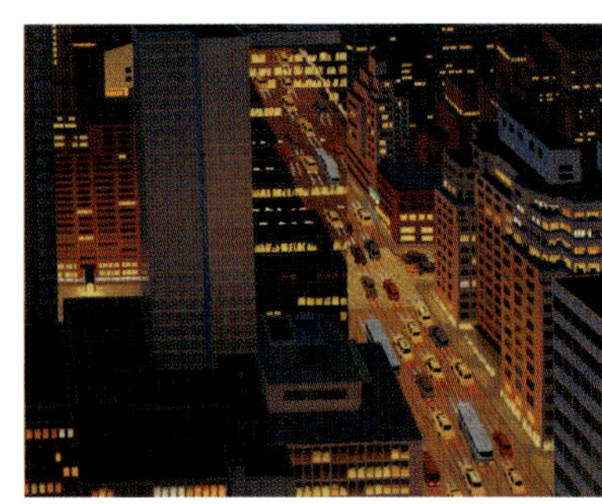

4A ABOVE RIGHT
Yvonne Jacquette
Third Avenue (with Reflection) II (detail), 2004
[see plate 32]

sparkles against the dark sky, prefiguring Jacquette's interest in nocturnal pattern and color.

Most resonant, perhaps, with Jacquette's perspective and subject were the many practitioners of graphic art and photography in the 20s and 30s. Hoover's 1930 *Manhattan Midnight*, with the towers of the Chrysler and Empire State buildings singled out above the crowd; Schutz's 1931 aquatint of *Lower Manhattan*, a gleaming, utopian apparition of the city floating on the East River; and Tittle's *Manhattan Minarets* of the same year, with a lone figure gazing upward in awe at the glowing peaks of some of the city's extraordinary behemoths, all investigate the same phenomena that interest Jacquette. In photography, improvements in equipment and processes had made possible crisp images of the illuminated city. Architectural photographer Samuel Gottscho, for one, in an aesthetic closely allied to Jacquette's, documented the nightly spectacle from perspectives both high and low [figures 9 and 10].[14]

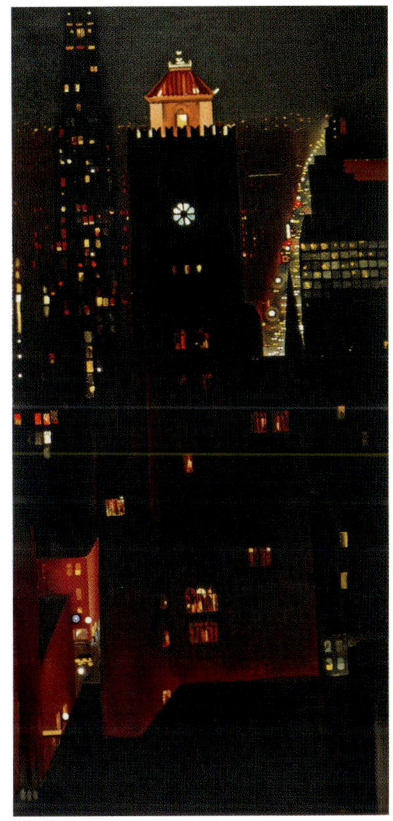

5 ABOVE LEFT
Georgia O'Keeffe (1887–1986)
New York, Night, 1929
Oil on canvas
40 x 19 inches
Sheldon Memorial Art Gallery and Sculpture Garden, University of Nebraska-Lincoln, NAA-Thomas C. Woods Memorial.
Photo © Sheldon Memorial Art Gallery

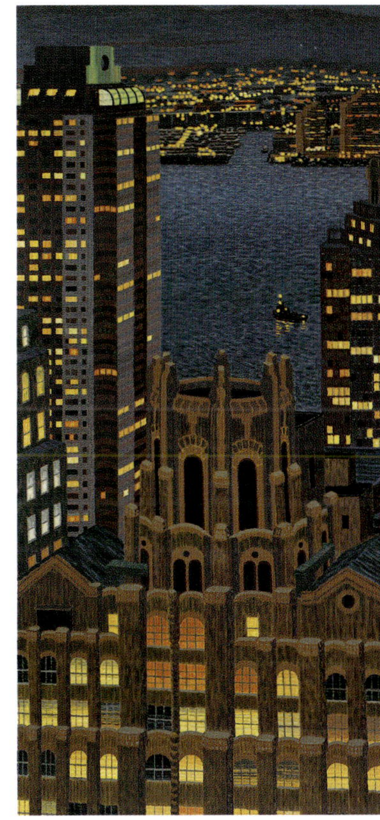

5A ABOVE RIGHT
Yvonne Jacquette
Lower Manhattan and New Jersey with Water Towers II (detail), 2005
[see plate 31]

THE ARTIST AND THE CITY

Born in Pittsburgh in 1934, Jacquette moved as a young child to Connecticut with her parents and six siblings.[15] As a private student of Robert Roché, her early training while still in high school was rooted in tradition, involving study of Old Masters and emphasis on careful rendering of simple forms like apples. Eventually Jacquette found Roché's antipathy toward modernism off-putting. When she went to the Rhode Island School of Design after high school in 1952, she received a sound foundation in the fundamentals of design, but after some exposure to the contemporary work being made and shown in New York City, Jacquette came to think the attitude at RISD was somewhat provincial. Given the times, Abstract Expressionism drew her attention, and she gave up on her fourth year at RISD to move to the city in 1955 and continue her education by studying the new art being shown in the galleries.[16] Jacquette immediately embraced the environment of New York: She has said it "absolutely impressed me the minute I got there . . . I wanted to do something with New York."[17] The idea must have percolated slowly, because it was many years before the city made an appearance in her paintings.

Her work of the 1950s, 60s, and early 70s—made in a minimal, reductivist style—focused on domestic interiors, cloud paintings, and eventually, daytime street scenes. Her shift to urban imagery was inspired in part by looking at the photography of Rudy Burckhardt (1914-1999), whom she met in 1961 and married in 1964, their son Tom born the

6 TOP LEFT
Ellison Hoover (1888–1955)
Manhattan Midnight, 1930
Lithograph
11 x 8 ¾ inches
Courtesy of Swann Galleries

7 BOTTOM LEFT
Anton Schutz (1894–1977)
Lower Manhattan Seen from 2 Montague Terrace, Brooklyn Heights, 1931
Color aquatint on yellow tinted paper
9 ⅞ x 13 ⅞ inches
Collection of The New-York Historical Society, James Boyd Collection of New York City Prints, negative #76183

8 BOTTOM RIGHT
Walter Tittle (1883–1966)
Manhattan Minarets, 1931
Drypoint
14 ⅝ x 9 inches
Collection of The New-York Historical Society, negative #76234

8A TOP RIGHT
Yvonne Jacquette
Chrysler Building Composite at Dusk II (detail), 1997
[see plate 20]

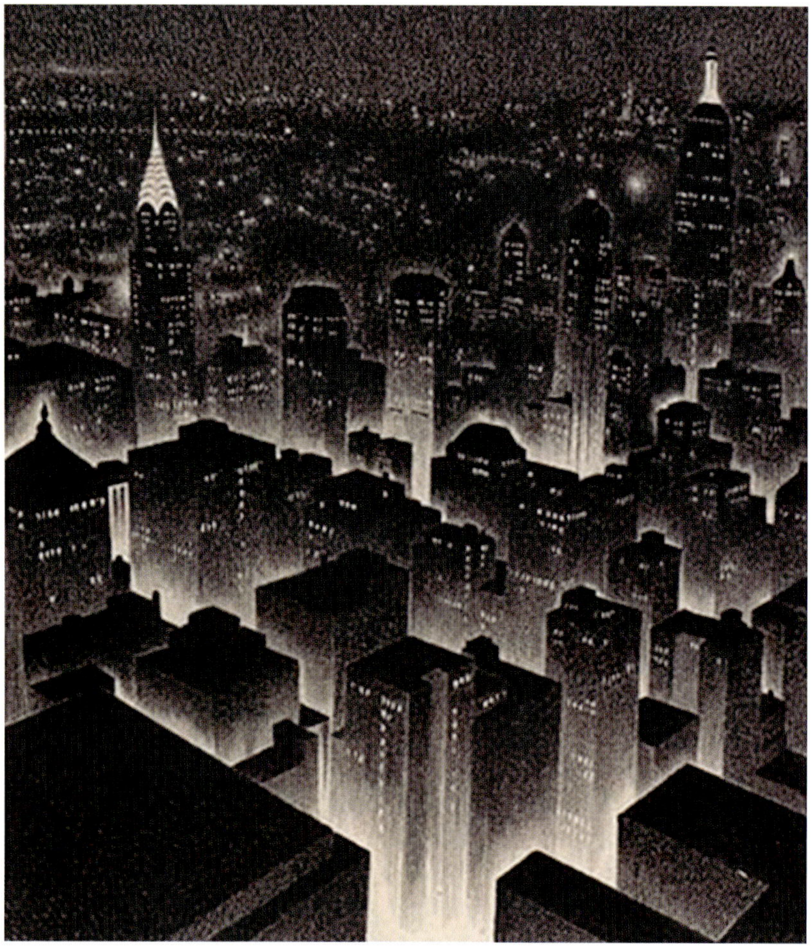

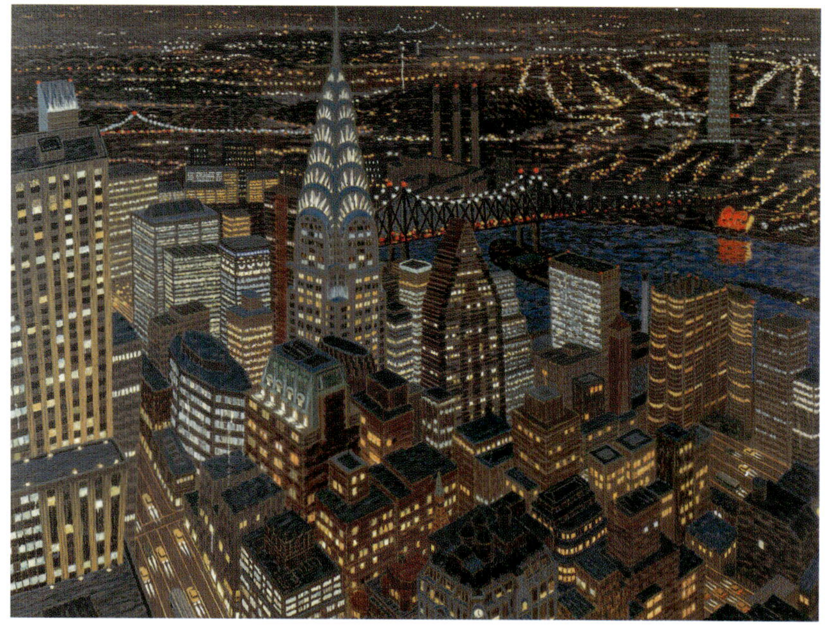

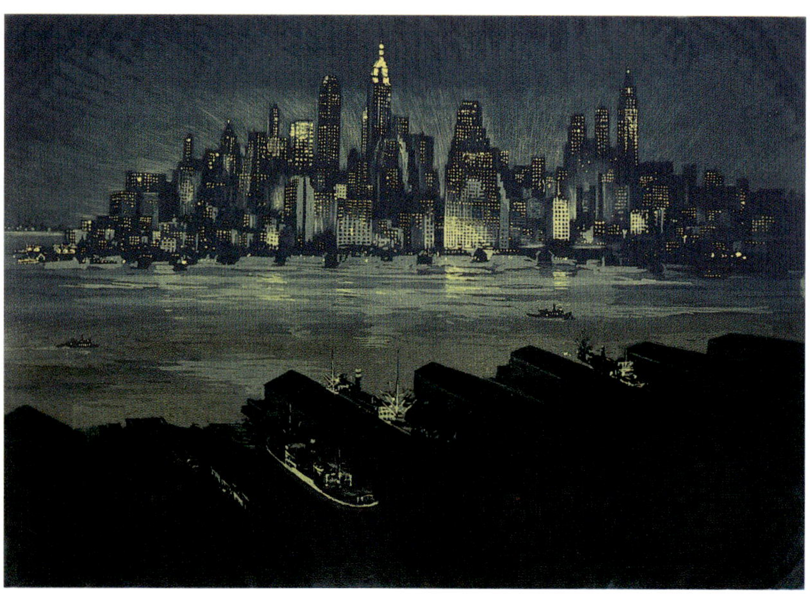

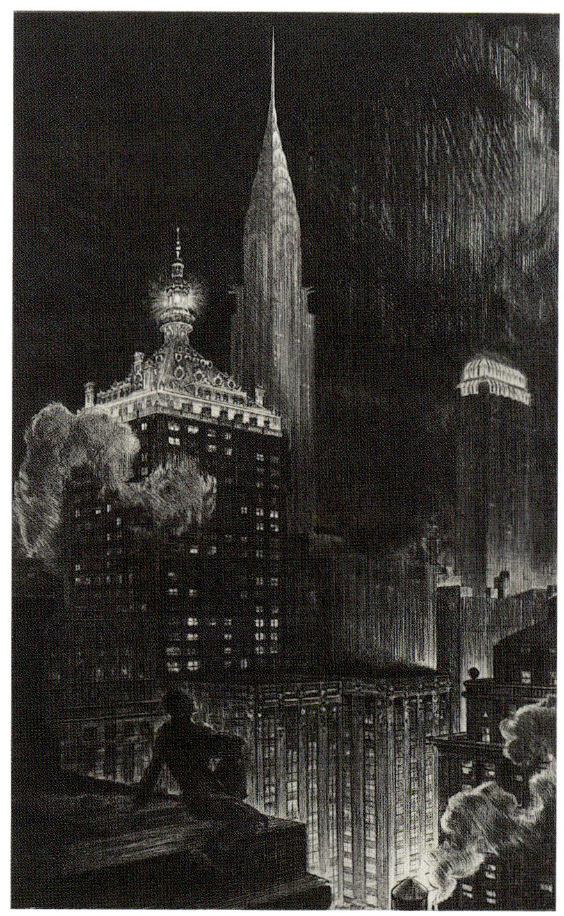

same year. Living with Burckhardt in Maine during the summers and New York during the winters, she became increasingly interested in exploring the city as subject matter during the half of the year spent there: "My husband Rudy Burckhardt's work was all along, I think, very influential, [particularly] his still photographs of New York [from the late 1930s and 40s]. I remember when I first met him those overwhelmed me, because he did in photographs what I would have liked to have done with New York."[18] Ultimately it was 20 years after her arrival in New York that she came to her primary subject of the city at night—its splendid architecture, neon signage, bridges, streets, and waterways—seen from aloft.

Jacquette's long exploration of the New York night began in 1976 during visits to Burckhardt's and her ailing friend Edwin Denby at University Hospital (now NYU Medical Center). Denby worried that she spent too much time at the hospital and not enough working, so she decided to work right in his room, first on the 17th and later the 15th floor.[19] Having first observed the view during the daytime, Jacquette says she "was shocked at how different the whole image was at night. I started a drawing there [*East River View at Night I,* (plate 1)], and I just kept working on it until it settled into something."[20] It settled into something important, as it turned out, since that chance experience led to her calling.

Jacquette has said that the "emotional turmoil [of Denby's grave illness] made the drawing more important to me."[21] She finished the pastel drawing back in her studio after he had recovered and been released from the hospital, and she soon found that visitors preferred it to all her other work. But it was so personal that when the Metropolitan Museum of Art wanted to purchase it for the collection she demurred, until a promise was offered to lend it to her if she ever wanted to make a painting based on the pastel. This very suggestion started her on the path of the night paintings. "I had no idea of how to think about the color in oil paint of dark colors. But since the drawing was so worked out, once I started the painting I found that it wasn't so difficult. My sister was an intern [at the hospital] at the time, so she could sneak me in, and I could go right back to the same room or a hallway nearby and sit there and get more information, and then just come home and work on the thing."[22] The result was her first painted nocturne, *East River View at Night II*, 1978 [plate 2].

The painting, like many of her early nighttime views, is sparely conceived with a shallow illusion of depth. Strongly asymmetrical, the

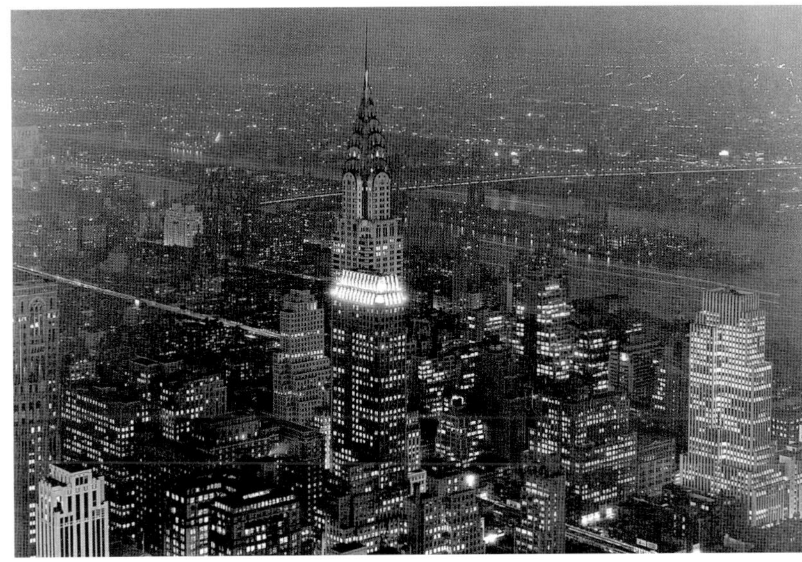

9 ABOVE
Samuel H. Gottscho (1875–1971)
View Looking Northeast from the Empire State Building with Chrysler and Chanin Buildings, 1932
Gelatin silver print
Museum of the City of New York,
Gift of Samuel H. Gottscho, 34.102.11

great dark emptiness of the East River is bordered at the top by the swagged lights of the 59th Street Bridge and at left by the streaming traffic of the FDR Drive. The meditative tenor is more pronounced in the painting than the pastel: the study's freer handling becomes more controlled in the painting, where the contrasts of light and color also deepen, and the expanse of water grows wider. When asked what night means to her in her work, Jacquette answers that it changes from painting to painting. Over time, night has suggested "compassion for the ill and vulnerable Edwin Denby and other souls clinging to life; erotic mystery; dramatic grandeur; loneliness; high energy; [and the] multiplicity and density of cities." [23]

Jacquette often says that she has a "literal mind." [24] This literal mind has led to a body of work based on observed reality, but the artist is aware that, while realism can make painting engaging and accessible, too much realism can make it uninteresting. In her assessment, some of the Photorealist work made in the late 60s and early 70s is "attractive for about 20 minutes. Your mind can't wander around in there." [25] Through such devices as fragmenting forms, composite views, and playing warm and cool colors against each other, Jacquette tries to slow down the viewer's perception precisely so that the mind is able to "wander around" in her paintings.[26] No one would mistake Jacquette's paintings for photographs; they do not share the hard, mirrorlike surfaces of hyperrealist works, and the hand and mind of the artist are always present.

Most conspicuous in the store of compositional techniques Jacquette uses to depict New York are the unusual angles of vision. Her signature aerial perspective both exploits the drama of scale and keeps the views, in her words, from being "trite." [27] The height has the effect of muting the city's volume and making the strident serene by lifting the viewer above the commotion. The lofty viewpoint also accounts for the unpopulated canvases: "From most of my heights, figures are not very obvious in the dark." [28] Although one may not see figures, this is no ghost town; the human presence can always be felt in the work. The hundreds of illuminated windows are in a sense symbolic substitutes for people; the lights left on after dark in the towers of Manhattan stand in for the day workers staying late at the office and the night shift arriving. The headlamps of each car on the congested streets and the navigation lights of each boat in the harbor serve the same end, both enlivening the surface and reminding us that people crowd the city.

The high vantage point—whether from skyscrapers, jets, or low-flying single-engine planes—gives the paintings compositional coherence as well, according to the artist: "Sometimes you find that things that look antagonistic to each other on the ground don't look that way in the air. A lot of things just fit into a pattern of the whole."[29] Altitude, she says, eliminates "some of the more trivial detail and gives unifying notes of color and texture."[30] By allowing us to tour the city by air, the paintings reveal views and configurations that are imperceptible at ground level, and distance brings grace and order to a city that can be jarring at close range.

Jacquette adjusts the prospect, depending upon the place from which the view was taken and the requirements of the scene. The perspective can vary from straight-down, vertiginous views (*South and West Views from the World Trade Center II*, plate 19, *East River View with Brooklyn Bridge II*, plate 7, *Flatiron Intersection II*, plate 3, *Oil Tanker near Battery Park II*, plate 4, and *Park Row Aerial II*, plate 6), to broad panoramas (*Chrysler Building Composite at Dusk II*, plate 20, *Lower Tip of Manhattan II*, plate 5, and *Two Bridges I*, plate 33), to soaring aerials (*Triboro Triptych at Night II*, plate 10, *George Washington Bridge at Night I* and *II*, plates 11 and 12, and *Night Wing: Metropolitan Area Composite II*, plate 15), to architectural close-ups (*Above Times Square II*, plate 27, *From World Trade Center, Mixed Heights II*, plate 21, and *Lower Manhattan and New Jersey with Water Towers II*, plate 31).

Among the works with a truly airborne perspective, some were begun from jets and some from small planes. In the days before 2001, when chartering private planes from Teterboro Airport to circle repeatedly over New York's rivers was still possible, Jacquette made studies for *George Washington Bridge at Night II* [plate 12] in this way. One of her most forceful paintings, the site is one little seen in her work—the upper reaches of Manhattan. The eastern tower of the bridge, with its graphically crisscrossed steel armature, appears to gaze down on the flaming vortices of traffic in Washington Heights. Cast in a cool green glow, the bridge tower—and Fort Washington Park and the Hudson below—are oases of calm against the sometimes overwhelming frenzy of urban life.

Among the precedents—some conscious, some not—for her compositions are the "floating world" prints of 19th-century Japan [figure 11], the works of Precisionist artists of the 1920s and 30s [figure 12], and photographs by her husband, Rudy Burckhardt [figures 13 and 14], Berenice Abbott, whom Jacquette cites as an influence [figure 15], and Andreas Feininger [figure 16].[31] Jacquette has said that "near and far don't matter

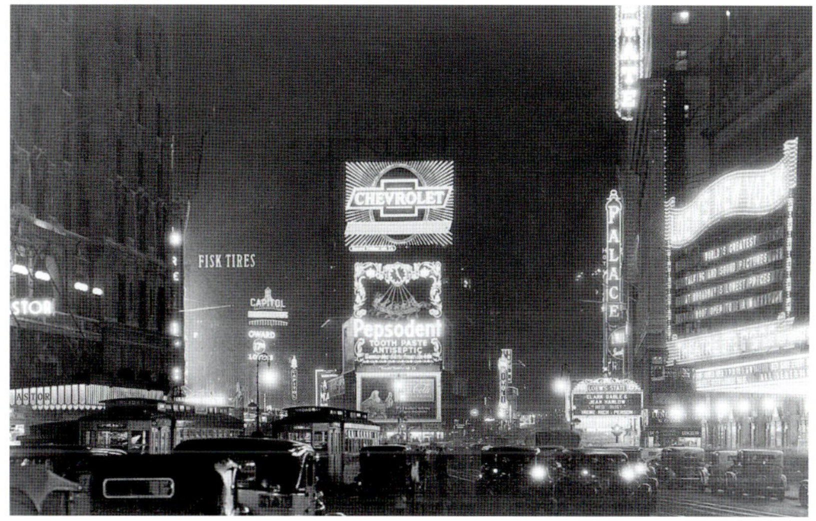

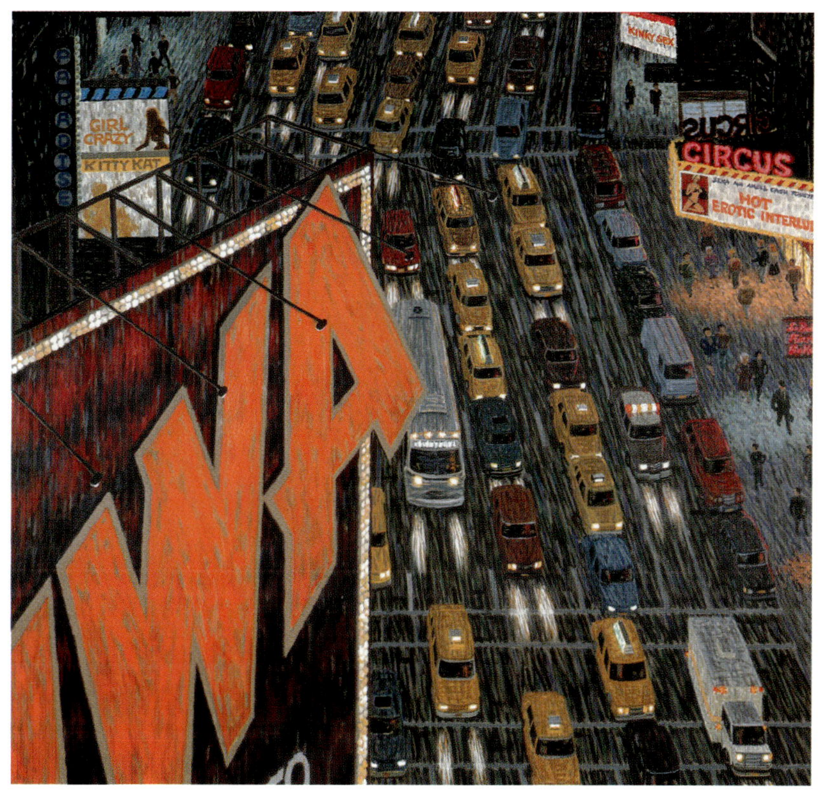

10 TOP
Samuel H. Gottscho (1875–1971)
Times Square at Forty-fourth Street, 1932
Gelatin silver print
Museum of the City of New York,
Gift of Samuel H. Gottscho, 34.102.10

10A BOTTOM
Yvonne Jacquette
Times Square Triptych II (detail), 1986–87
[see plate 9]

so much" in her work because "objects just lie on the plane," reflecting a Japanese approach to perspective, in which forms stack vertically on the picture plane, rather than recede into illusionistic space.[32] This Japanese device affected many Western artists at the time the prints became known in Europe—most strongly van Gogh, Manet, and Whistler—and the latter in turn had enormous influence on the next generations of painters and photographers in America. All shared an interest in exploring flatness and alternative angles of vision in place of traditional spatial recession.

The scale of Jacquette's paintings contributes to their power on the wall. They range from about 4 by 6 feet for the smallest single-canvas painting to 7 by 20 feet for the largest triptych. Her interest in working big began early. She has said that because of the large scale of Abstract Expressionist paintings she was seeing in the galleries in New York, as well as those by her close friend Alex Katz, she thought, "Well, why not?" As her vantage point changed from the ground, looking up, to the sky, looking down, she needed more canvas to accommodate the view. She also felt that with greater scale the "viewer could feel they were *in* the painting . . . [they could] have the painting wrap around them a little."[33] Given the amount of visual information in her large New York aerials, the canvas size allowed her to take a passage merely indicated on a "small study and really make something quite interesting, once you see five more inches of it."[34]

Another of Jacquette's formal stratagems is to create a void at the center of her compositions, as seen in *Flatiron Intersection II* [plate 3], *East River View with Brooklyn Bridge II* [plate 7], and *Pier A at Battery Park III* [plate 30]. One of the many examples of how Buddhist philosophy has left its mark on her work, the void, she says, is not really empty, but pregnant with possibility. She came to Buddhism, an interest shared with her husband, through meditation, first Transcendental Meditation, then "more serious meditation later." For her, meditation was about "looking for a more expanded view of the world."[35] In regard to the void, Jacquette also mentions the work of Jules Olitski, in whose abstract paintings slim figurative elements appear at the edges of the work, leaving the center as an expansive field of color.[36]

Contrasting the empty center in *Flatiron Intersection II*, other forms are cut off at the edges—the street lamp at top right, the taxi at lower left, the truck and car at top and bottom—making the view appear

11A TOP
Yvonne Jacquette
East River View at Night II, 1978
[see plate 2]

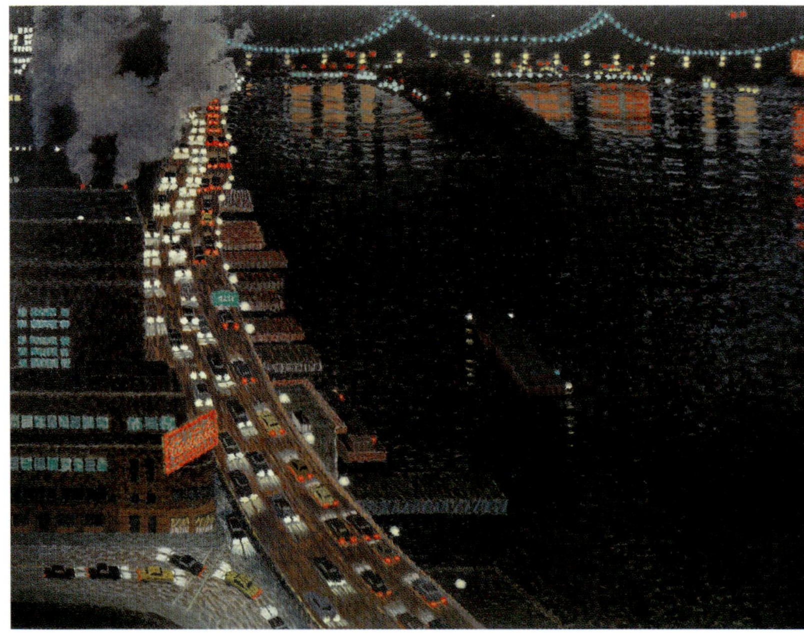

11 BOTTOM
Utagawa Yoshitora (active c. 1840–1880)
Station 21: Kanagawa (from *The Tokaido*), 1863
Woodblock print
15 x 10 inches
Published by Sanoya Tomigoro
Image courtesy of Horst Graebner

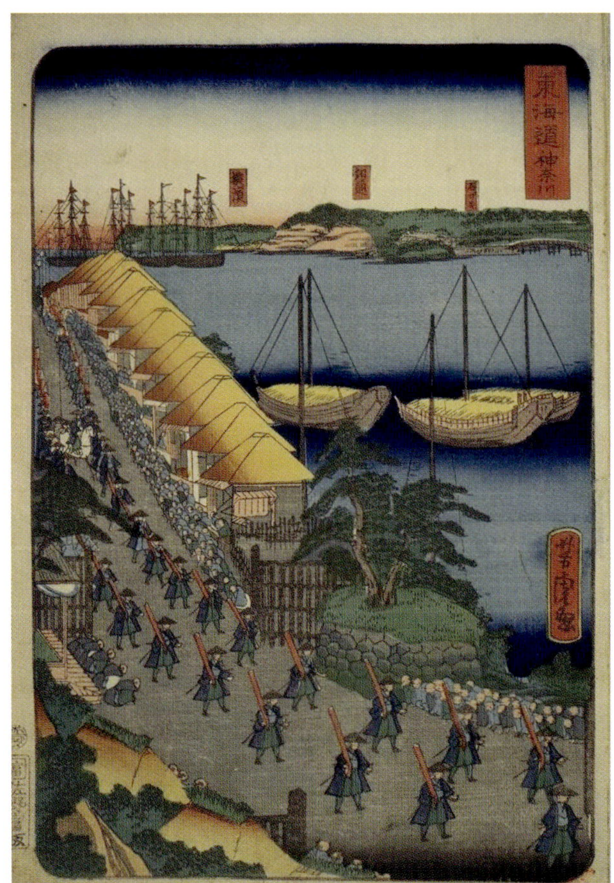

12A TOP LEFT
Yvonne Jacquette
Chelsea Composite II (detail), 1995
[see plate 18]

12 TOP RIGHT
Armin Landeck (1905–1984)
North River Vista, 1932
Two-color lithograph
16 x 11 ¼ inches
Courtesy of The Old Print Shop, New York, with permission from the Landeck Estate

13 BOTTOM
Rudy Burckhardt (1914–1999)
Chelseascape, New York, 1947
Gelatin silver print
Courtesy the Estate of Rudy Burckhardt and Tibor de Nagy Gallery, New York

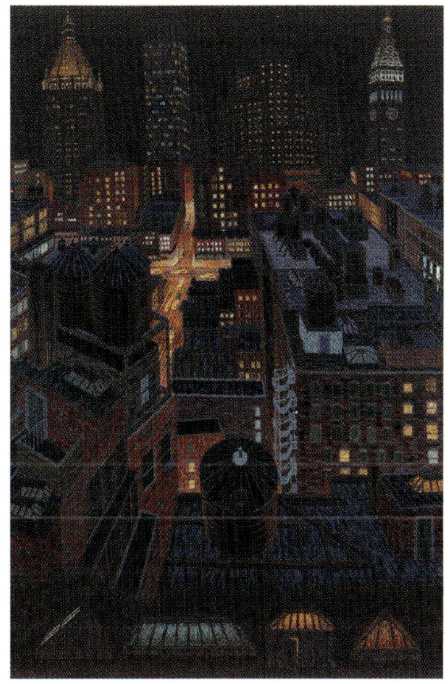

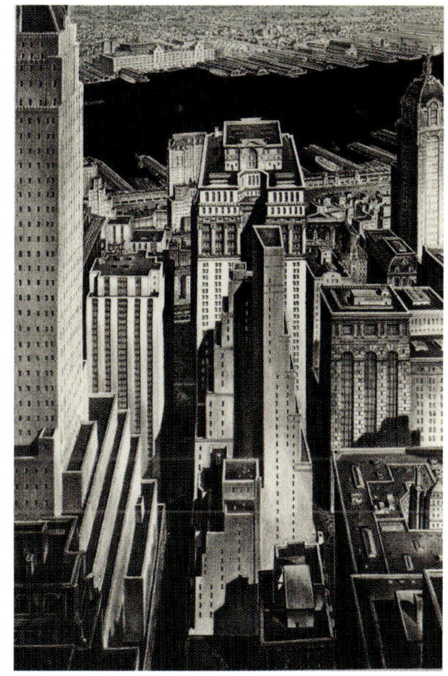

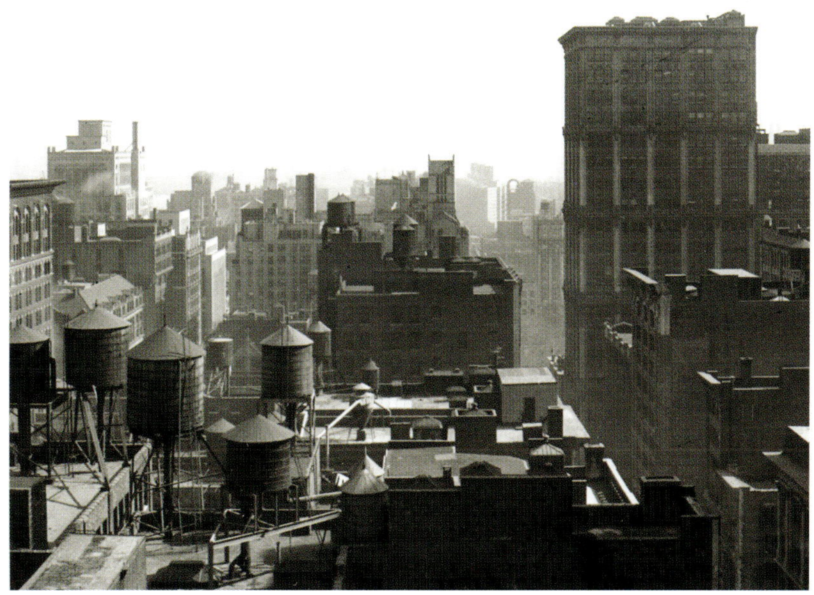

randomly selected. The possibility of change, as Jacquette suggests, is soon to be fulfilled by the approach of these two vehicles. The void here is made more pronounced by the radical angle of vision, which is nearly 180 degrees straight down. By eliminating both the horizon and any hint of sky, the painting has a vertigo-inducing impact; the viewer is in essence dangled head first over the street, disoriented by not being able to tell which way is up.

Those who search for block-by-block accuracy in Jacquette's aerial depictions of New York will find their efforts frustrated. Many of her works are synthetic images—the places are real enough, but the order is invented. In these composites, she confounds cartographical expectations by mixing up adjacencies, heights, and directions through her use of documentary photographs and drawings made from different floors of the same building, and even different buildings. Though the architecture is rendered with a fidelity that allows individual buildings to be easily recognized, their rearrangement is perplexing to anyone trying to make order of the city view.

Jacquette has said that the composite views also grew out of her Buddhist studies, which led her to a less "solid" concept of reality, a reality in which "things aren't settled and permanent in space."[37] Among the works with a composite structure is *Chrysler Building Composite at Dusk II*, 1997 [plate 20]. Nowhere more than in this painting does Jacquette's work remind us of a marvelous urban jigsaw puzzle. The pieces have been thrown in the air by the artist, and when they land, though they fit back together seamlessly, they have fallen into an entirely new pattern than the one they occupy in reality. Buildings sit on the wrong avenues, avenues travel in the wrong directions, and distances are both compressed and exaggerated.

The fracturing of views was carried even farther when Jacquette worked from the World Trade Center. Though she had made studies from the public observation deck in earlier years, in 1998 she had studio space in the towers through the Lower Manhattan Cultural Council's World Views program, in which artists were given access to unoccupied offices where they could work. Moving from one tower to another facilitated her composite paintings: "I found that I could start a drawing in Tower One then go over to Tower Two and go a little higher. Sometimes I could see the same building, but from a different angle, and it would become a different size in the drawing. I then started putting these things together . . . [to make] composites. I almost

14 TOP
Rudy Burckhardt (1914–1999)
Singer Building, New York, 1948–53
Gelatin silver print
Courtesy the Estate of Rudy Burckhardt and Tibor de Nagy Gallery, New York

14A BOTTOM
Yvonne Jacquette
Above Times Square II (detail), 2003
[see plate 27]

didn't think. I would ram these things together. Then I thought, these are kind of interesting."[38]

From World Trade Center, Mixed Heights II, 1998 [plate 21], with the top floors and distinctive mansard roof of Cass Gilbert's 90 West Street building repeated from two different angles, illustrates this method of recording the view from multiple vantage points and combining the results on a single canvas. During her residency with the Lower Manhattan Cultural Council, Jacquette was occupied with two commissions in her own studio in Chelsea, limiting the time she had to spend working downtown. She says she had keys to seven or eight spaces scattered through the two towers, and she would rush among them and "draw like mad."[39] (The landmark Gilbert building was the immediate neighbor to the south of the World Trade Center and sustained extensive damage from falling debris during the collapse of the towers, its copper roof completely destroyed by fire. The building was hailed as the "miracle survivor of 9/11" by *The New York Times* and has been thoroughly restored, now housing residential space.) The effect of the repetition of architectural elements, especially combined with the tilted viewpoint, is to make the vista—familiar as it is—seem strange and new.

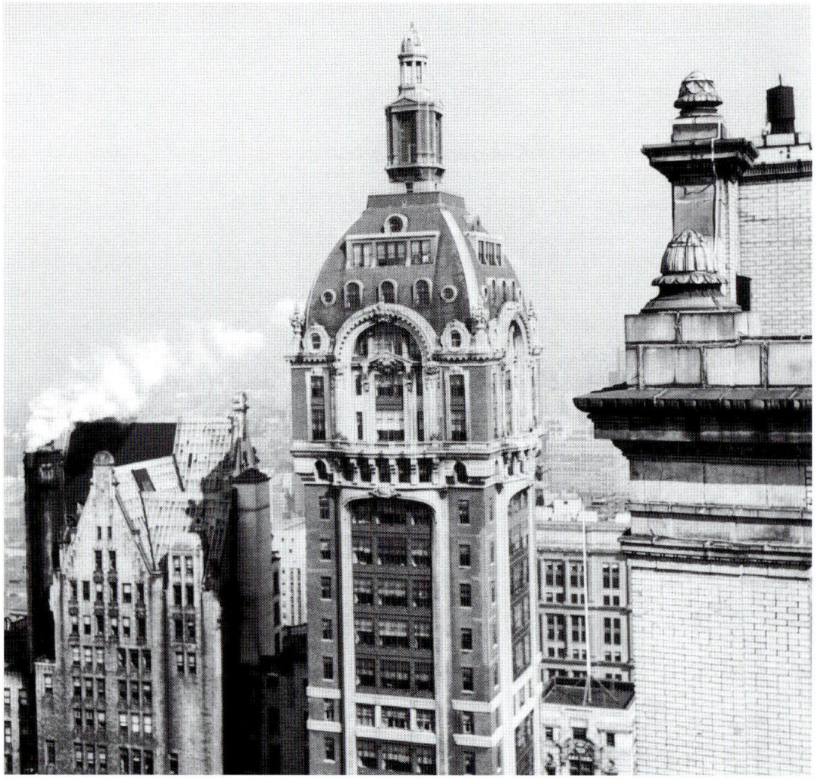

Many artists have found New York to be a sublime spectacle but were unable to imagine a way to "contain" it in a painting. "It is madness to think of employing such a subject artistically. One admires it humbly, and that's all," wrote French modernist painter Fernand Léger.[40] The city's vastness from the vantage points Jacquette chooses is surely a representational challenge, but with the "ordering and picturing eye of the artist," she subdues the immensity of the view by selectively breaking it into manageable chunks.[41]

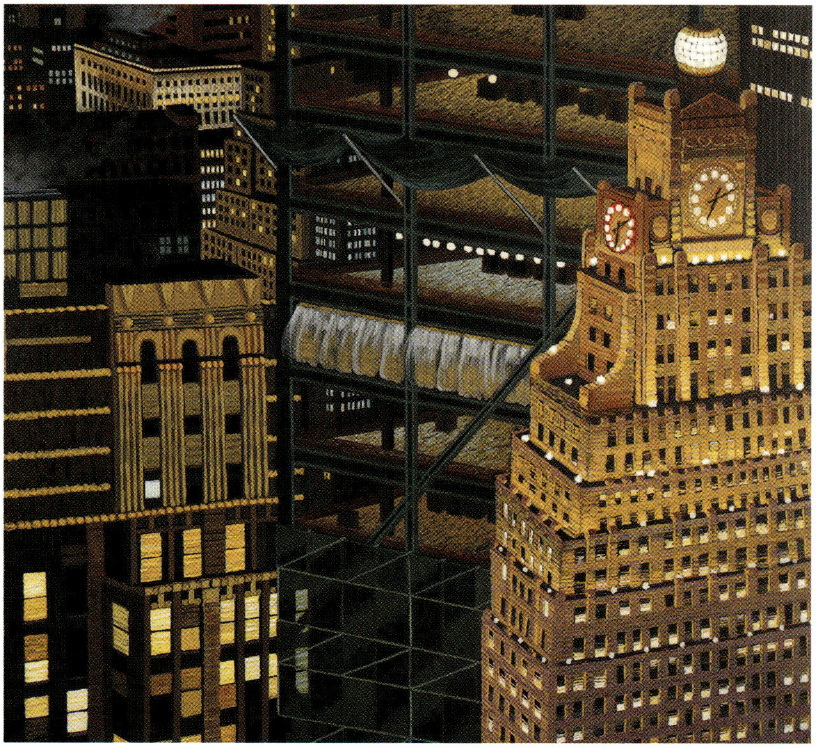

Stylistically, Jacquette strives for liveliness in her paintings of New York, a quality difficult to elicit from the very rectilinear subject matter of the built environment: "It made me very nervous for a while to have to deal with all those verticals and linear elements in the city landscape. Sometimes the work can get very stiff because of all those lines."[42] The concern was resolved in 1973 when she began to use pastel.[43] "At first the pastels seemed completely fat and unwieldy, but after I got the touch and made separate marks rather than blending . . . I got very excited by what the colors did. In a sense, it was like the Impressionists' touch—a kind of a breakdown." Pastel drawings made on-site eventually came to serve as studies for the large paintings, beginning with the first pastel and painted night views of New York in 1976 [plates 1 and 2]. To be able to perceive enough light while looking out at the darkened city to make a drawing, the light inside must be very low as well, because the eyes cannot easily switch between a bright interior and the dark view. Of her first night pastel, Jacquette says "I had to work in very dim light, doing the drawing with a flashlight, and hope that the next day in the daylight I could correct any mistakes." She found that she could "do certain things at night and other things in the day, to get the buildings to stand up in the day and to get the color right at night."[44] The pastel drawing also became important as a "color plan." Jacquette found she "could quickly get this sensory quality of the color in a kind of rough pastel, and then correct it in terms of drawing later." The kind of marks necessitated by the medium of pastel led to freer stroking in her paintings, as well. "By making my marks in a more intuitive manner, it gradually broke up the stiffness . . . I try to work as fast as I can, and as intuitively as I can, about how the marks are made. And often I find that the little [pastel] drawing is the key for how to make the strokes when they get larger [in the paintings]."[45]

This intuitive marking results in the characteristic exuberance of Jacquette's brushwork—the purposeful wiggle of the stroking, though this is visible mostly at close range. At a distance, the paintings appear more linear, but the animated touch keeps the surfaces supple and vibrant. Jacquette lays down each bit of color carefully with discrete strokes, recalling the brushwork of Seurat or van Gogh, two artists she cites as having influenced her approach. Her stroking varies considerably from painting to painting, and over time. In the early *Flatiron Intersection II*, 1979, [plate 3], the brushstrokes are larger and patchier, and her device of alternating matte and shiny strokes—accomplished through the introduction of varnish in the shiny parts—is very noticeable. In *Park Row Aerial II*, 1982 [plate 6], the central street loop is covered with hundreds of individualized strokes of varying color: "I want a certain kind of energy of the action of these cars moving up this road . . . an energy flow. I never saw those lines on the street, except I did see headlight markings as the cars go by . . . that gave me an idea for the kind of strokes, these crisscrossing strokes."[46] In the panoramic *Chrysler Building Composite at Dusk II* of 1997 [plate 20], the handling is looser and more painterly than in many of her paintings that are more restricted in scope. The variety of stroking—vertical, horizontal, and exaggeratedly wavy for the passages of reflection—in the 2004 *Third Avenue (with Reflection) II* [plate 32] makes for a very dynamic surface. By contrast, in the recent semi-monochromatic paintings [plates 28 and 30], the canvas seems smooth and even, with little visible stroking, but even here textures of two colors close in value—two blacks, for example—admit slight texture.

Since Jacquette began to explore aerial views of New York at night in 1976, she has developed a customary working process. Each view is treated in several stages, resulting in a finished pastel, a colored oil painting, sometimes a print, and recently a second, nearly monochromatic version of the painting.[47] She starts by making a colored pastel drawing on paper, looking down at the city from the window of either an airplane or a tall building. The pastels are drawn on paper that she has coated with colored acrylic paint—mixed with a bit of fine pumice to give "tooth" to the paper and to help hold the pastel—and she keeps many of these sheets on hand in various colors. From the vantage point used for the pastel, she also takes lots of documentary photographs with print film to supplement her memory of the view when working on the painted version that will follow.[48] When the pastel is complete, she takes a slide of it and projects it on canvas, marking the contours with charcoal (and very recently, with colored pencil). The support used is Belgian linen, which she buys already prepared with a white ground. Working around the charcoal lines, the canvas is next covered in an underpainting color, which relates to the color of the paper used for the pastel. The charcoal is brushed away, leaving a monochromatic painting. (At this stage, when the underpainting is complete for the colored painting—the canvas has a dark ground, and shapes are indicated by linear areas of bare white canvas—Jacquette takes another slide, which she uses as a guide for single-color woodcuts. When a print is made, it is generally after she has finished the painting, and prints are not made of all views.) Referring back to the pastel as a guide for both color and stroke, and to the photographs for more exhaustive information about the view, she finishes the oil painting. In the last year, Jacquette has begun to work the view into an additional state, which she calls the "underpainting as overpainting" version [plates 28 and 30]. These monochromatic paintings have the economy of means and graphic punch of a print, with their natural emphasis on line. A slide of the finished oil painting is projected on a new canvas for this state, and Jacquette makes changes in detail and tone as she paints [see plates 29 and 30 for alterations between states].

Beginning with the first night pastel, Jacquette created a numbering system to indicate the order in which states of each view were made: the pastel is version I, the full-color oil painting is generally version II,

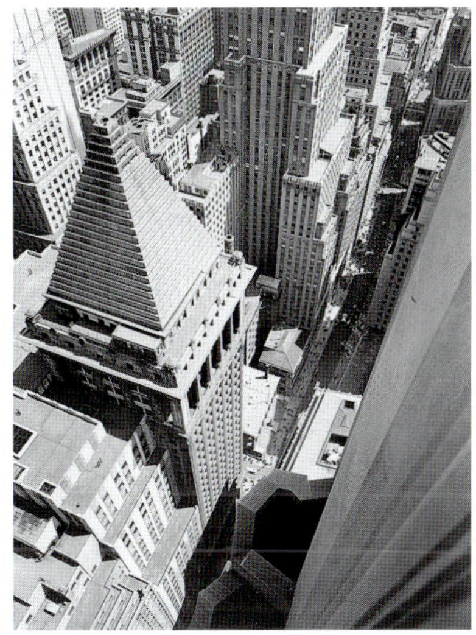

15 TOP LEFT
Berenice Abbott (1898–1991)
Wall Street District, 1938
Gelatin silver print
Museum of the City of New York, Museum purchase with funds from the Mrs. Elon Hooker Acquisition Fund, 40.140.274

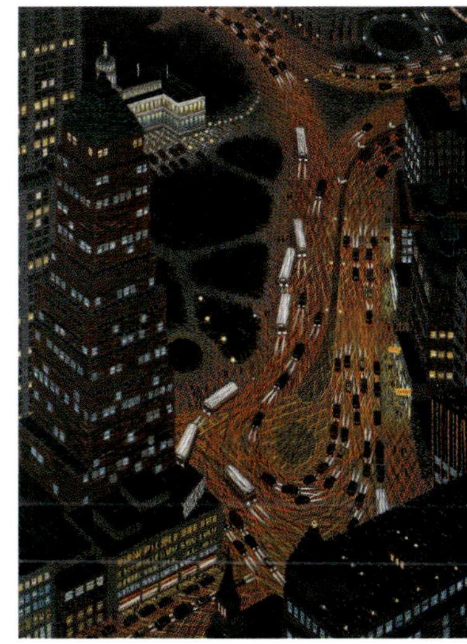

16A TOP RIGHT
Yvonne Jacquette
Park Row Aerial II, 1982
[see plate 6]

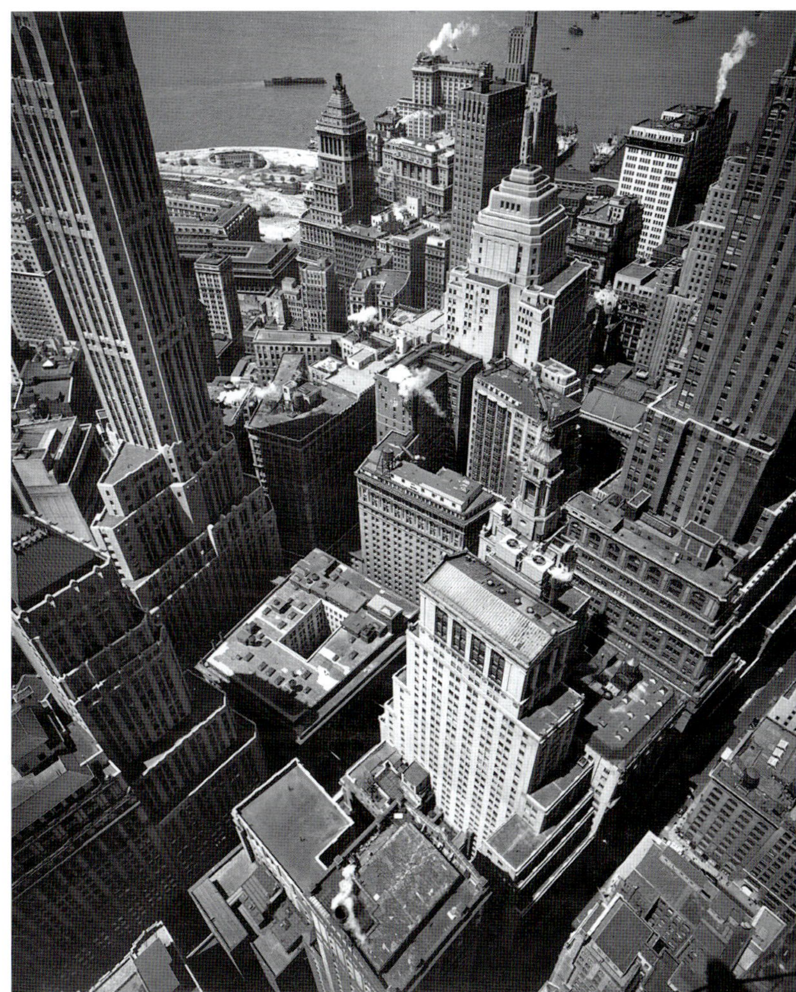

16 BOTTOM
Andreas Feininger (1906–1999)
Untitled [Skyscrapers and Battery Park], c. 1941
Gelatin silver print
Museum of the City of New York, Gift of the photographer, 55.31.129

and the new monochromatic paintings, version III. (In the 1970s she occasionally made several pastels before beginning the painting, making its number higher than II.) She estimates that the pastels require three days and nights of on-site work, and often several more days of work in the studio. A large, detailed painting takes two or three months, working on nothing else.[49] Since the 1980s when she enlarged the size of her paintings and began to make some work on commission, she has used an assistant for such prep work as color mixing—based on swatches provided by the artist—and painting background areas.[50]

Mood in Jacquette's New York nocturnes has many shades, but most palpable are a sense of humor and of mystery in the paintings, often side by side in the same piece. The buoyancy often commented upon in her work is achieved in part through the inherent festivity of bright light and color against the night sky, making the hundreds of illuminated windows look like neatly arranged confetti suspended over the city streets. Immense discrepancies in scale add to the distinctive humor, too: cars appear so small from the air they might as well be toys, utterly out of proportion with the enormous buildings around them. Jacquette has likened the incongruities of size in her paintings to Robert Wilson's avant-garde theater pieces, in which "something huge and grand is next to something small."[51] The playfulness in her work also derives from human and animal shapes detectable among the elements of the urban scene, like the giant eye along the shore in *Mixed Heights and Harbor From World Trade Center II* [plate 22]—in reality a stretch of curved boardwalk in Battery Park—or the silhouettes of toy giraffes at the upper edge of *Southeast View from World Trade Center II* [plate 25], actually mammoth container cranes outlined in lights at Brooklyn's Red Hook Terminal. Jacquette also says "Buddhism has a lot to do with [the buoyant mood in her work]. A positive view is part of Buddhism."[52]

Balancing the mischievous wit of the paintings is an enveloping aura of mystery. Again, inherent in the night view as a genre are the competing presences of glamour and danger, romance and loneliness. In *Ola II*, 1994 [plate 17], for example, amidst the pulsating signage that advertises familiar products (Fuji film, Canon cameras, and Coca-Cola) in Times Square, Jacquette has included at the lower right a sinister partial image of a female face, covered by and suspended over a spider web. The ambiguity of this passage, next to all the vividly straightforward neon signs, suggests that Jacquette included this logo for the 1993

Broadway production of *Kiss of the Spider Woman* both to balance the glaring commercialism of the district and to introduce an element of mystery. She has said that of the many meanings of night in her work, one is erotic mystery.[53] "Night is a time of dreaming, of freeing repressed libidinal energies," and the psychological suggestiveness of the painting speaks to the sometimes perilous seductiveness of the city after dark.[54]

Pulling together the threads of humor, mystery, and melancholy is *Southeast View from World Trade Center II*, 2001 [plate 25]. Falling as it does in Jacquette's oeuvre not long after her husband's death, the painting, with its dark barge at upper right, calls to mind the last lines from the 1928 Brecht/Weill song "Pirate Jenny" from *The Threepenny Opera:*

> And the ship, the black freighter,
> disappears out to sea,
> and on it is me.

This painting is also the last to record the panorama from the World Trade Center before the buildings and their view were lost in 2001. The ghostly cylinder off the northern end of Governor's Island (a ventilation tower for the Brooklyn-Battery Tunnel) and the puffs of steam across the lower center now register as elegiac notes in the painting. The painting's meditative mood also speaks to the loneliness Jacquette sometimes feels working by herself at night in deserted office buildings or empty hotel rooms.[55]

A SHARED SENSIBILITY

Yvonne Jacquette and Rudy Burckhardt were creative and personal partners for nearly 40 years, from the time of their meeting in 1961 until Burckhardt's death in 1999. They sometimes collaborated, usually on films, but mostly each pursued independent work. Despite this independence, their approaches to representing the city share visual and philosophical parallels. Among the affinities between their New York work are an interest in pattern (seen in architectural detail, cast shadows, and clothing fabrics in his work and in the directional stroking and arrangement of illuminated windows in hers); an interest in language and text (seen on his billboards and storefronts and in her neon signage); in famous New York icons (the Flatiron Building and Brooklyn Bridge); in cropped views; in elevated perspectives (from rooftops in his case, often from greater altitude in hers); in compositions that seem uncomposed; in conveying intimacy despite the city's grandeur; in an approach unaffected by political or social commentary; and in the pleasure of looking and seeing. Balancing all the correspondences between their work are the obvious, though more insignificant, differences in their city imagery: the prominence of figures in his photographs, her use of color, and her preference for night scenes over day.

Burckhardt's New York works, particularly his still photographs of the 1940s, served as lasting exemplars for Jacquette. "When I first met him, I was very interested in his views of Chelsea . . . from high-rise buildings looking down onto the street or across to water towers. I just love those. They were very interesting, because you would think that you would get a very distanced, detached view, but they were very friendly. They had an intimacy and warmth to them."[56] Certain photographs—sometimes made 40 years earlier—were important as stylistic ideals: "The aerial photograph of Astor Place with the Coca-Cola billboard [plate 66] was a strong example to me of a way one could be high above the street but still avoid some grandiosity."[57] Sometimes the specifics of subject matter come to Jacquette directly from either films or photographs by Burckhardt. "In *Times Square Triptych II* [1986–87, plate 9], my figures recall his films of people walking in Times Square. I deliberately chose to do my versions of the Flatiron Building [1979, plate 3] and Brooklyn Bridge [1983, plate 7] influenced by him."[58]

Burckhardt's work was significant not only in style, perspective, and subject for Jacquette, but as a link to photography in general, and to earlier generations of photographers who looked at the city by day and night. The parallels are many between Jacquette and Burckhardt and another great creative partnership: As O'Keeffe found things that resonated when she looked at the photographs of her husband Stieglitz, so Jacquette and Burckhardt had an ongoing exchange between painting and photography (and film). In the years since Burckhardt's death, Jacquette's career and life have moved forward, but their long dialogue—both personal and artistic—left valuable marks on their work.

Describing the way their relationship informed their work, Jacquette has said:

> I hoped that his sense of the poetry of N.Y. would creep into my work. I did choose some views that he had used, such as the Brooklyn Bridge, although I usually opted for the night view when he used the daytime. Later we collaborated on the film *Night Fantasies*, which joined our visions. He was usually very supportive of my painting. When I owned a studio on 38th Street, he came there to paint from the 11th floor windows. Before that I think he gained patience from watching me do elaborate city views for a long oil from our loft on 29th Street, even painting all the bricks on the adjacent roof walls. He taught me technical knowledge about photography. I assisted him in many small ways with films: acting, making costumes or hairstyles, giving "crits" of films in progress, suggesting music (as in *Night Fantasies*). I could give him "crits" of his paintings, but he was very clear about his photography in still work. I may have encouraged his close-up landscapes in painting, but he probably already had discovered it in still photography.[59]

When asked about how her husband's death affected her work, she says, "If my work has changed since 1999, it's lacking his comments and encouragement. New areas have opened up for me he might have been surprised about (the work from helicopters [in Maine]). Going to Rome [in the fall of 2007 to work at the American Academy in Rome] will evoke his presence and his work in Mediterranean cities."[60]

* * *

It has been said that "New York schematized as energy and engineering was an artistic construct."[61] This modernist vision of New York—a symbolic synopsis that reduced the city to a densely built grid of soaring skyscrapers, blazing with electricity—persists to this day. Willingly—consciously—or not, Jacquette inherits the mantle of an illustrious line of New York artists who sought to make sense of the environment around them by depicting its constant metamorphosis. It is a challenge she embraces: "Change is constant in New York City! I hope to be open to new views, but more importantly, to discover new means to indicate how I see and how painted color can reveal new perceptions."[62] The fascination and awe that New York's skyline elicited when it first began to rise in the early decades of the last century linger still, and the relentless cycle of demolition and construction continues to transform the city, giving Yvonne Jacquette endless material for her painted rhapsodies on the New York night.

1
F. Scott Fitzgerald, *The Great Gatsby* (New York: Scribner's, 1992), 73.

2
Ellen Harris, et al. *Precisionism in America, 1915–1941: Reordering Reality*, (New York: Abrams, in association with the Montclair Art Museum, 1994), 34. When Jacquette was first searching for a way to paint New York, she looked at the artists of the period: "I discovered the Precisionists and looked at those people." Quoted in Kate Horsfield, "On Art and Artists: Yvonne Jacquette," *Profile* vol. 2, no. 6 (November 1982): 16.

3
Anna C. Chave, "Who Will Paint New York?," *American Art* vol. 5, nos. 1–2 (Winter/Spring 1991): 88.

4
Ezra Pound, *Patria Mia* (Chicago: R. F. Seymour, 1950), 32–33. Originally published in the London journal *New Age*, 18 September 1912.

5
Correspondence with the author, 30 May 2007.

6
Interview with the author, 30 May 2007.

7
Correspondence with the author, 30 May 2007.

8
Quoted in William Sharpe, "New York, Night, and Cultural Mythmaking. The Nocturne in Photography, 1900–1925," *Smithsonian Studies in American Art* (Fall 1988): 3.

9
Peter Conrad, *The Art of the City: Views and Versions of New York* (New York: Oxford University Press, 1984), 132.

10
Merrill Schleier, *The Skyscraper in American Art, 1890–1931* (Ann Arbor, MI,: UMI Research Press, 1986), 77.

11
The first images of the earth's surface from space were taken from an unmanned rocket in 1946, and other partially illuminated images followed from the voyages of *Apollo 8* and *11*, among others, but none received the coverage of the *Apollo 17* photographs.

12
Critic John Ruskin condemned *Nocturne in Black and Gold* in the London press, accusing Whistler of "flinging a pot of paint in the public's face," and resulting in the notorious libel suit.

13
Correspondence with the author, 30 May 2007.

14
Interestingly, Gottscho approached the challenge of night images with a technique not unlike Jacquette's own, described on page 29 of this essay, in which she examines the view for her pastel drawings both at night, for color and light, and in the daytime for the structure. Gottscho's night images are made up of two exposures, one made at dusk to record shapes with adequate light, and one made after dark to capture the illuminated signs and windows (see Donald Albrecht, *The Mythic City: Photographs of New York by Samuel H. Gottscho, 1925–1940*, [New York: Princeton Architectural Press and The Museum of the City of New York, 2005], 30).

15
See Chronology, page 240, for biographical details. The most comprehensive source of information about Jacquette's work and life is Hilarie Faberman, *Aerial Muse: The Art of Yvonne Jacquette* (New York: Hudson Hills Press, 2002).

16
Horsfield, 3–5.

17
Horsfield, 6.

18
Horsfield, 12.

19
Artist's statement, dated November 1978, Metropolitan Museum of Art object file for *East River View at Night I*.

20
Quoted in David Cohen, "Canaletto of the Skies," *Artcritical.com* (Summer 2003): no page numbers.

21
Horsfield, 24.

22
Horsfield, 24.

23
Correspondence with the author, 30 May 2007.

24
Interview with the author, 30 May 2007.

25
Interview with the author, 30 May 2007.

26
Correspondence with the author, 30 May 2007.

27
Jacquette, quoted in Cohen, no page numbers. Harris, 55, associates a similar angled perspective with the Precisionist artists of the 1920s and 30s.

28
Correspondence with the author, 30 May 2007.

29
Horsfield, 21.

30
Correspondence with the author, 30 May 2007.

31
Jacquette discussed the importance of "oriental influences" in her 1978 statement about the pastel study for this work; see note 19. Abbott photographed from some of the same buildings that Jacquette has worked in, including the Empire State Building. Interview with the author, 30 May 2007.

32
Interview with the author, 30 May 2007.

33
Interview with the author, 30 May 2007.

34
Horsfield, 17.

35
Interview with the author, 30 May 2007.

36
Interview with the author, 30 May 2007.

37
Quoted in Cohen, no page numbers, and correspondence with the author, 30 May 2007.

38
Quoted in Cohen, no page numbers.

39
Panel discussion of artists from the World Trade Center residency program, sponsored by the Museum of the City of New York and the Lower Manhattan Cultural Council, at the Museum, 24 May 2005, author's notes.

40
1931 essay, quoted in Chave, 104.

41
Alan Trachtenberg, "Image and Ideology. New York in the Photographer's Eye," *Journal of Urban History* vol. 10 (August 1984): 461–62.

42
Horsfield, 18.

43
Faberman, 40.

44
Horsfield, 24–25.

45
Horsfield, 17–18, 25–26.

46
Horsfield, 25–26.

47
Information about Jacquette's working method from correspondence with the author, 23 August 2007 and interviews with the author, 22 March 2007 and 30 May 2007.

48
Jacquette uses a 50mm lens for long-range photographs from airplanes and high buildings, where speed is important. When she is able to use a tripod in a building, she sometimes uses a telephoto lens for detailed close-ups; see note 48.

49
Correspondence with the author, 24 August 2007.

50
Correspondence with the author, 23 August 2007 and interviews with the author of 22 March 2007 and 30 May 2007.

51
Interview with the author, 30 May 2007.

52
Interview with the author, 30 May 2007.

53
Correspondence with the author, 30 May 2007.

54
Sharpe, 11.

55
Interview with the author, 30 May 2007. Jacquette describes on the one hand the lonely isolation of working in such situations and on the other the pleasure and relief of being able to work freely—a heightened creativity.

56
Quoted in Cohen, no page numbers.

57
Correspondence with the author, 2 August 2007.

58
Correspondence with the author, 2 August 2007.

59
Correspondence with the author, 30 May 2007.

60
Correspondence with the author, 30 May 2007.

61
Wanda M. Corn, "The Artist's New York: 1900–1930," *Budapest and New York: Studies in Metropolitan Transformation, 1870–1930,* (New York: Russell Sage Foundation, 1994): 298–99.

62
Correspondence with the author, 30 August 2007.

1
East River View at Night I, 1976–77
Pastel on paper
18 ¾ x 23 inches
The Metropolitan Museum of Art, Purchase, Friends of the Department Gifts and matching funds from the National Endowment for the Arts, 1978 (1978.199)

2
East River View at Night II, 1978
Oil on canvas
56 x 74 inches
Leola and Robert S. Macdonald

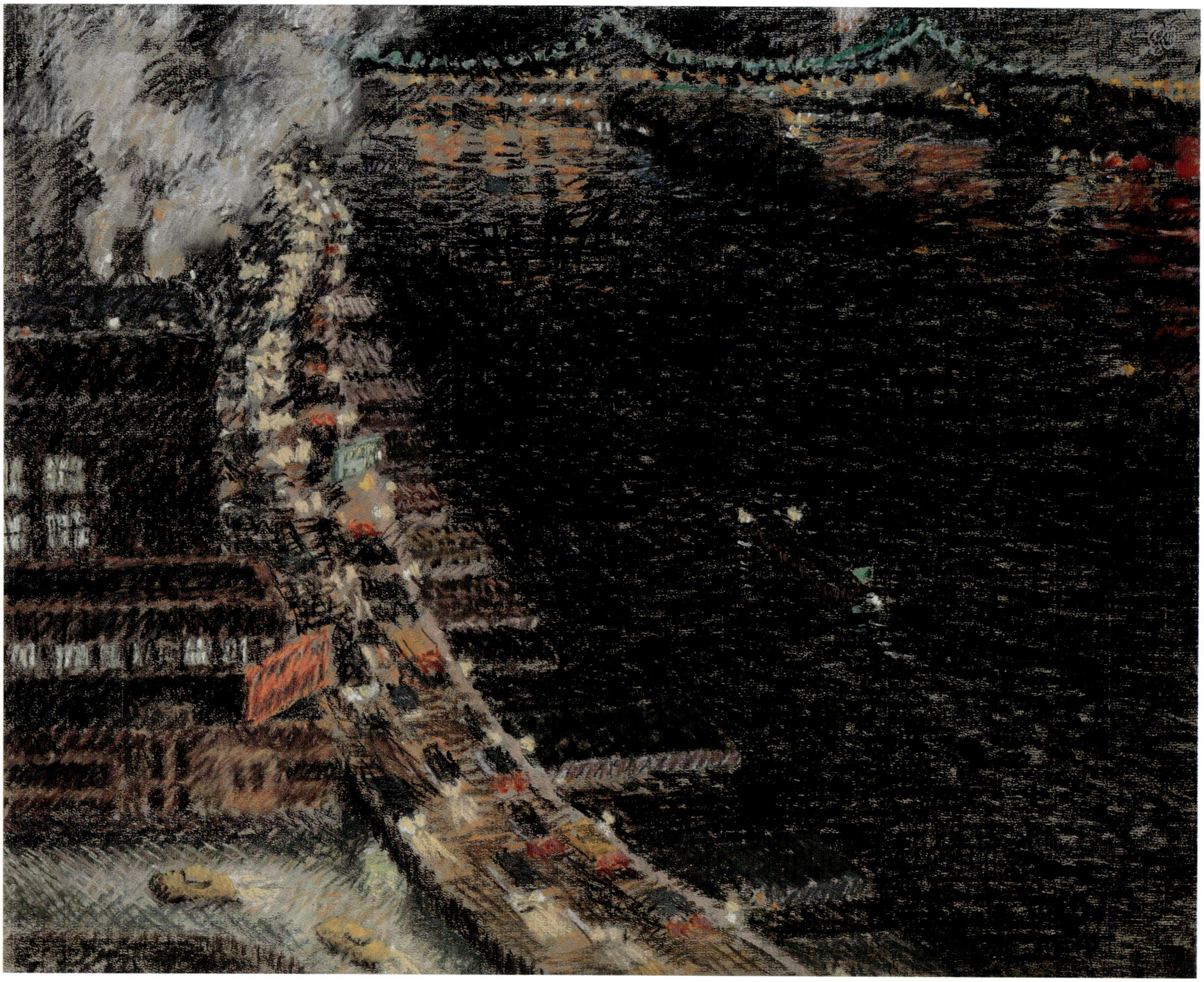

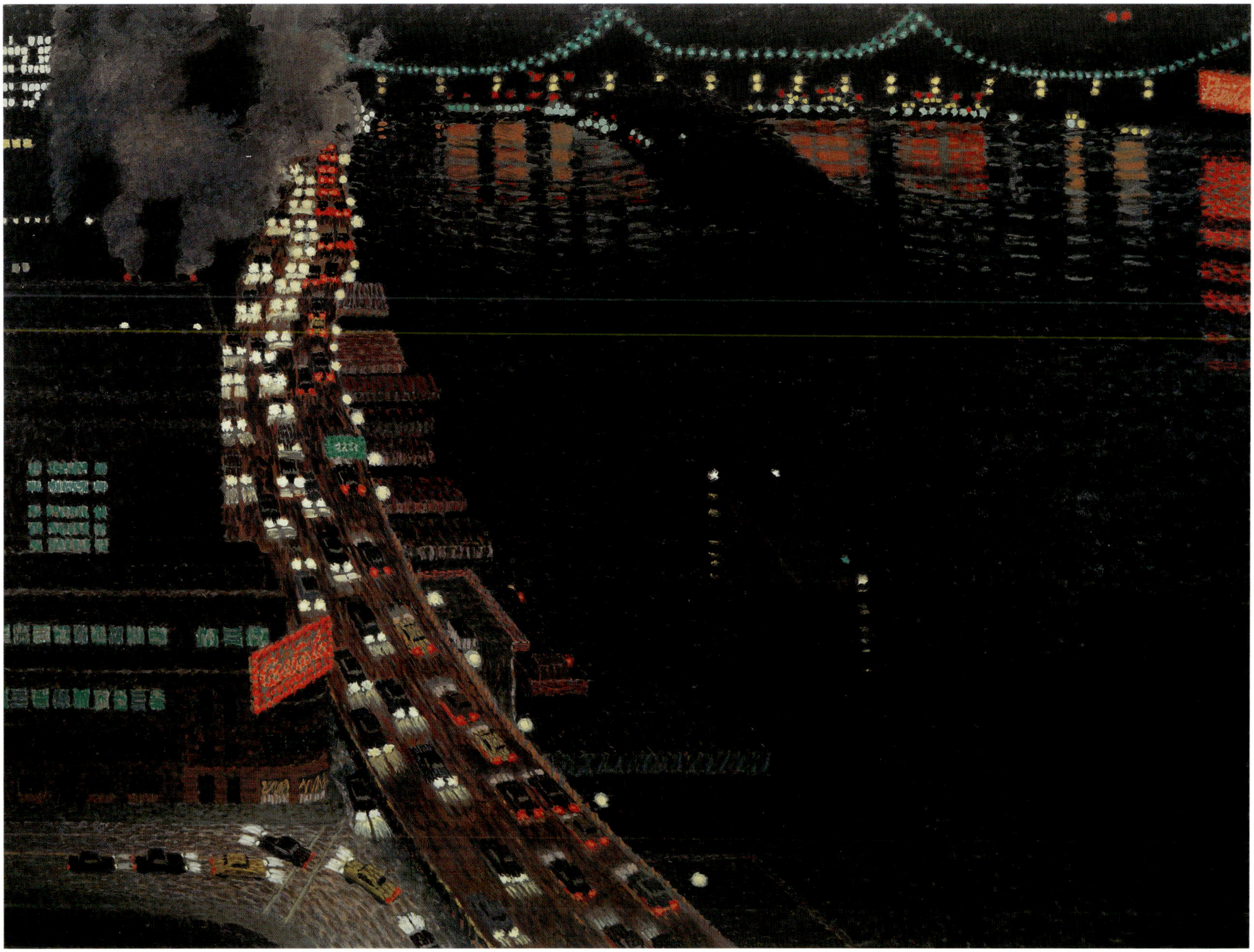

3
Flatiron Intersection II, 1979
Oil on canvas
60 x 80 inches
Private collection

4
Oil Tanker near Battery Park II, 1981
Oil on canvas
76 x 62 inches
Tom Burckhardt and Kathy Butterly

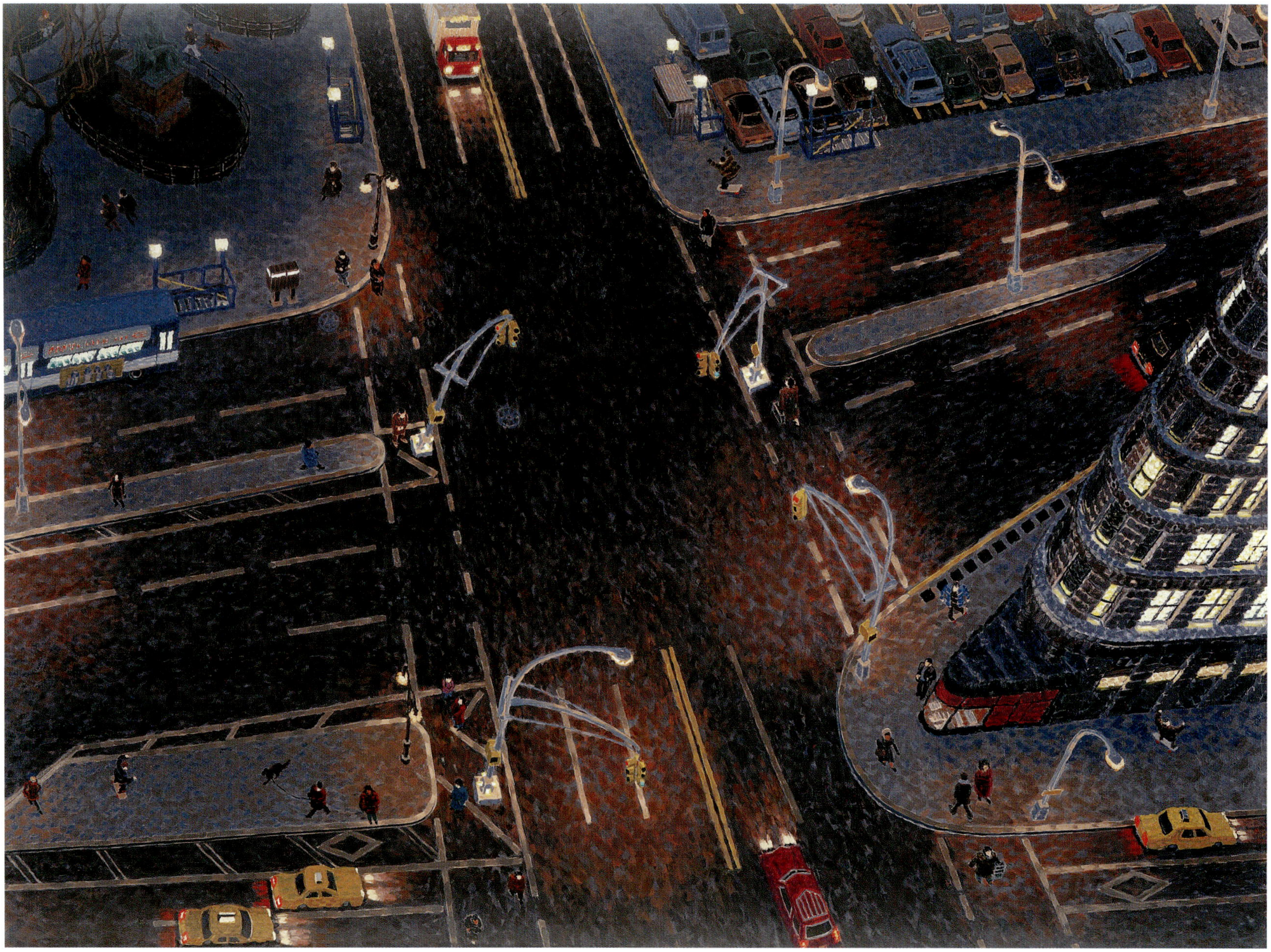

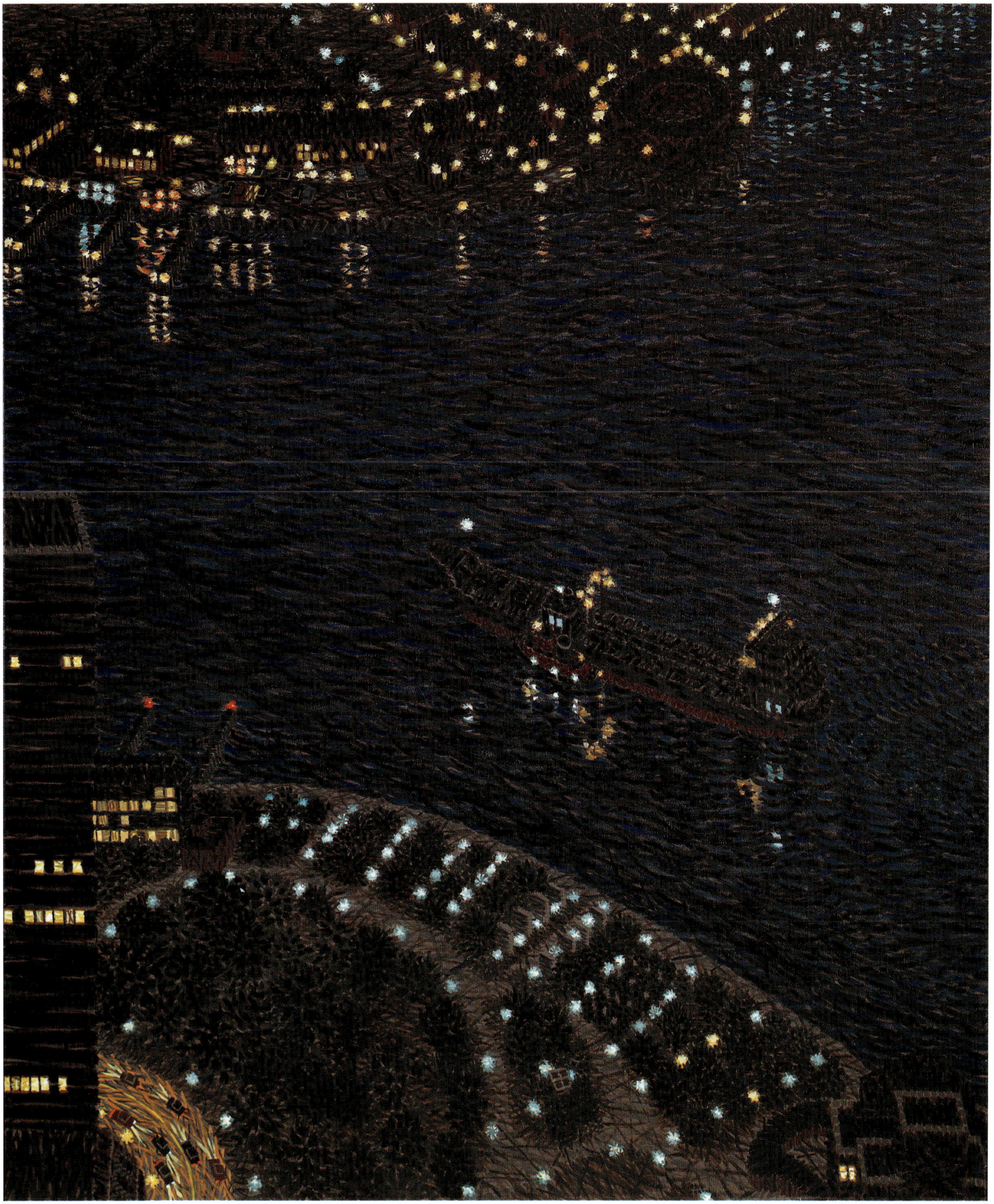

5
Lower Tip of Manhattan II, 1981–82
Oil on canvas
90 x 168 inches
Private collection, Texas
Not in exhibition

6
Park Row Aerial II, 1982
Oil on canvas
90 x 70 inches
Collection of Harry W. and
Mary Margaret Anderson

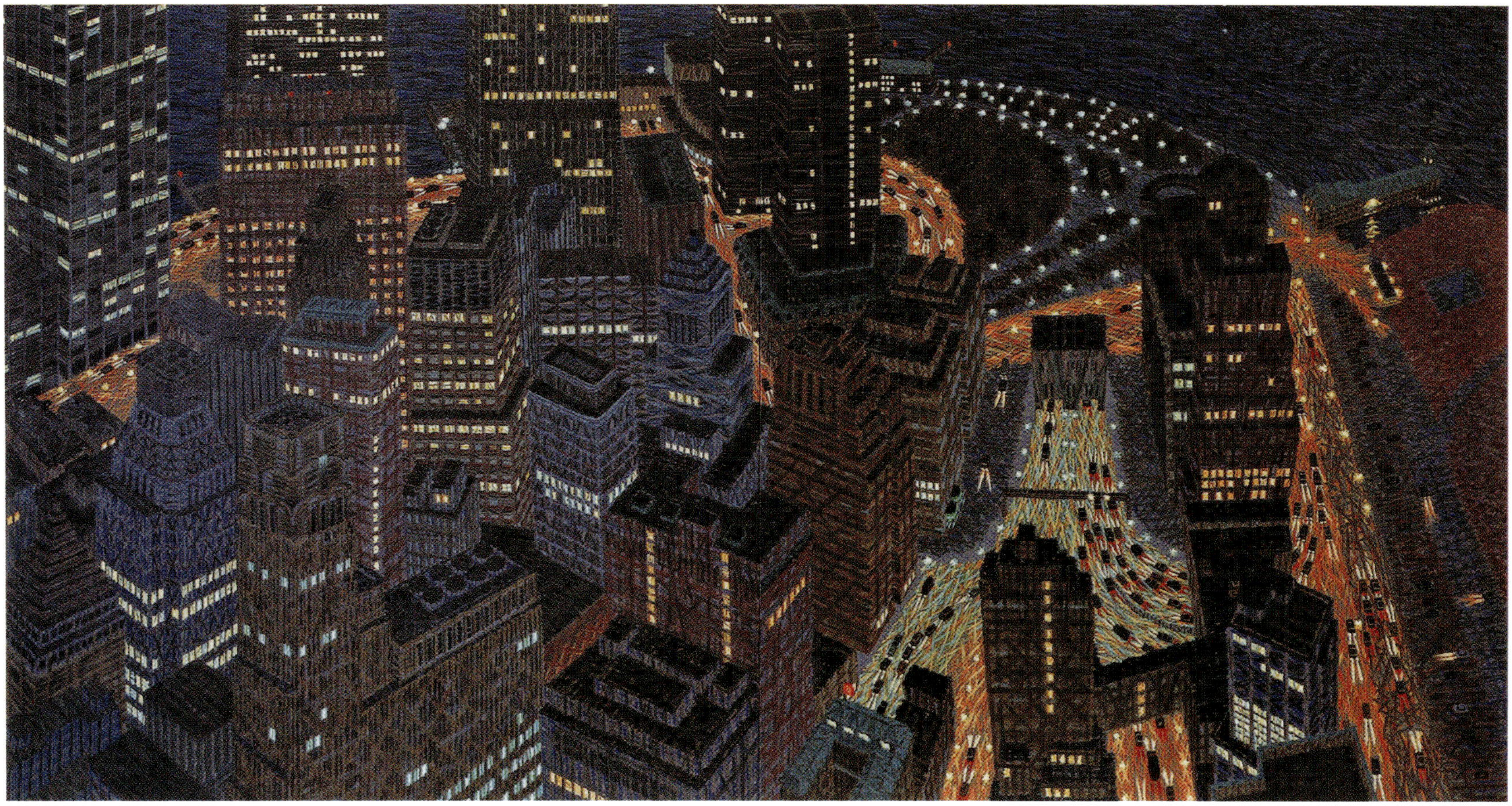

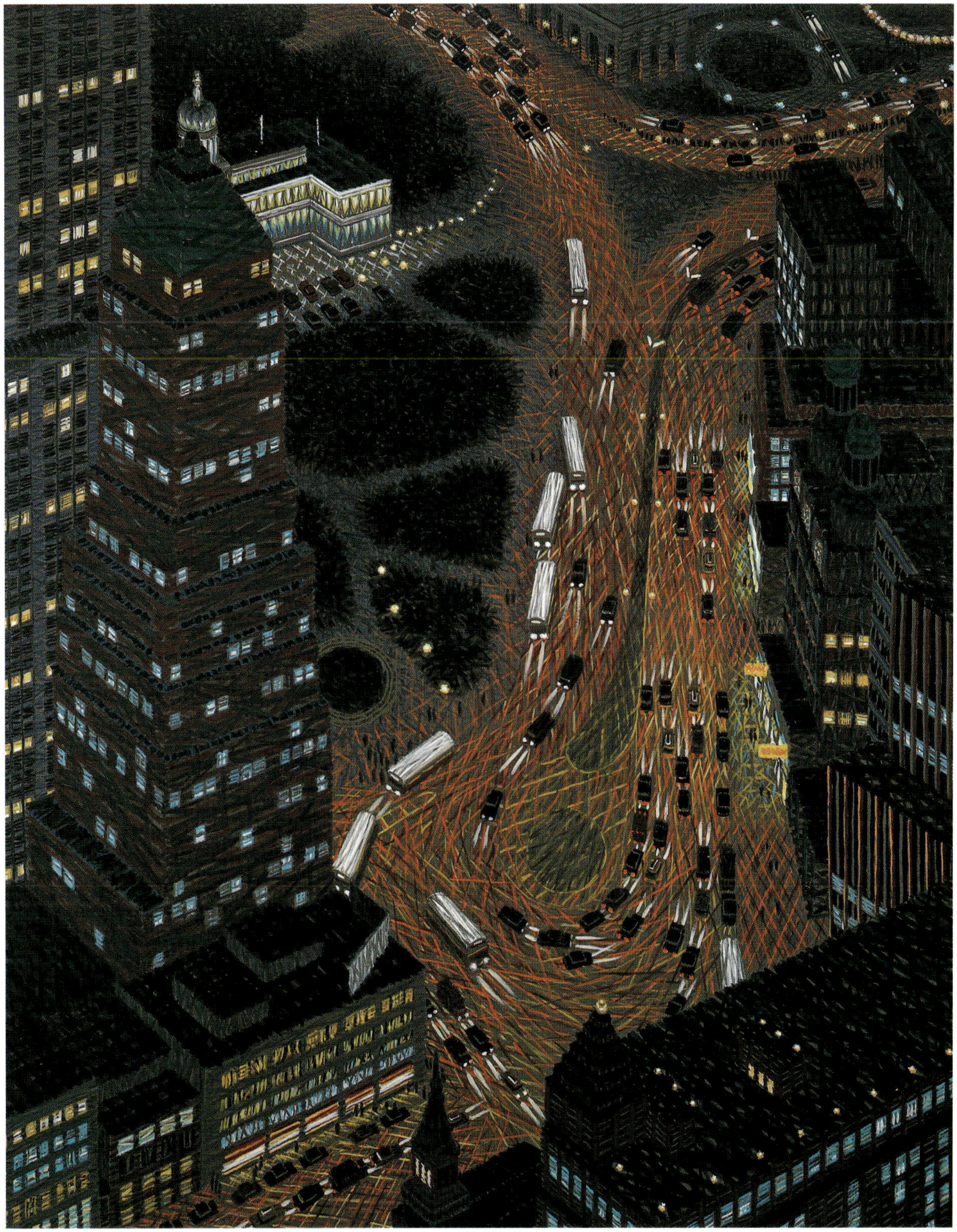

7

East River View with Brooklyn Bridge II, 1983
Oil on canvas
96 x 128 inches
Brooklyn Museum, Purchased with funds given by the Landowne-Bloom Foundation in memory of Louis Landowne and the Dick S. Ramsay Fund, 83.84

8

Fifth Avenue Traffic I, 1984–88
Pastel on paper
15 x 17 ¾ inches
Collection of Sullivan & Cromwell, LLP

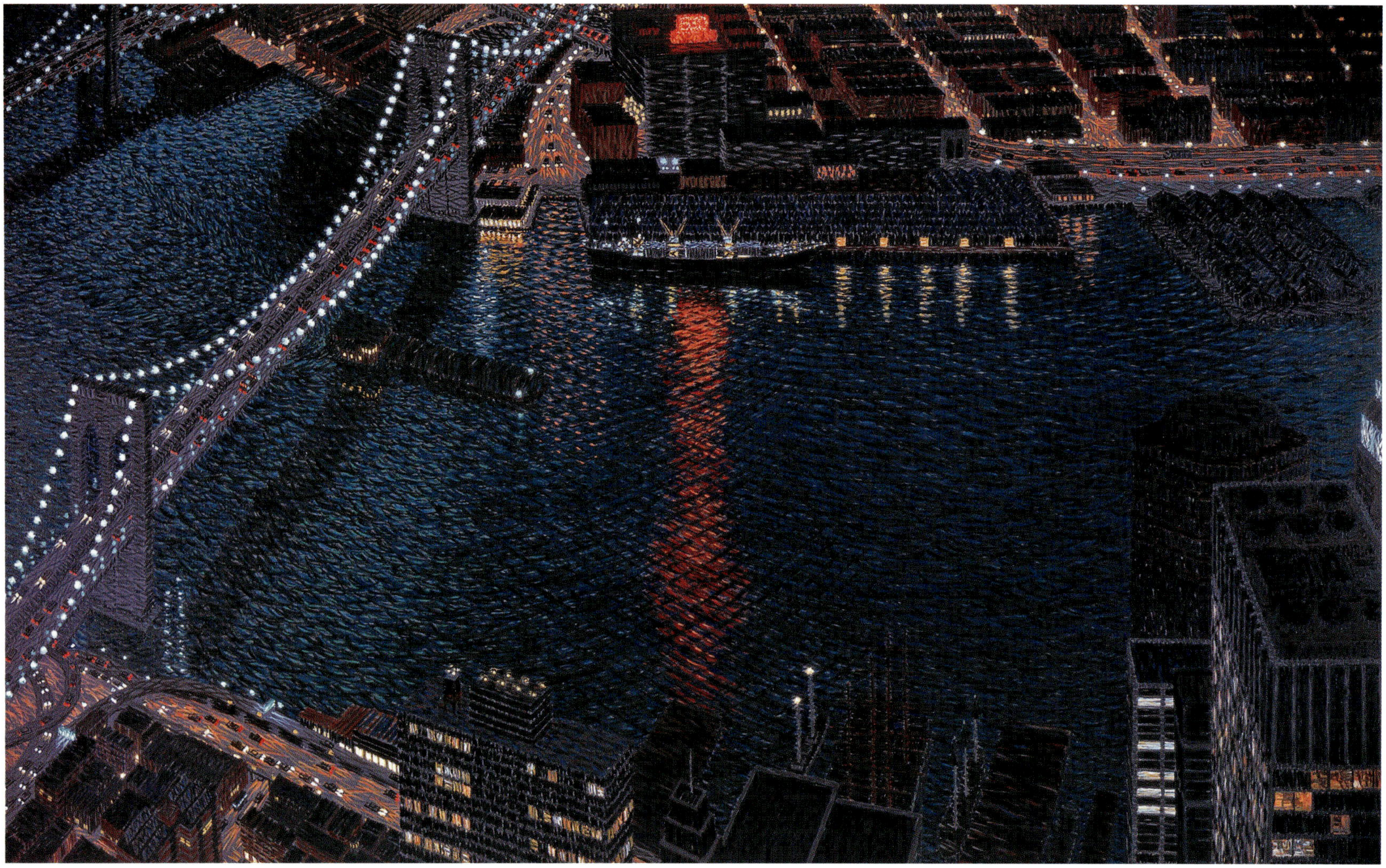

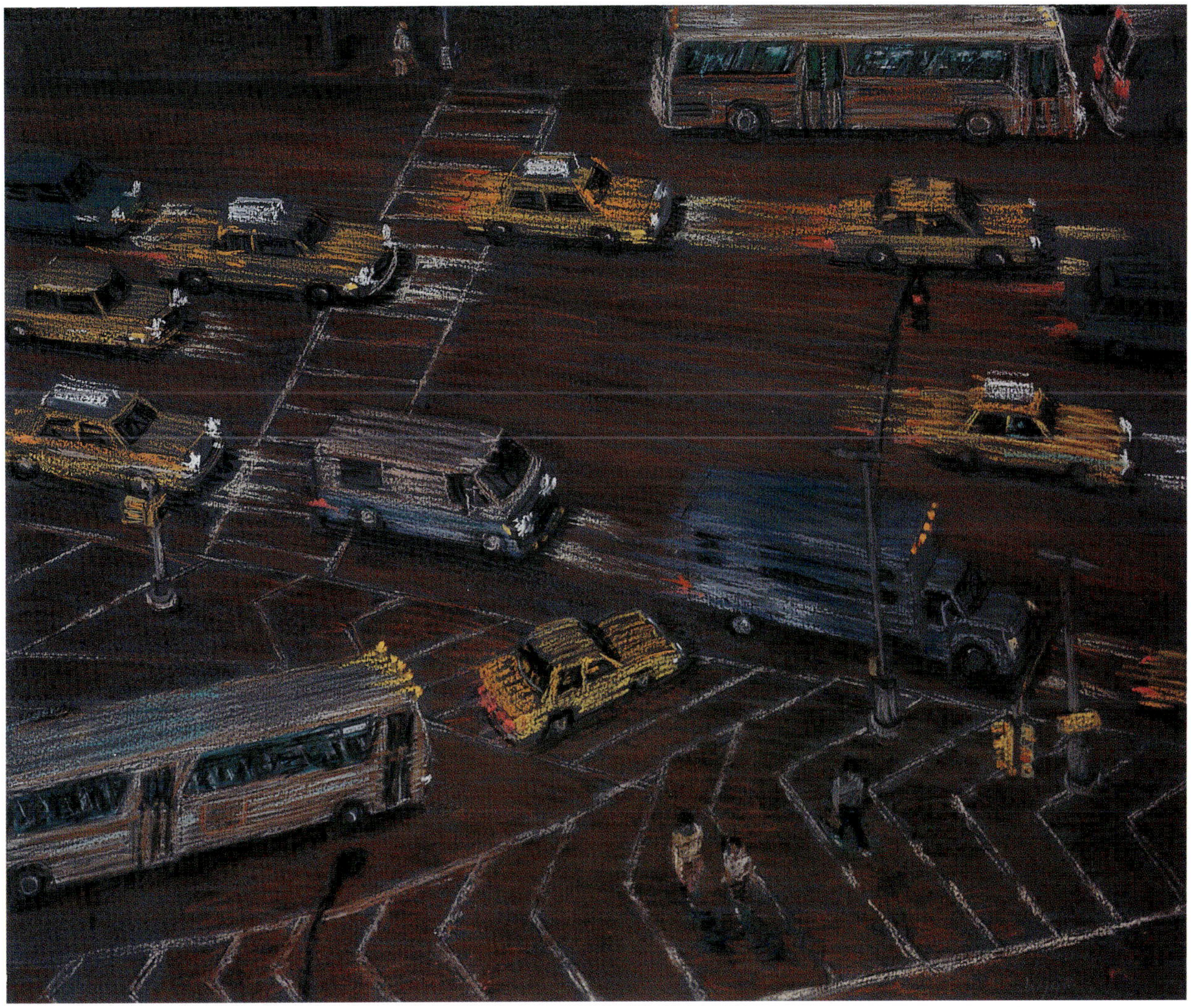

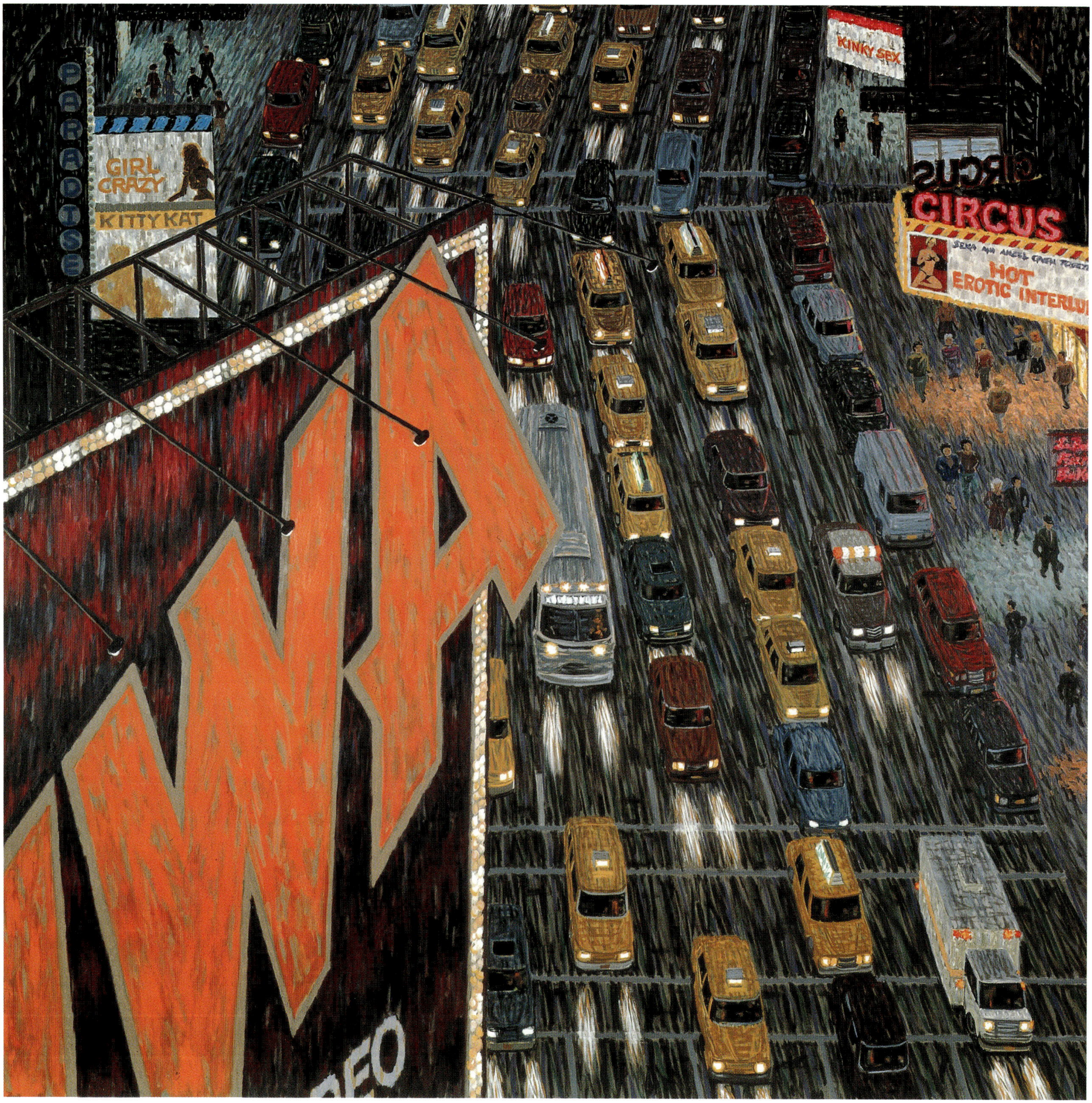

9

Times Square Triptych II, 1986–87
Oil on canvas
Three panels, 80 x 80 inches each
Courtesy of the artist and DC Moore Gallery, New York

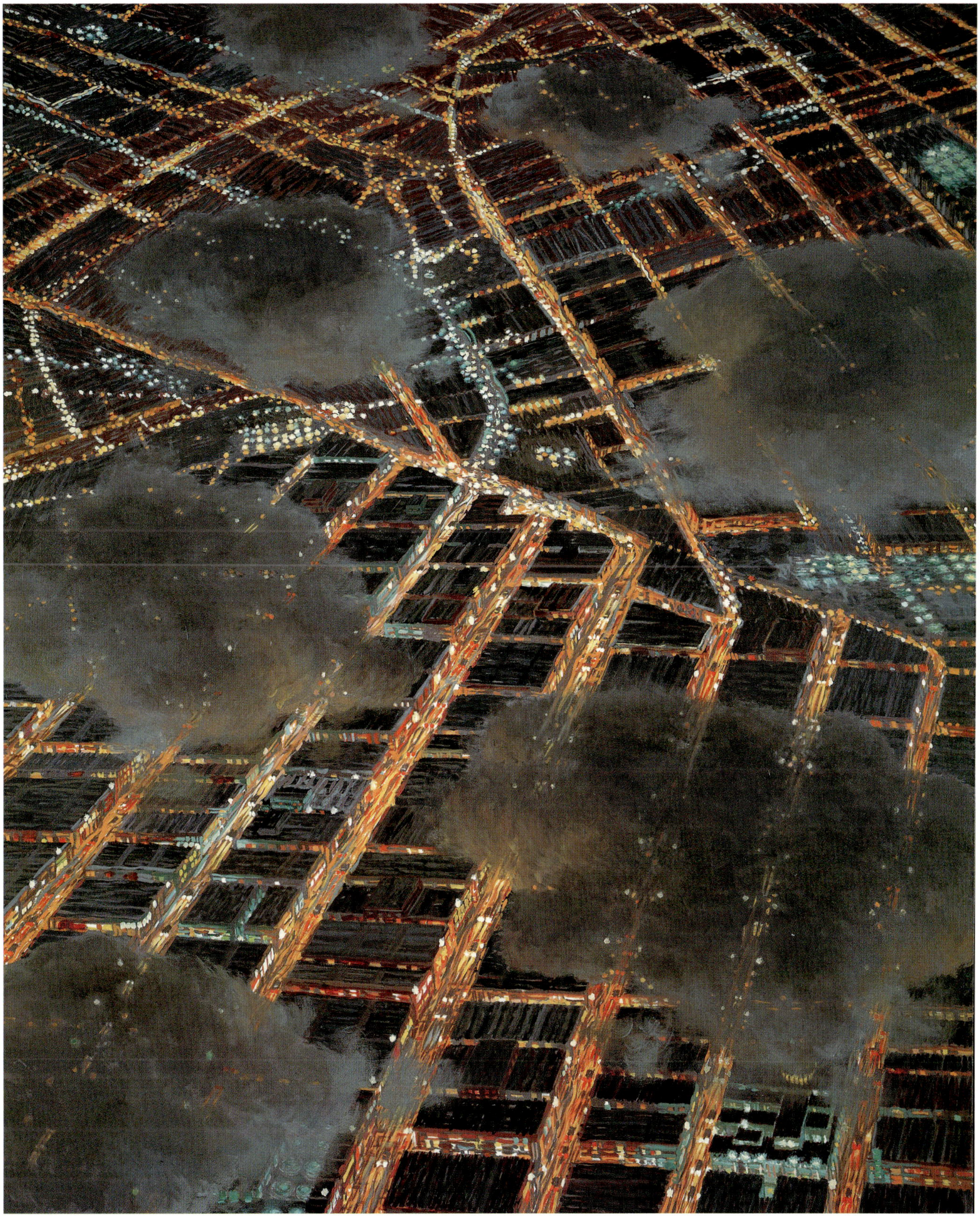

10

Triboro Triptych at Night II, 1987–88
Oil on canvas
Three panels, 78 x 64 inches each
Courtesy of AT&T

→

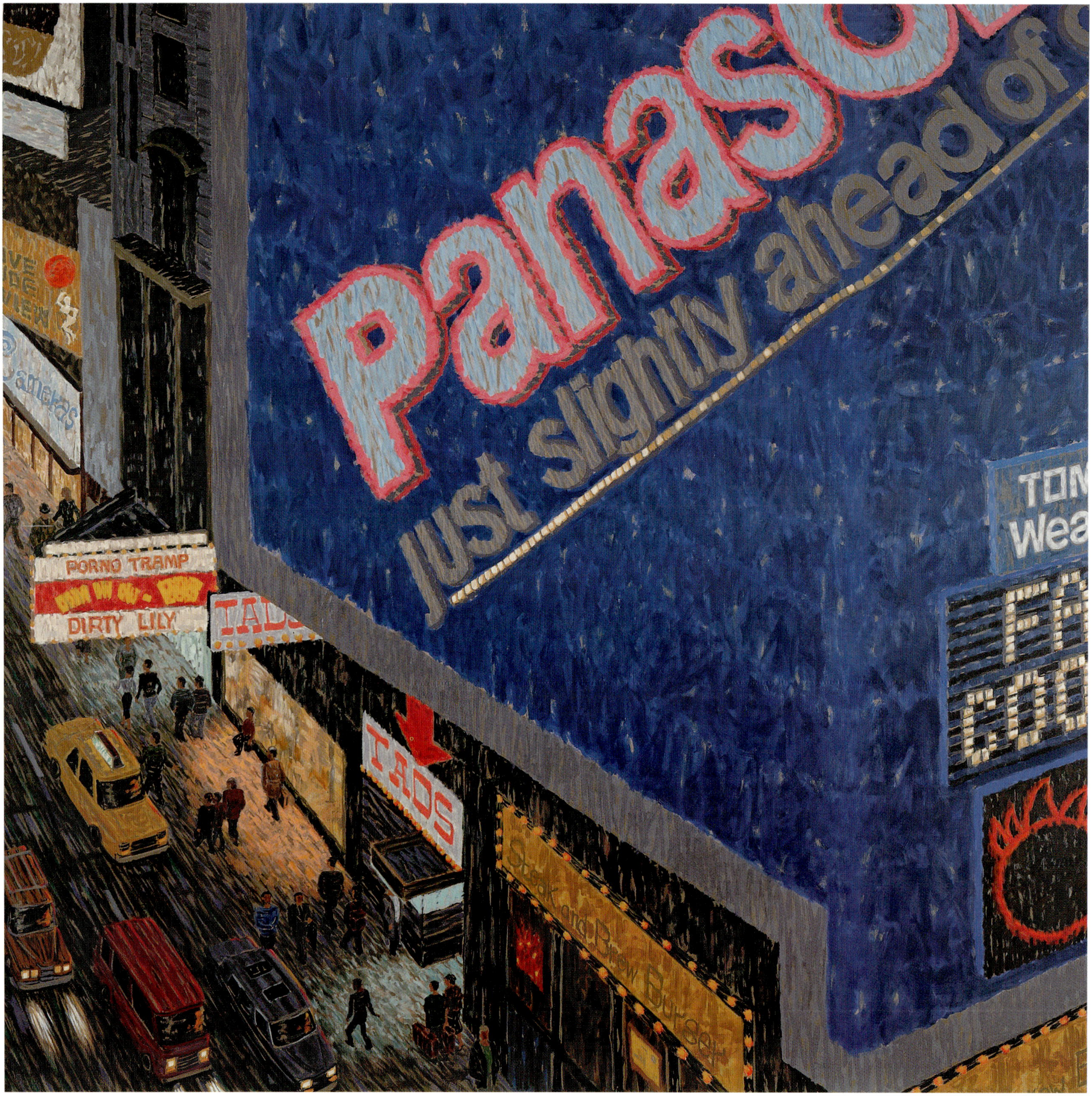
just slightly ahead of
PORNO TRAMP
DIRTY LILY
TADS
TADS
Steak and Brew Burger

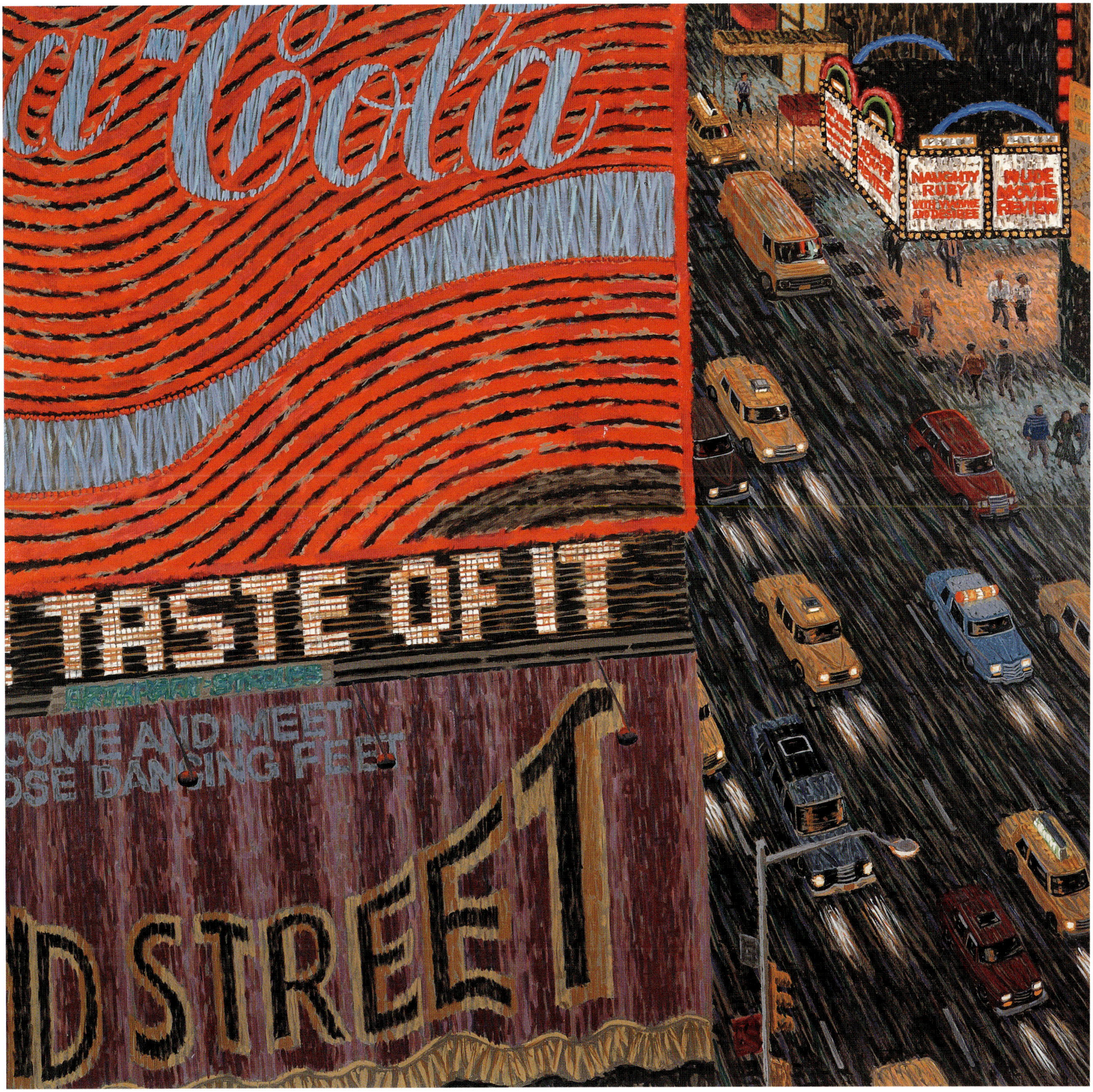
Cola
TASTE OF IT
COME AND MEET
OSE DANCING FEET
D STREET
NAUGHTY RUBY
NUDE MOVIE REVIEW

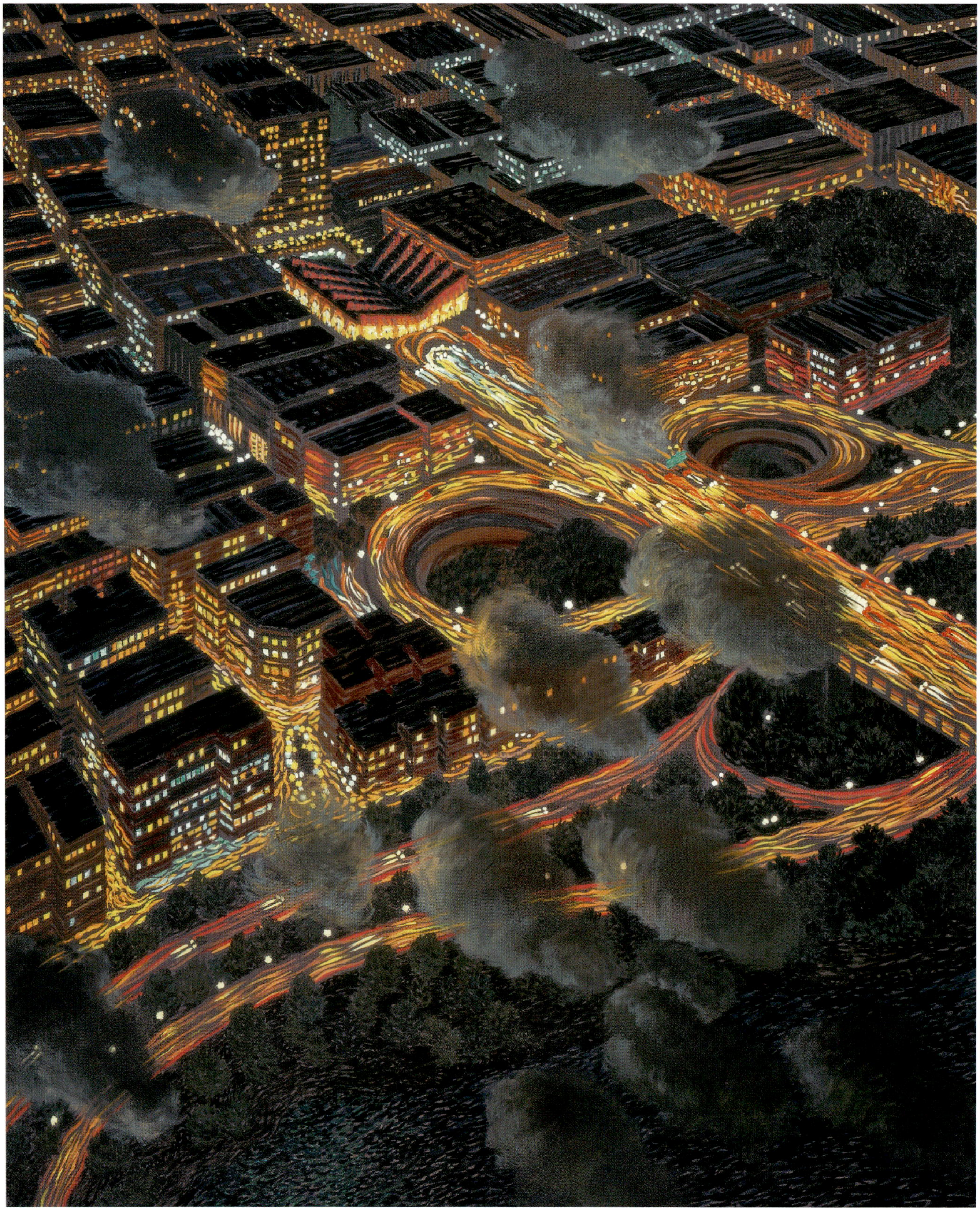

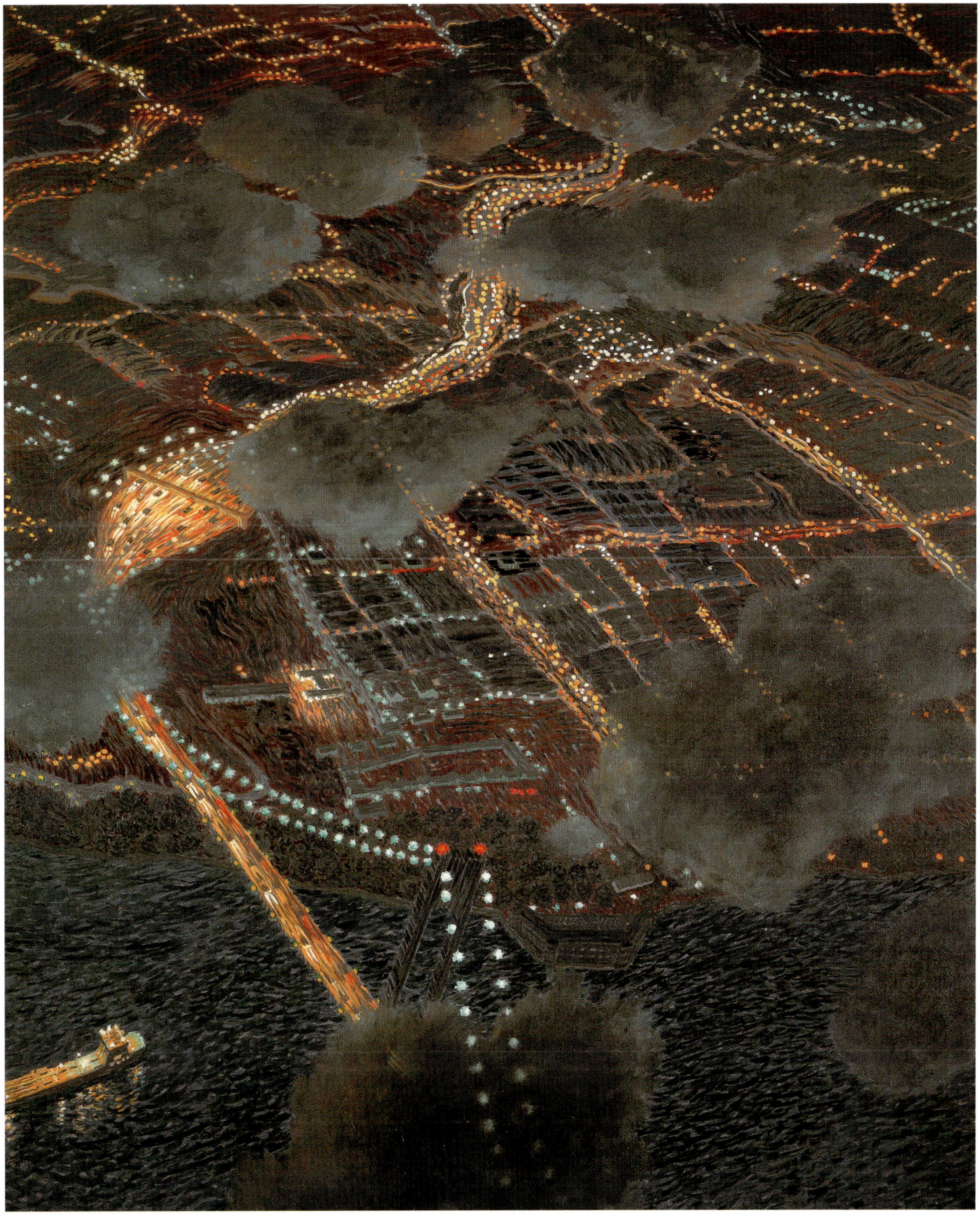

11
George Washington Bridge at Night I, 1988
Pastel on paper
13 5/8 x 15 7/8 inches
Private collection

12
George Washington Bridge at Night II, 1988
Oil on canvas
69 13/16 x 79 3/8 inches
Private collection

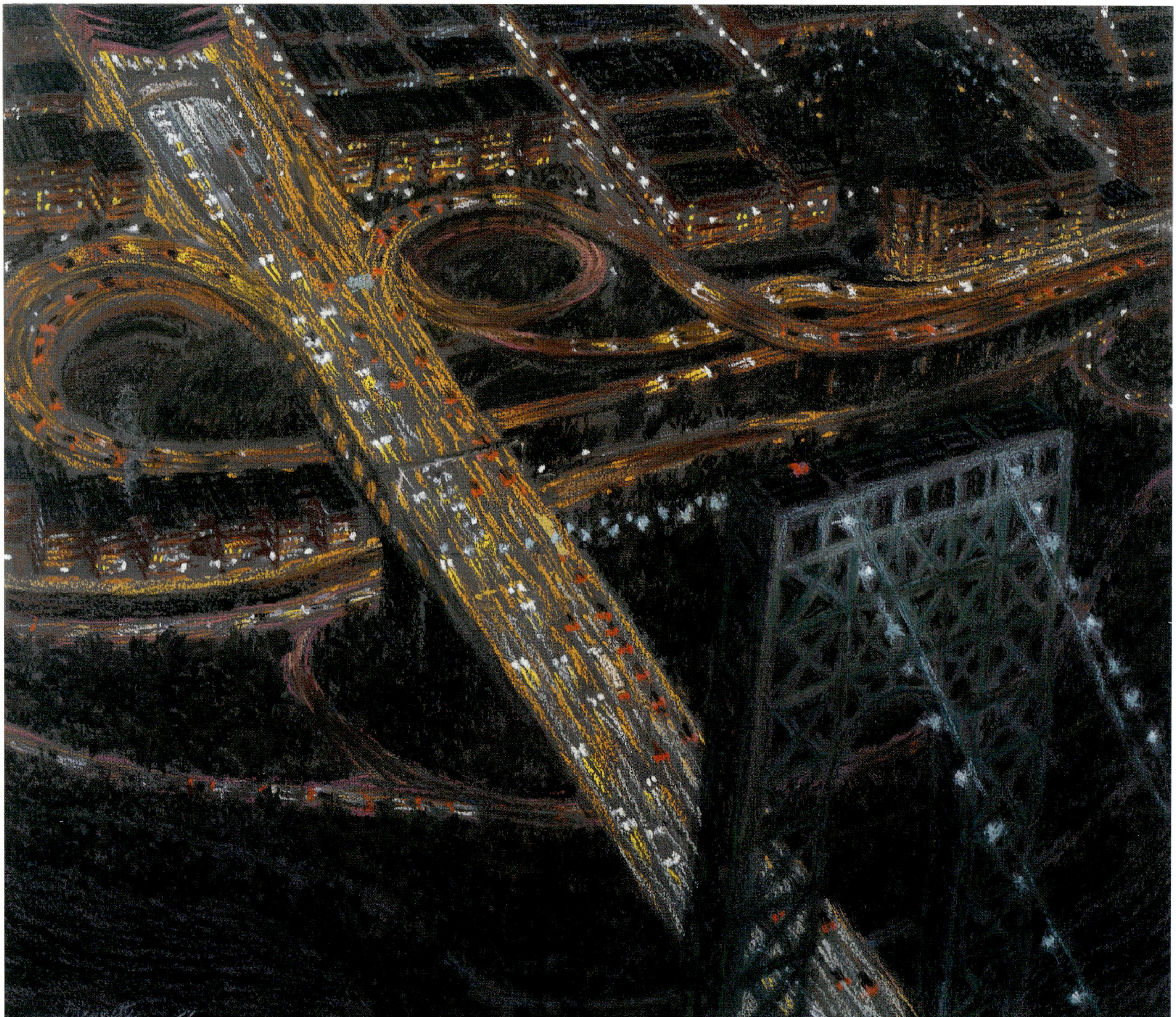

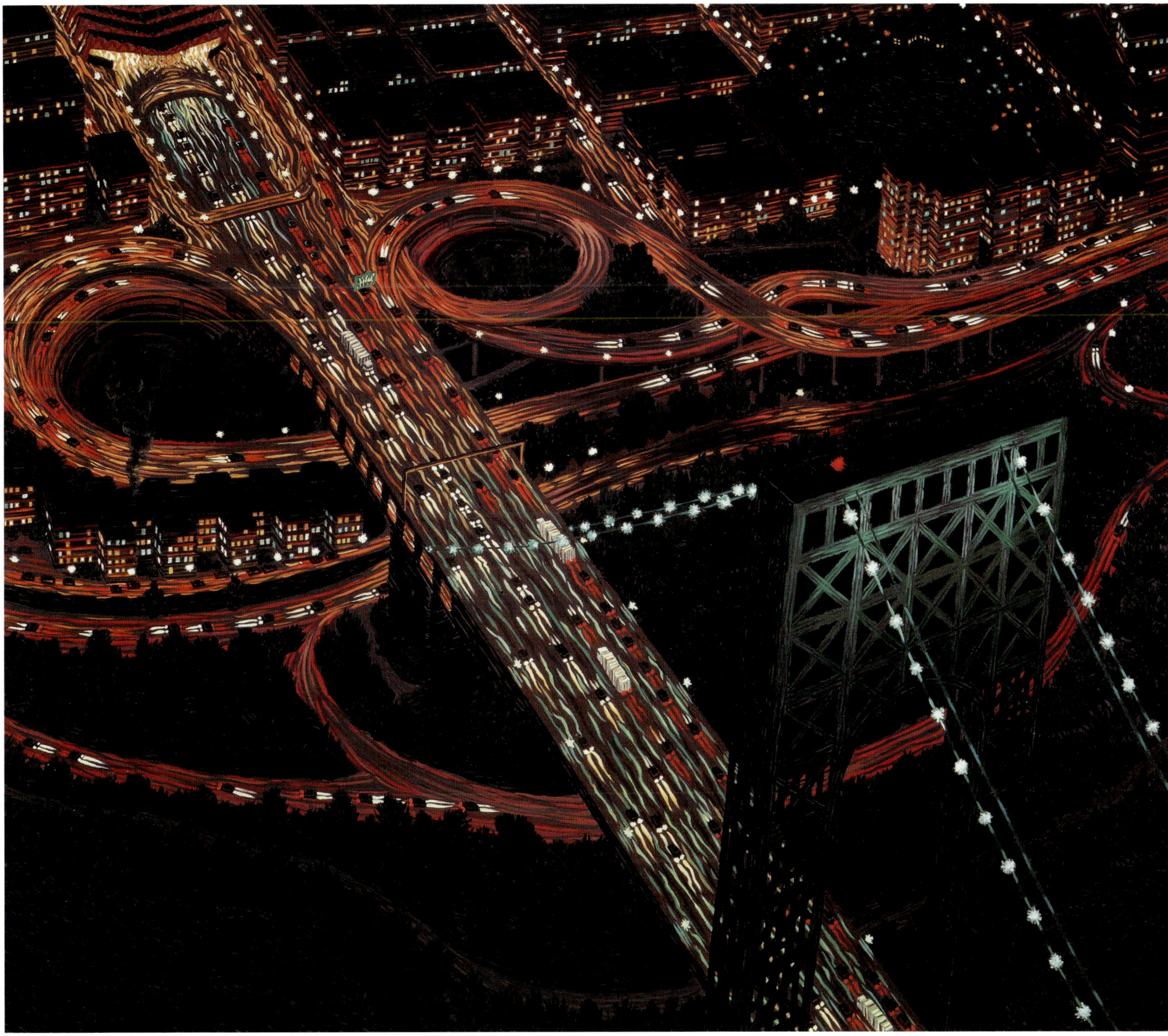

13
Manhattan Nocturne:
Late Evening Traffic II, 1988
Oil on canvas
87 ⅝ x 69 15/16 inches
Private collection, Texas
Not in exhibition

14
Herald Square Composite II, 1993
Oil on canvas
76 ½ x 65 ¼ inches
Courtesy of the artist and
DC Moore Gallery, New York

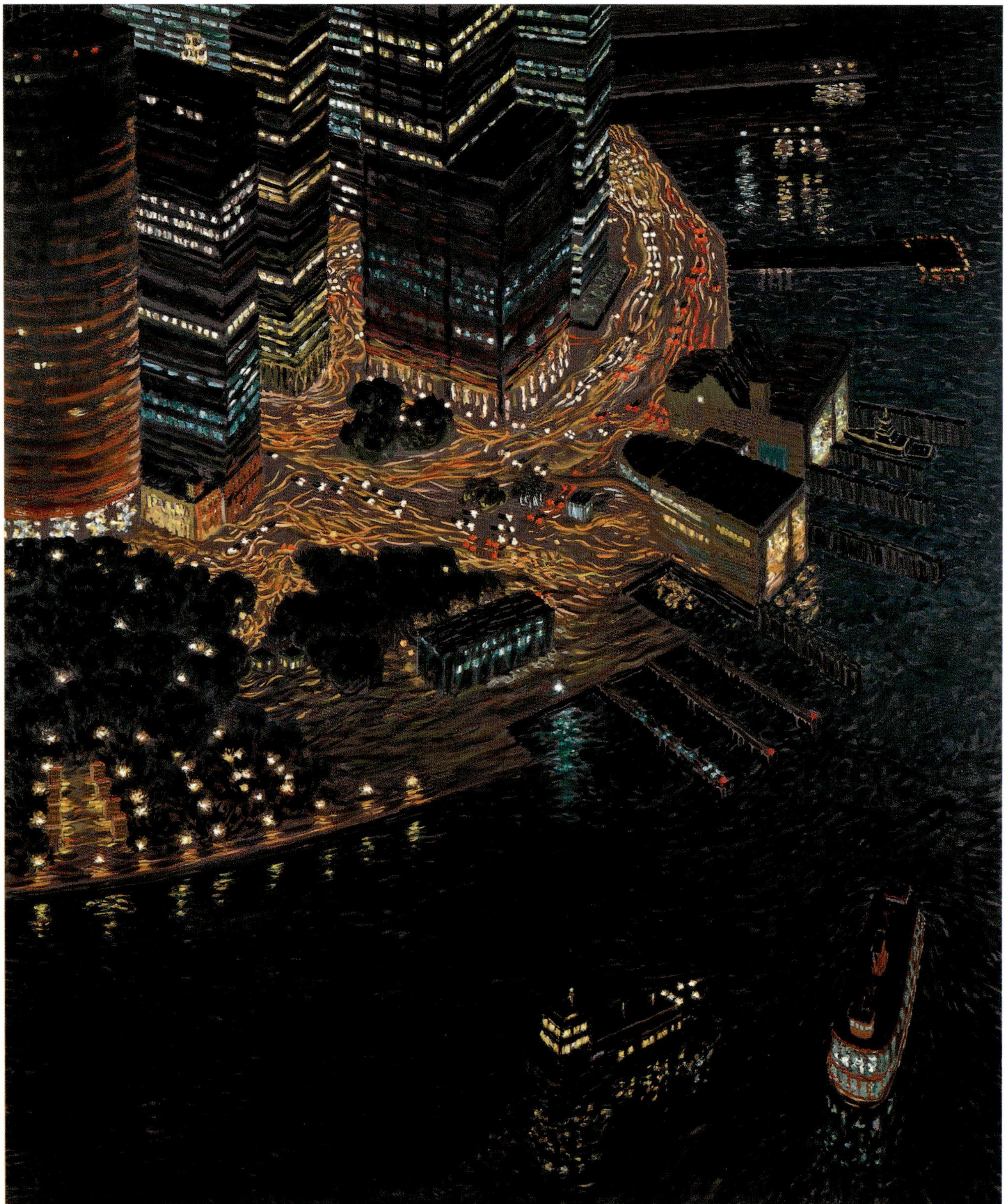

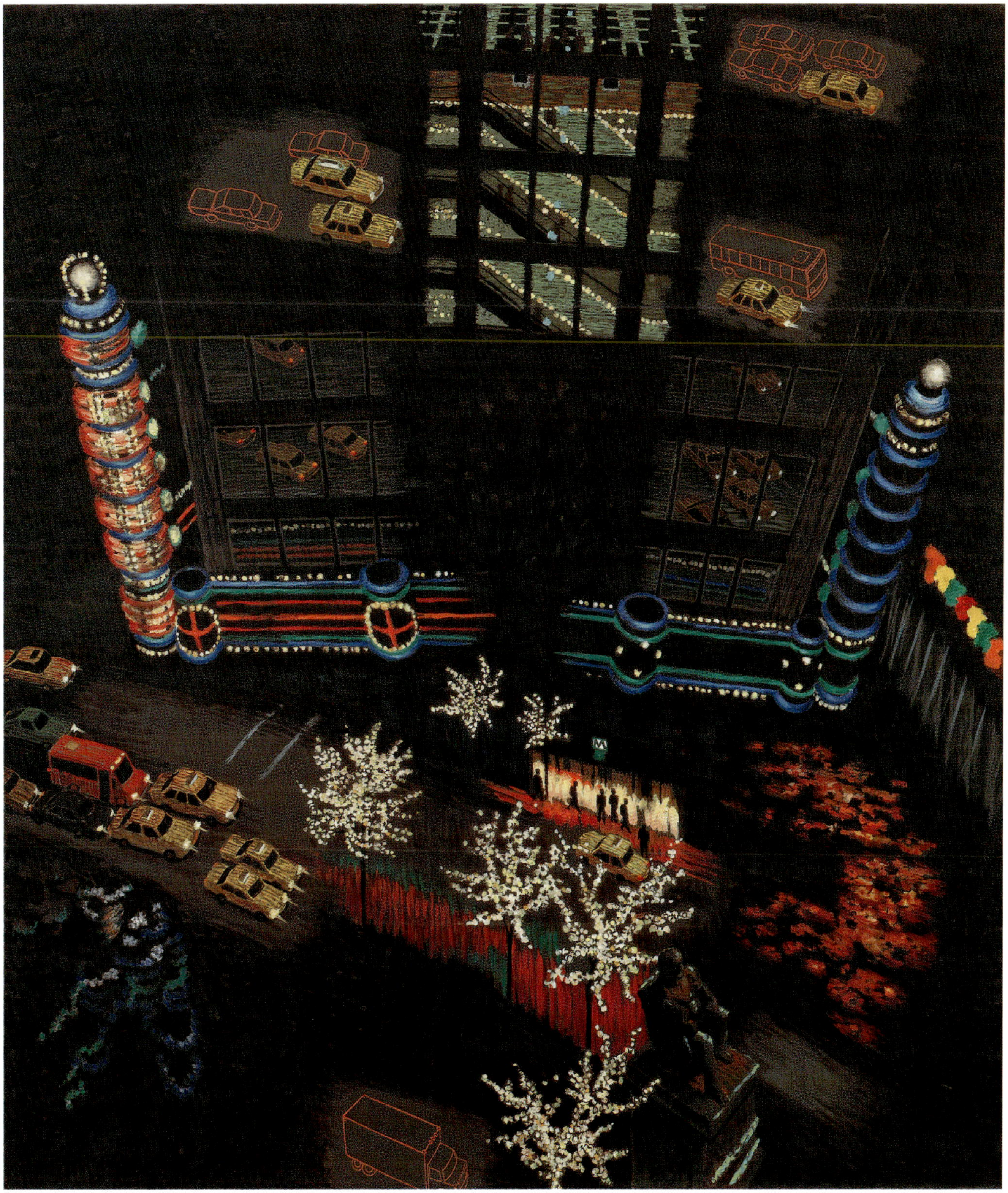

15
Night Wing: Metropolitan Area Composite II, 1993
Oil on canvas
80 5/8 x 56 3/4 inches
North Carolina Museum of Art, Raleigh, Purchased with funds from the North Carolina State Art Society (Robert F. Phifer Bequest)
Not in exhibition

16
Night Jet Wing, Pink Clouds I, 1995
Pastel on paper
17 1/8 x 14 inches
From the collection of Michael and Susan Rich

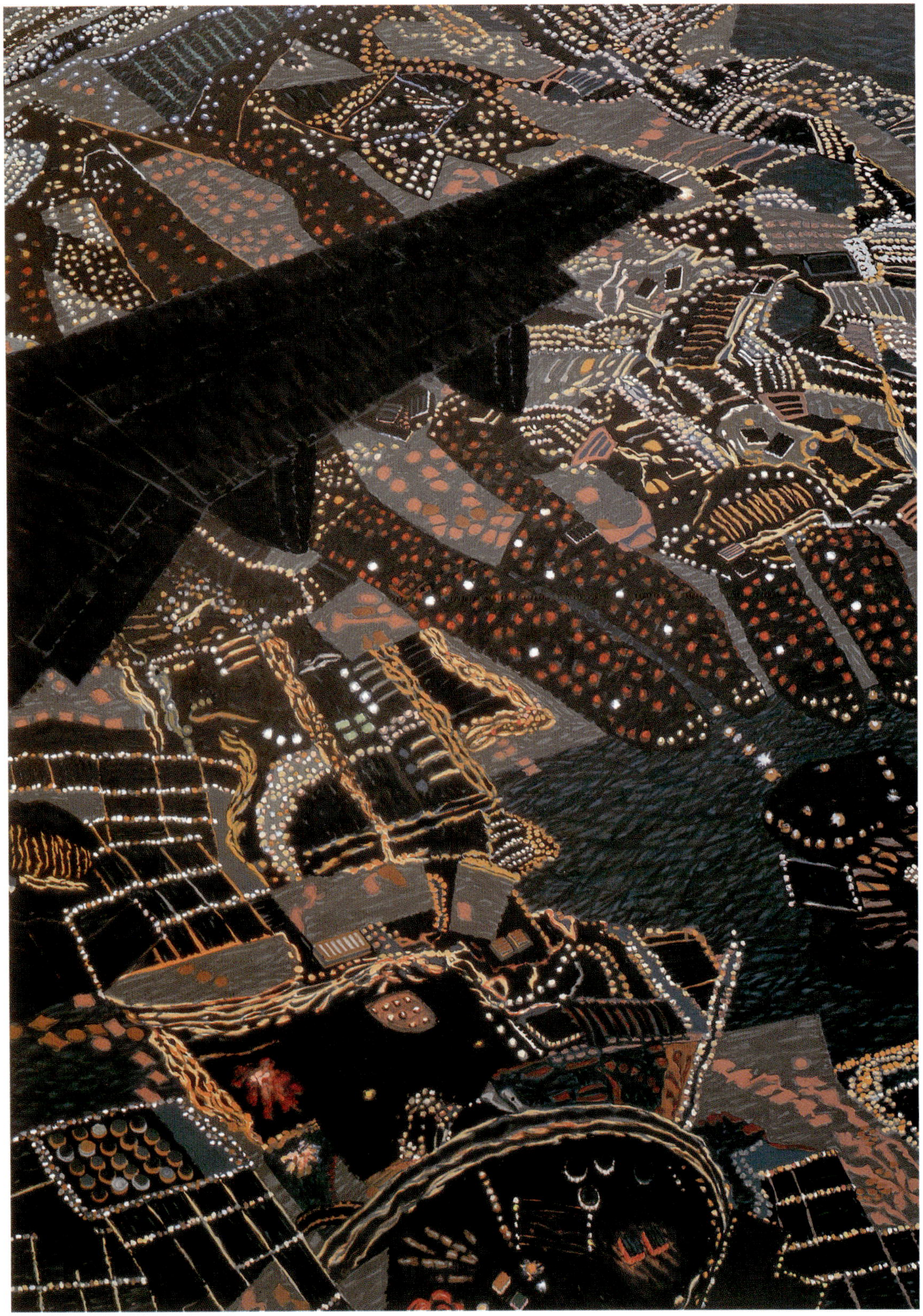

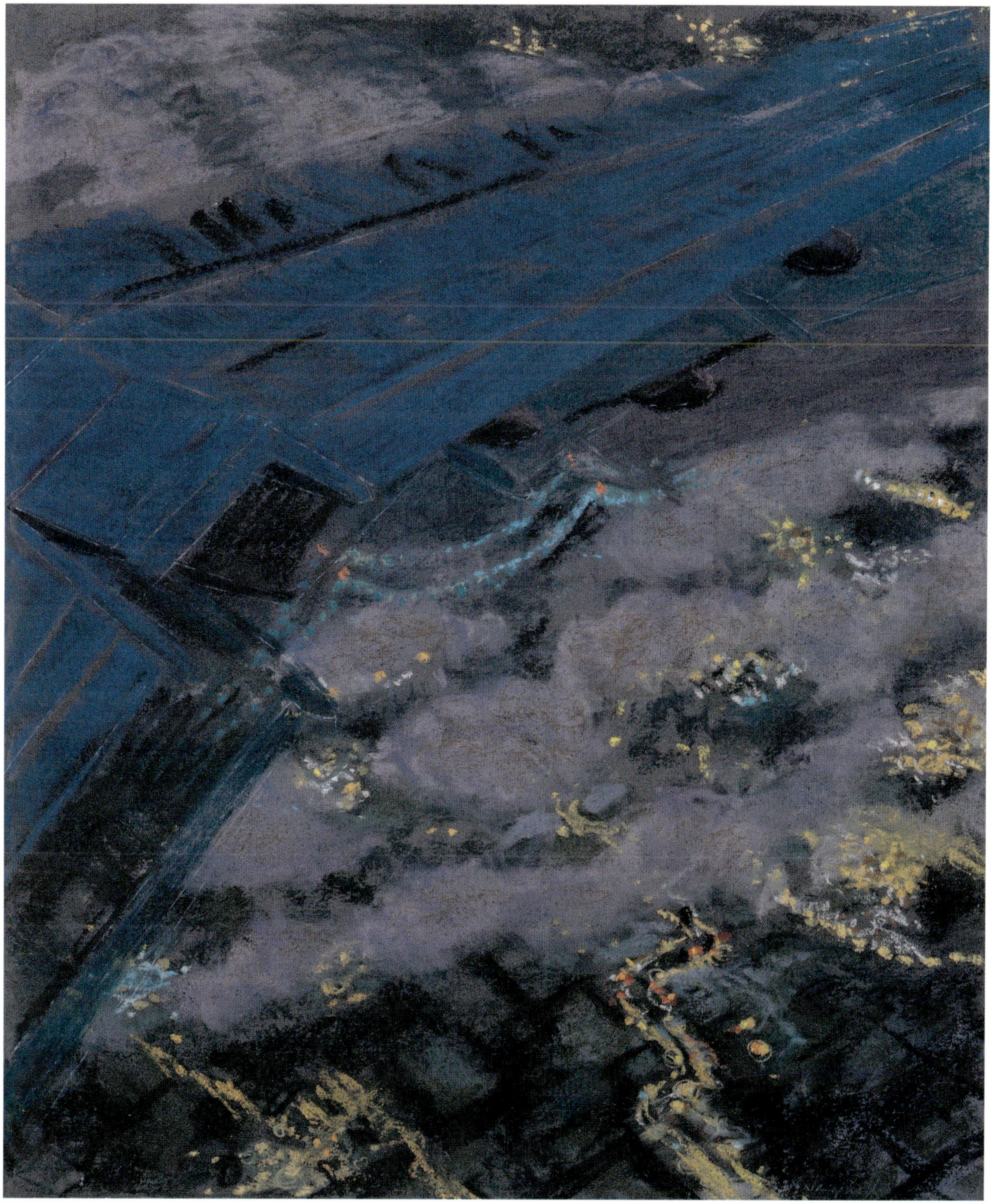

17
Ola II, 1994
Oil on canvas,
77 x 59 inches
Collection of Robb and
Mary Ann Peglar

18
Chelsea Composite II, 1995
Oil on canvas
80 x 59 inches
The Samuel P. Harn Museum of Art,
University of Florida, Museum purchase,
gift of Mary Ann P. Cofrin

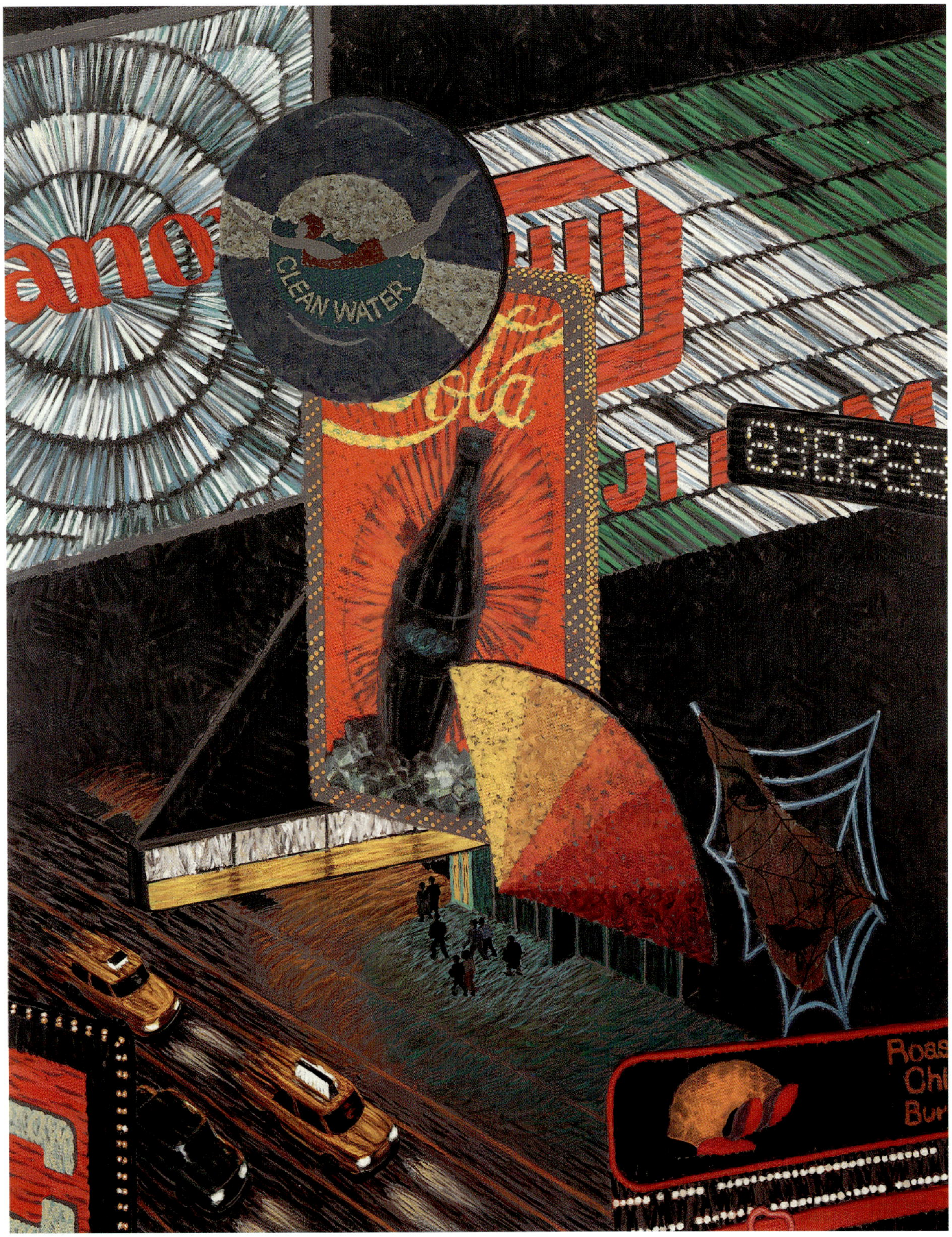

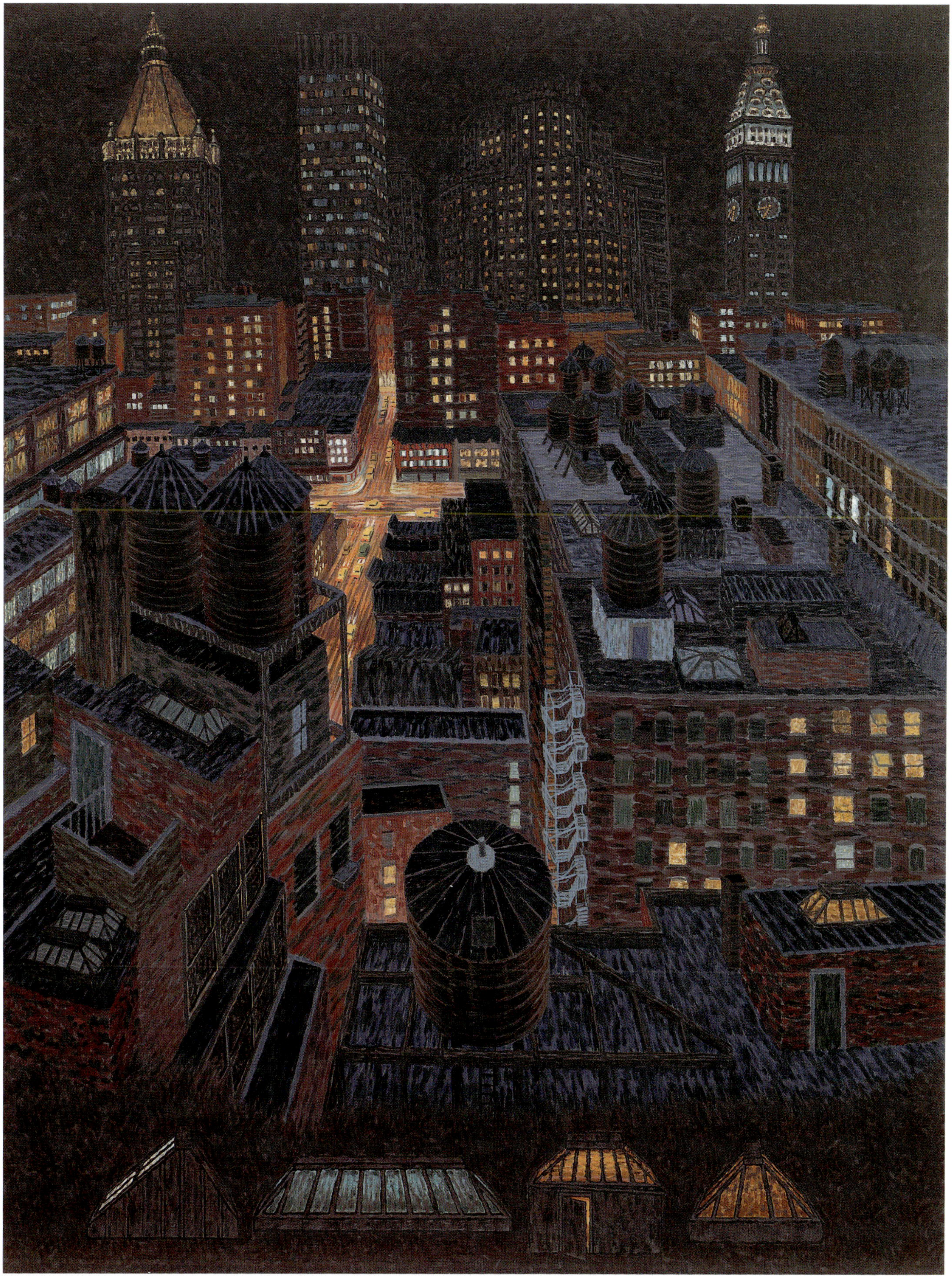

19

South and West Views from World Trade Center II,

1996

Oil on canvas

Two panels, 53 x 72 inches each

Private collection

Not in exhibition

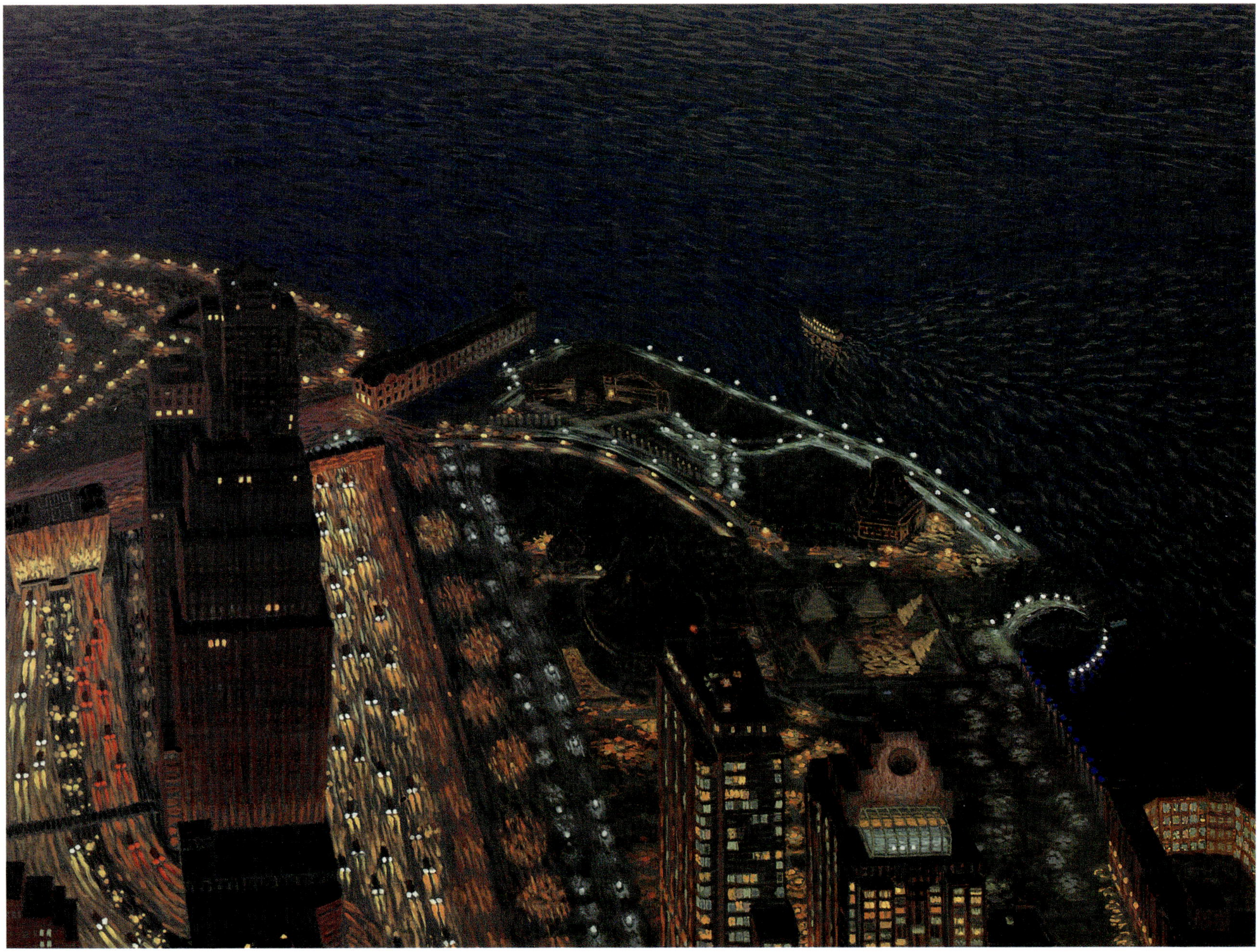

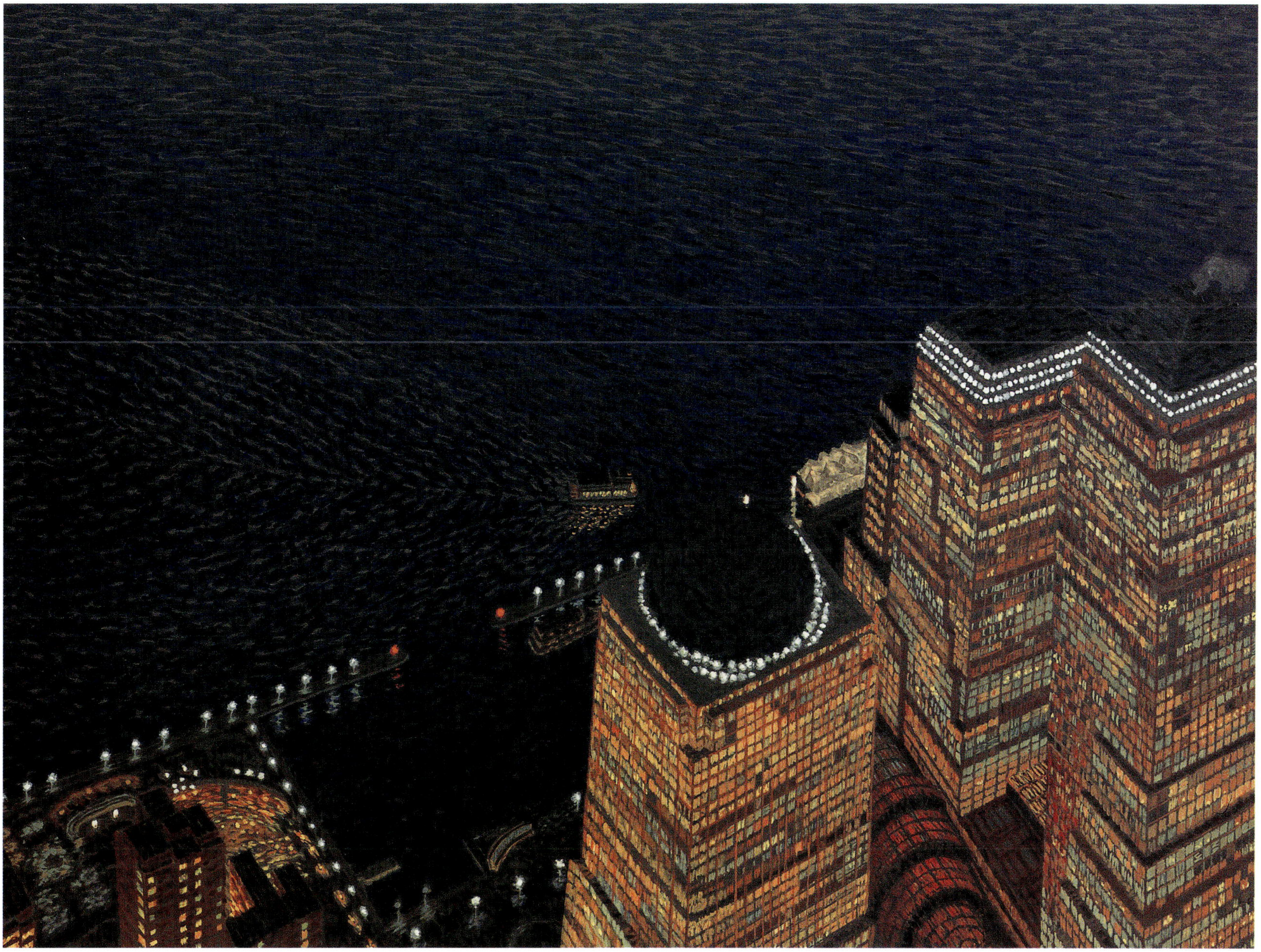

20

Chrysler Building Composite at Dusk II, 1997

Oil on linen

75 ½ x 86 inches

Collection of Rose and Morton Landowne, New York, New York

21

From World Trade Center, Mixed Heights II, 1998

Oil on canvas

79 ¾ x 59 ⅜ inches

The New-York Historical Society, museum purchase, 2001.297

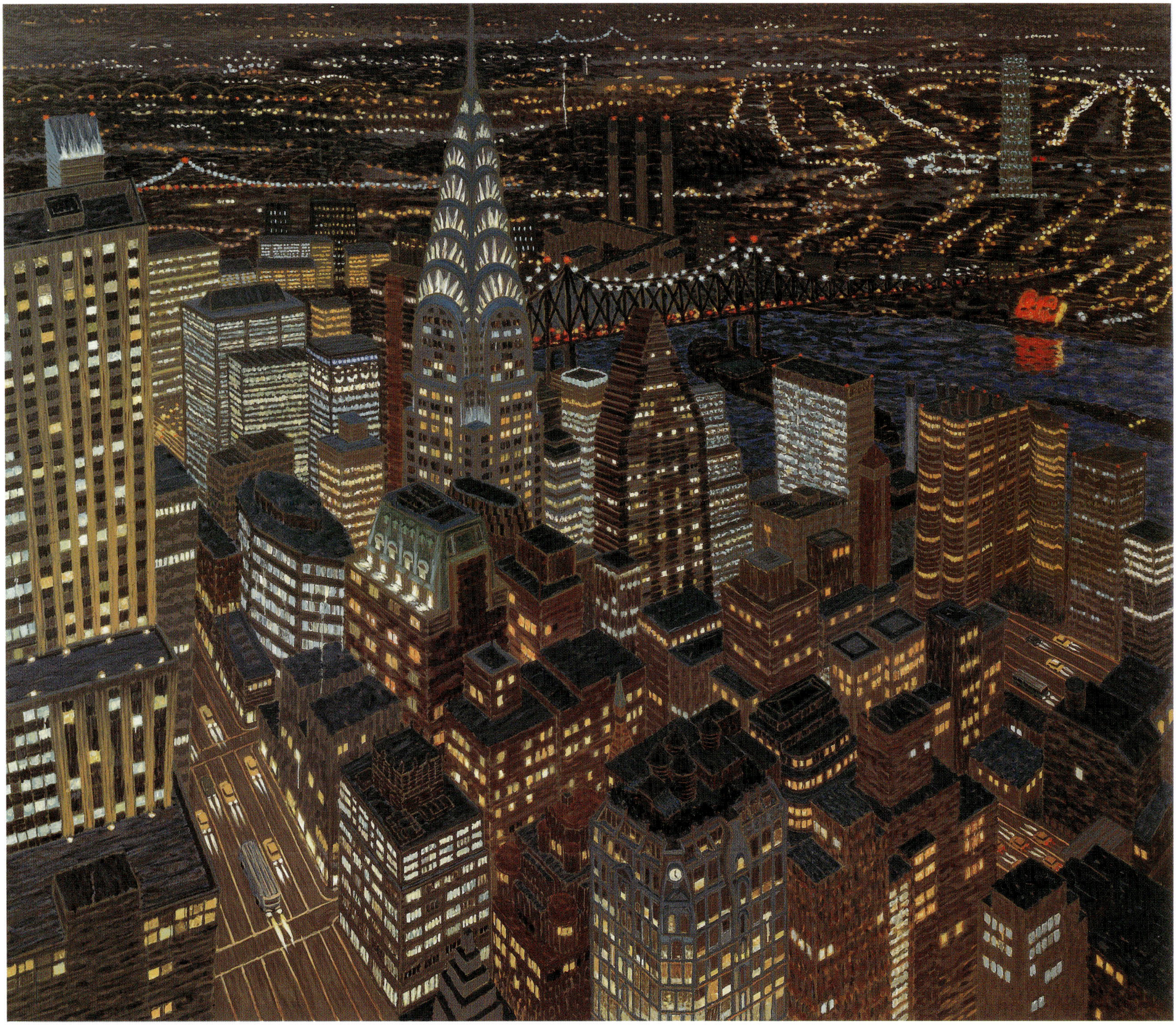

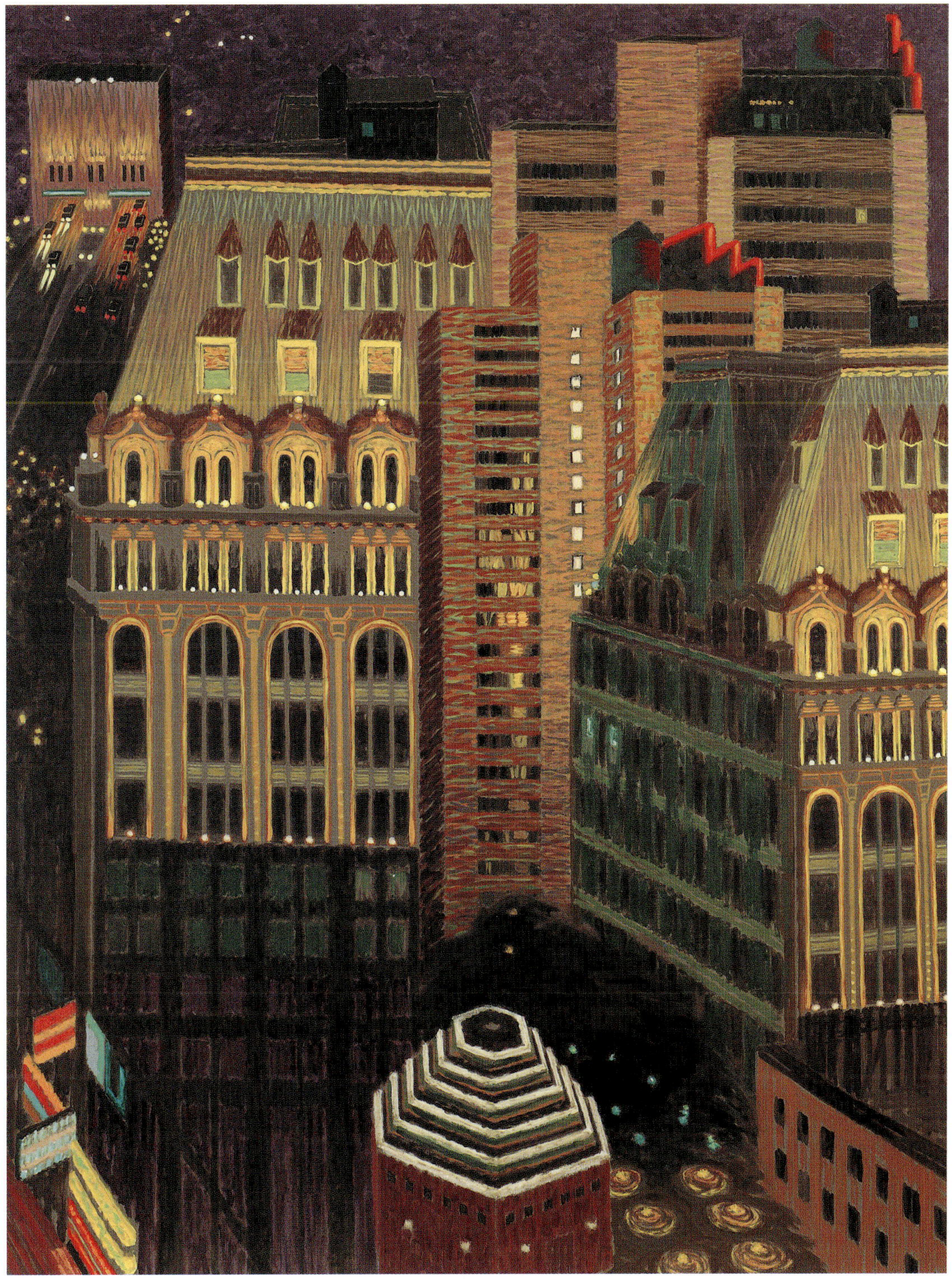

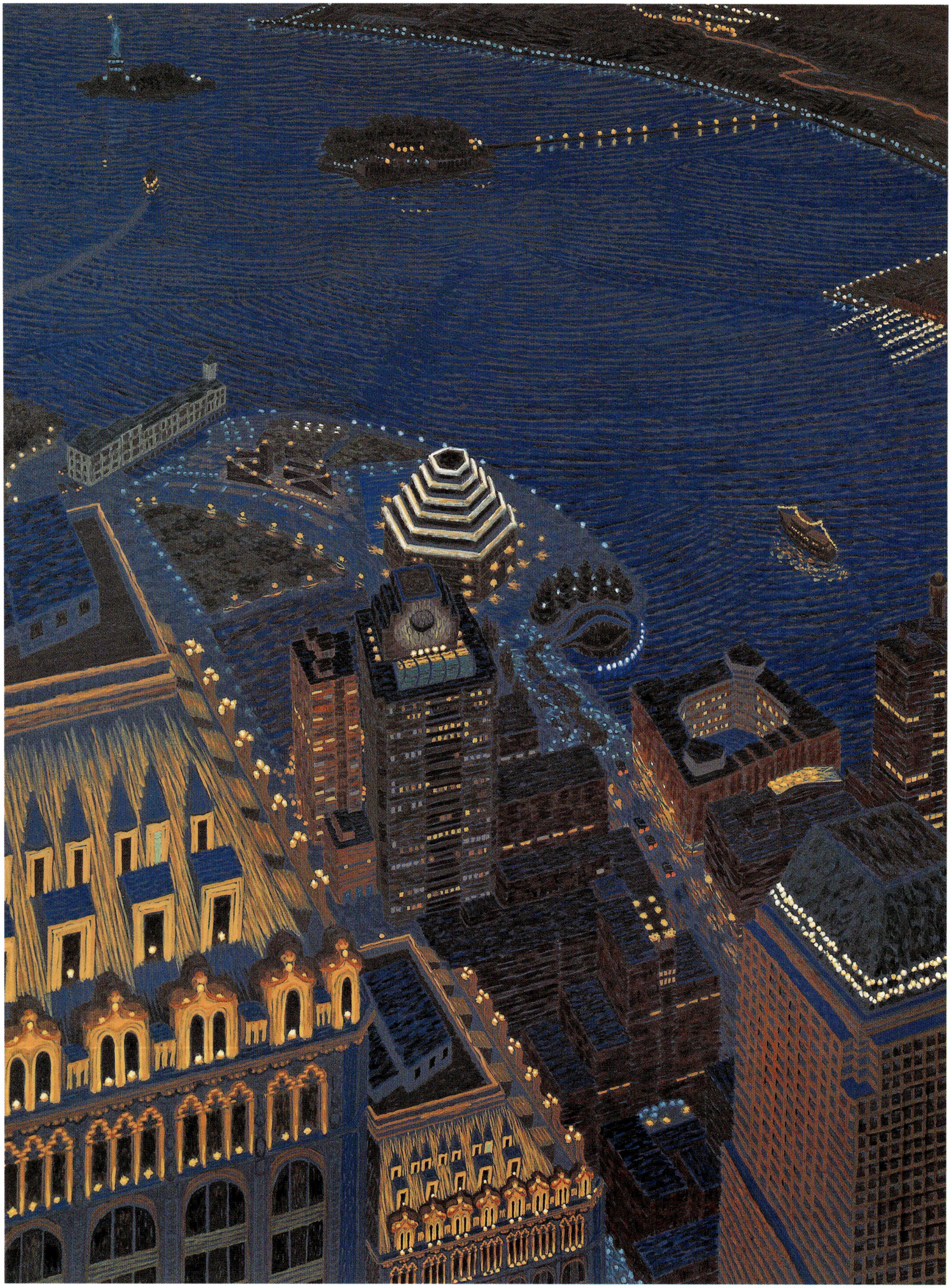

22
Mixed Heights and Harbor from World Trade Center II, 1998
Oil on canvas,
79 ¼ x 58 ⅜ inches
Collection of Thomas and Jean Pederson

23
From World Trade Center, Mixed Heights and Harbor I, 1998
Pastel on paper
30 x 22 inches
Mr. and Mrs. Judson P. Reis

24
New York Harbor View with Crown of Statue of Liberty I, 2001
Pastel on paper
18 ⅛ x 15 inches
Collection of Helen and Paul Anbinder, New York

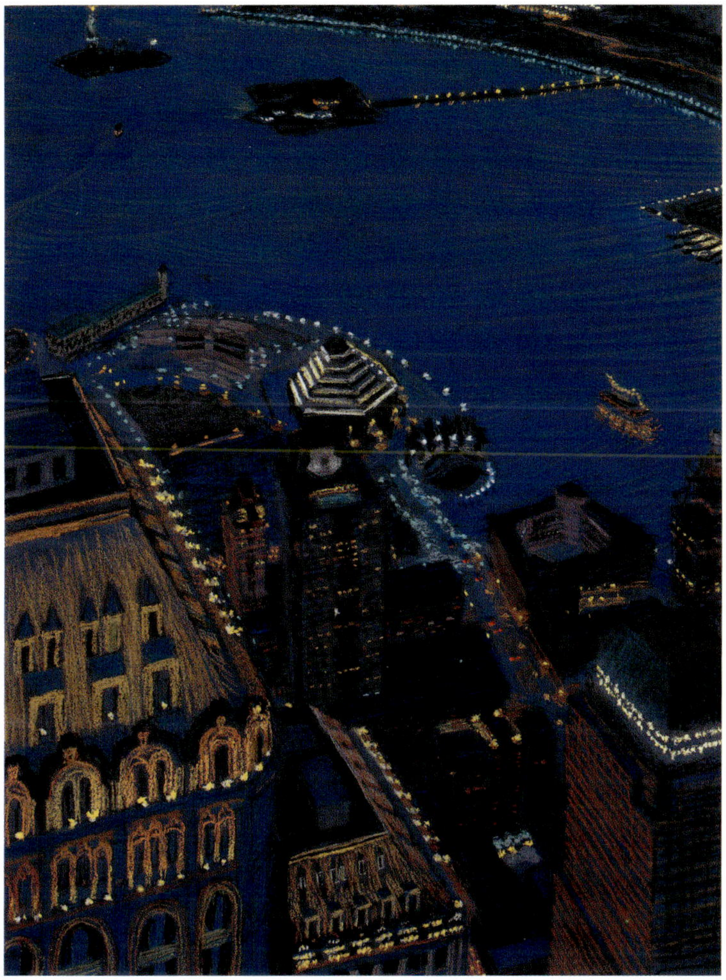

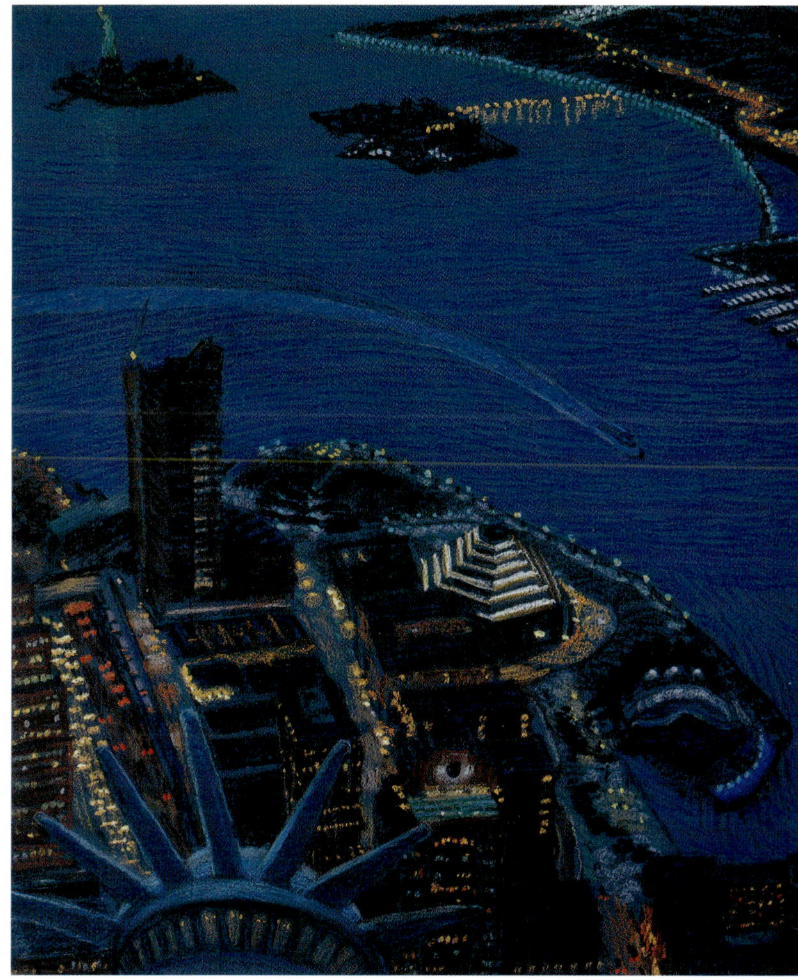

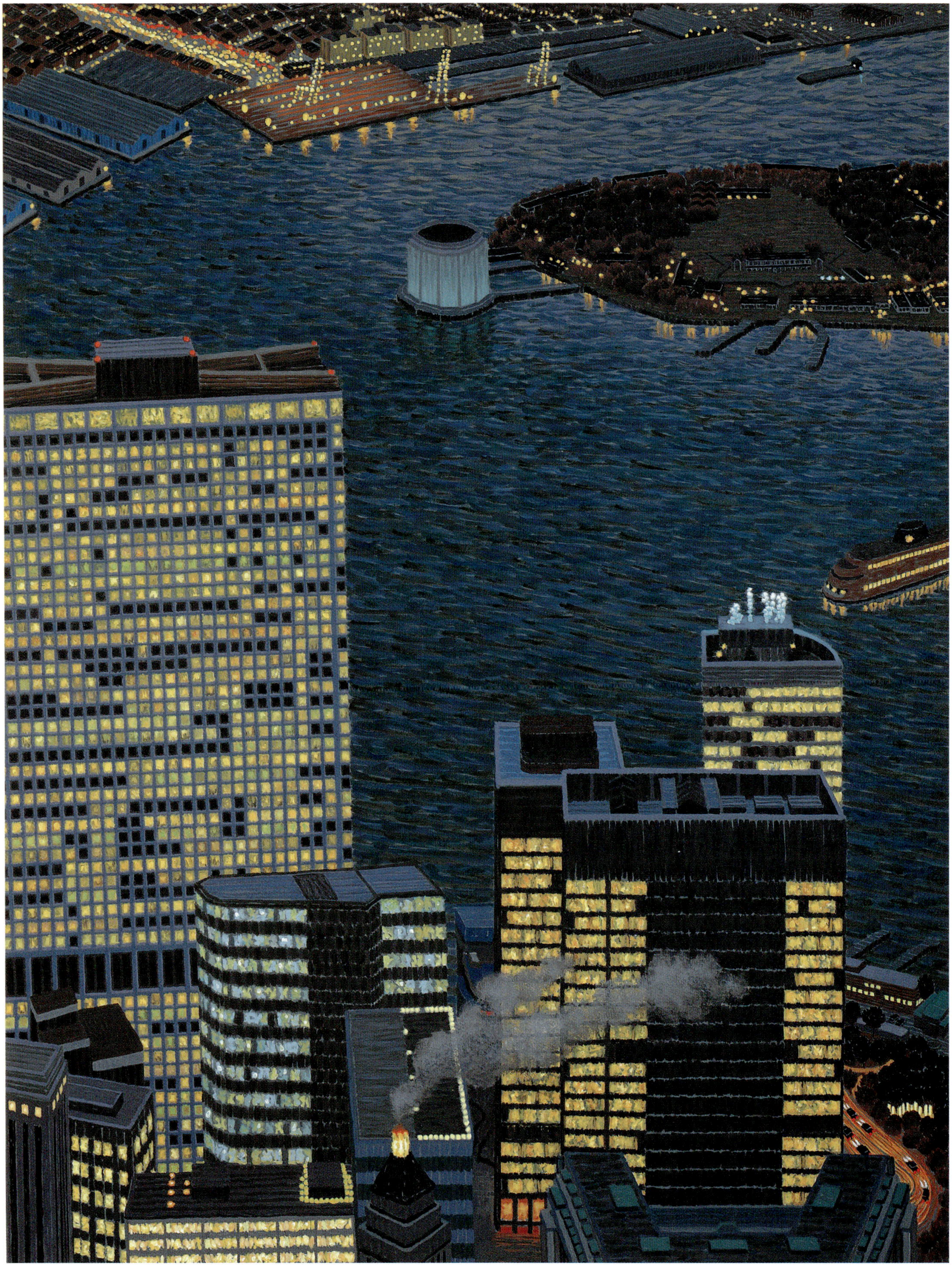

25
Southeast View from World Trade Center II, 2001
Oil on linen
73 x 54 inches
Yale University Art Gallery, Janet and Simeon Braguin Fund

26
Queensboro Bridge, Autumn, with Police Boat I, 2002
Pastel on paper
15 ¾ x 28 ⅛ inches
Collection of Stephen Godchaux

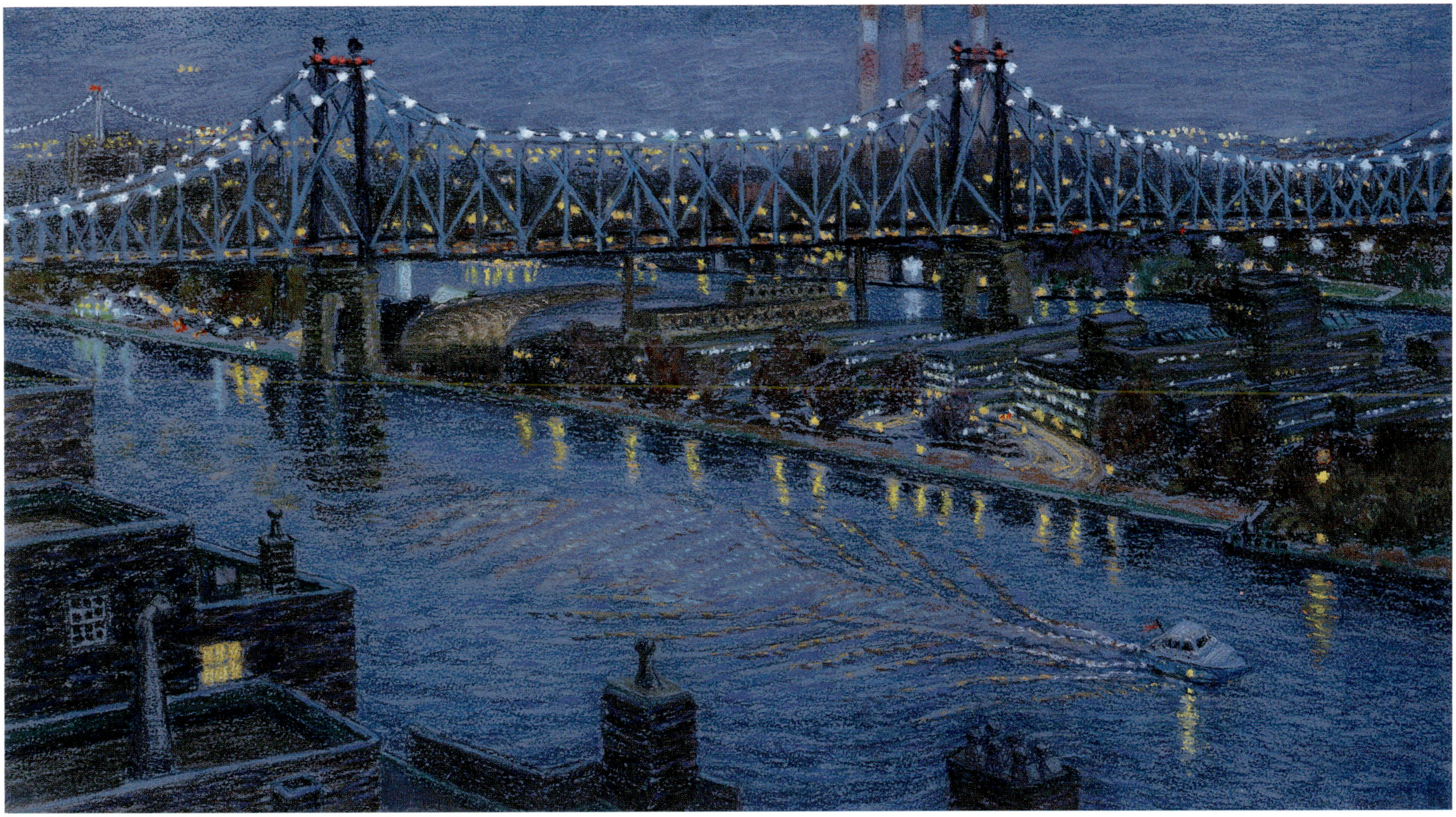

27
Above Times Square II, 2003
Oil on canvas
63 x 72 ½ inches
Courtesy of the artist and
DC Moore Gallery, New York

28
Above Times Square III, 2007
Oil on canvas
49 x 56 inches
Courtesy of the artist and
DC Moore Gallery, New York

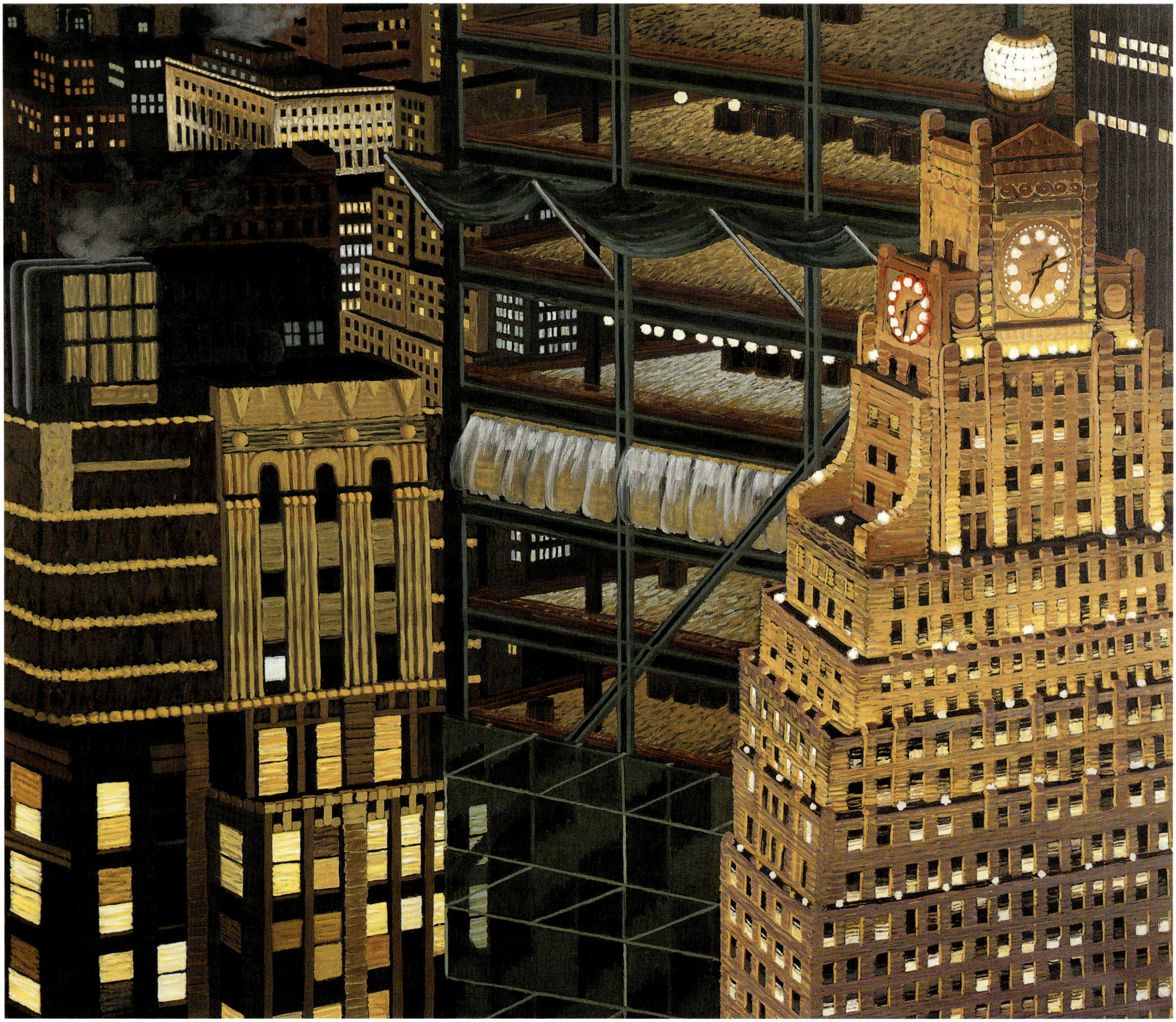

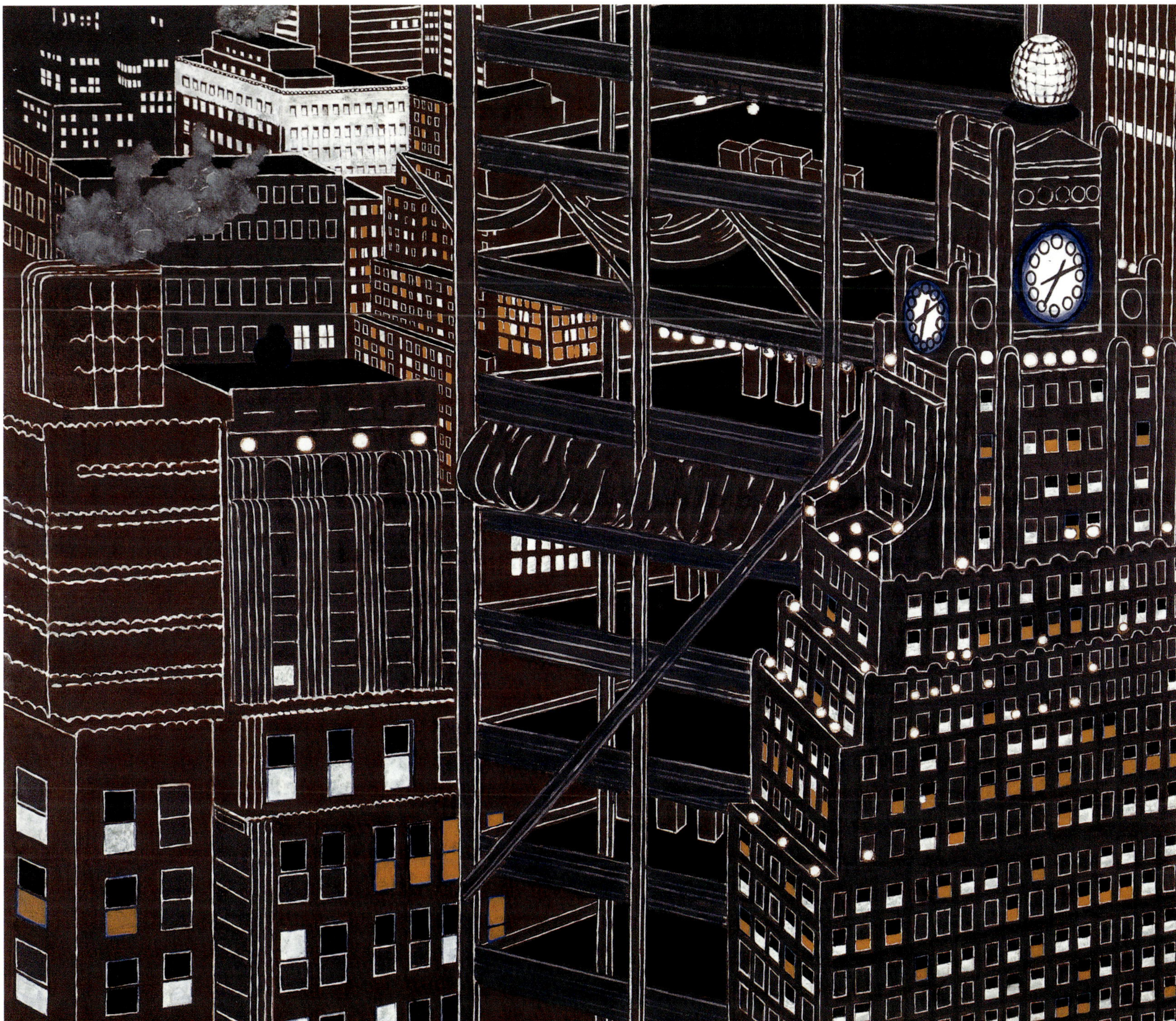

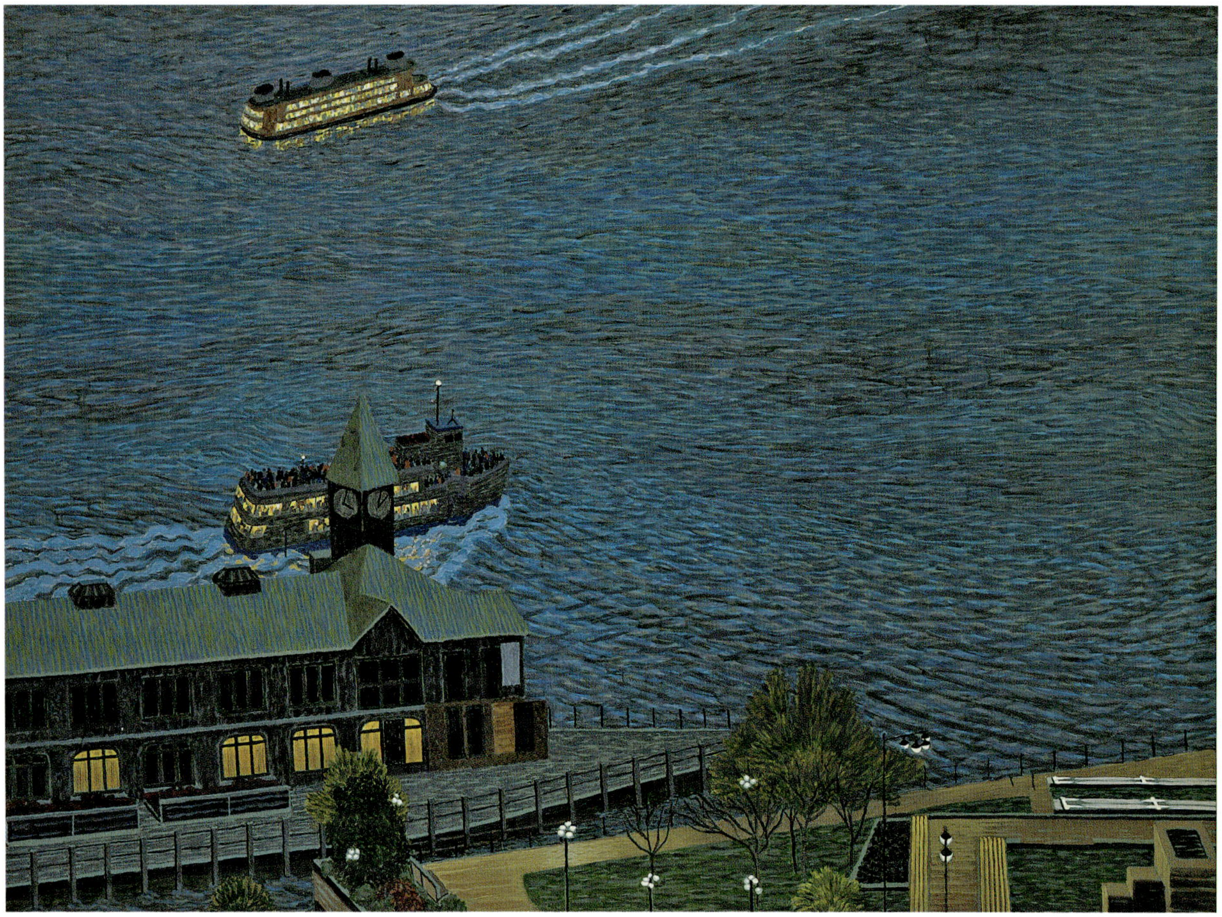

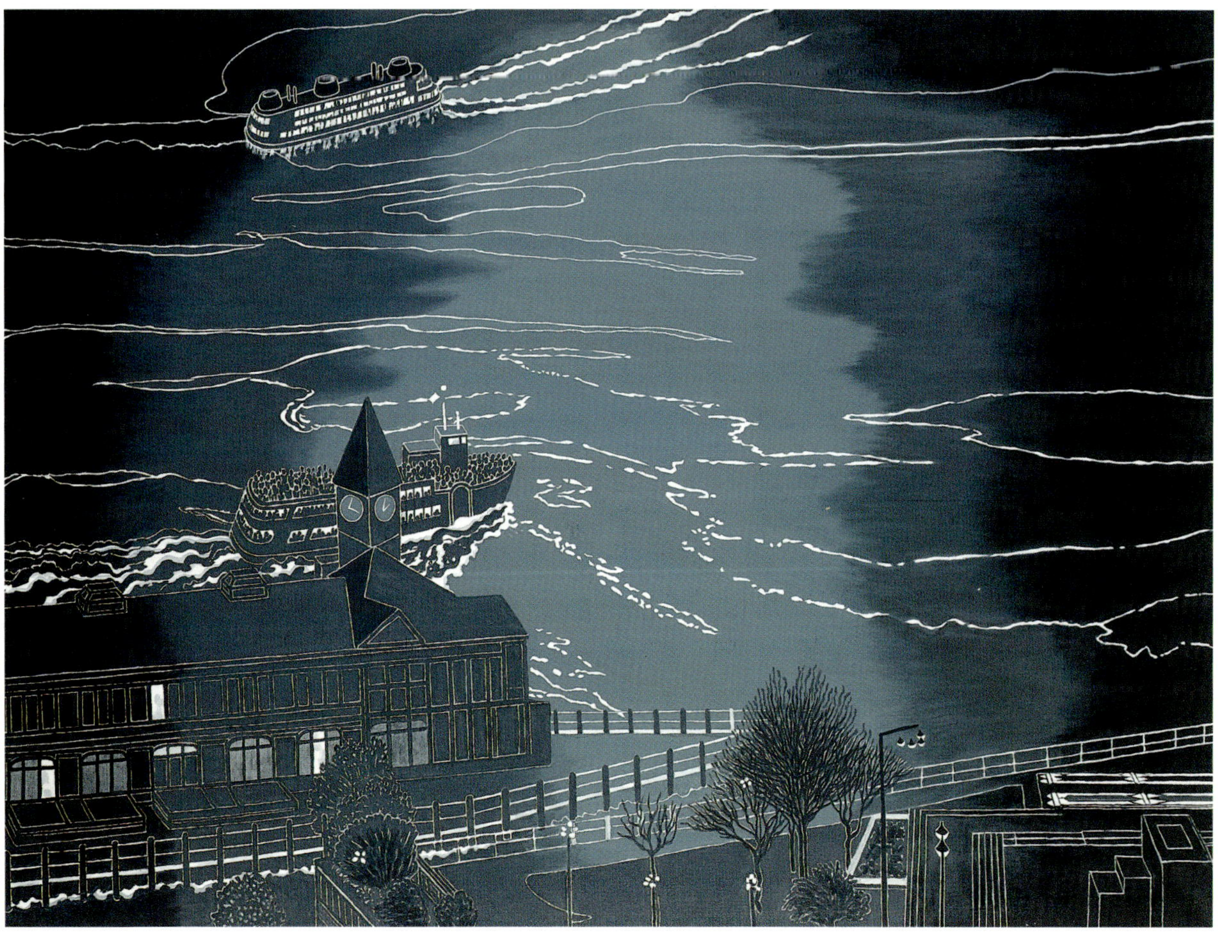

29
Pier A at Battery Park, Overcast Eve II, 2005
Oil on canvas
56 ½ x 75 inches
Collection of Shelley and Ruvan Cohen, New York
Not in exhibition

30
Pier A at Battery Park III, 2007
Oil on canvas
50 x 60 inches
Courtesy of the artist and DC Moore Gallery, New York

31
Lower Manhattan and New Jersey with Water Towers II, 2005
Oil on canvas
71 ⅛ x 62 ⅝ inches
Private collection, Irvington, New York

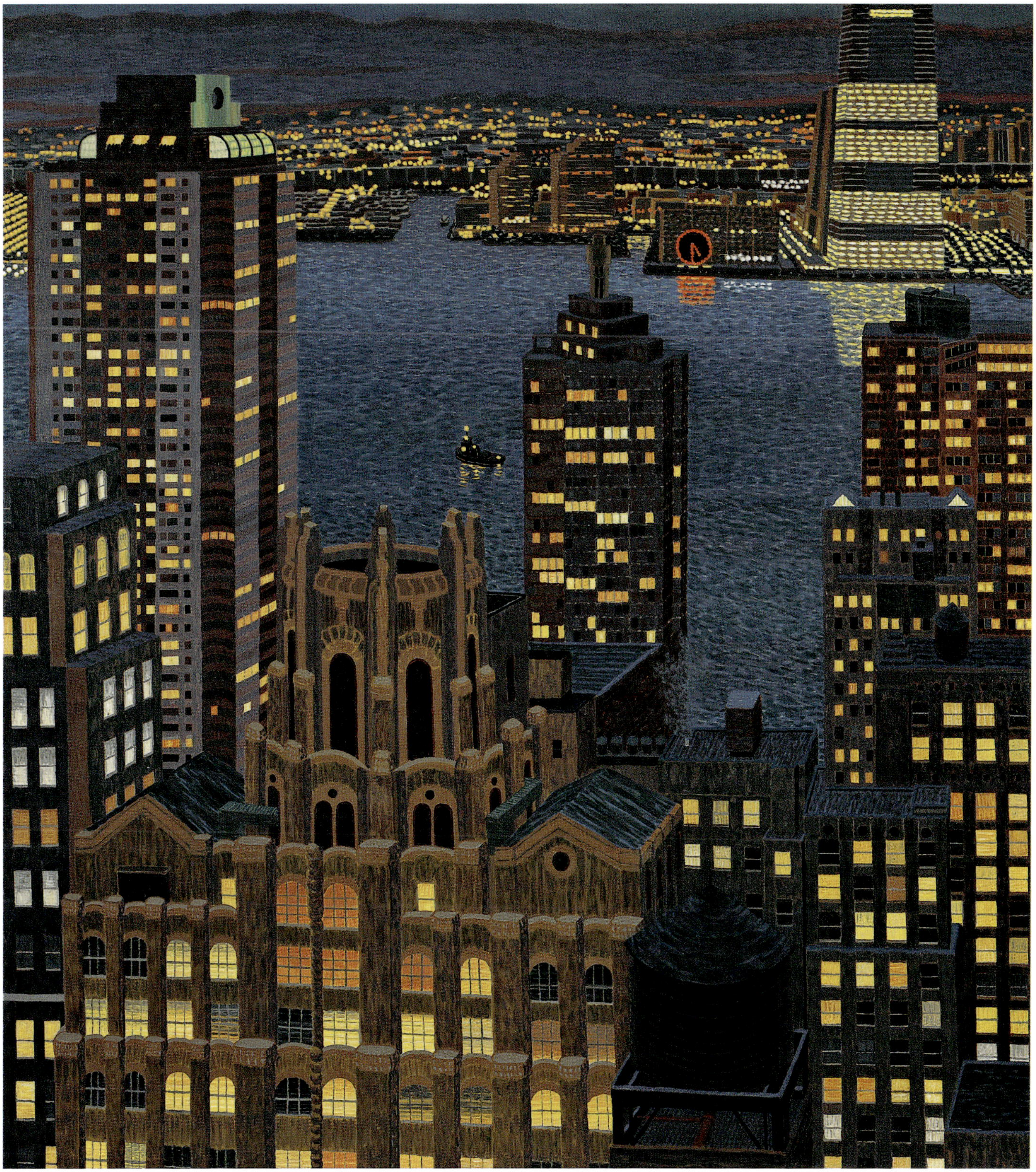

32
Third Avenue (with Reflection) II, 2004
Oil on canvas
63 x 77 inches
Collection of Time Warner, Inc.

33
Two Bridges I, 2007
Pastel on paper
29 ½ x 22 ½ inches
Courtesy of the artist and
DC Moore Gallery, New York

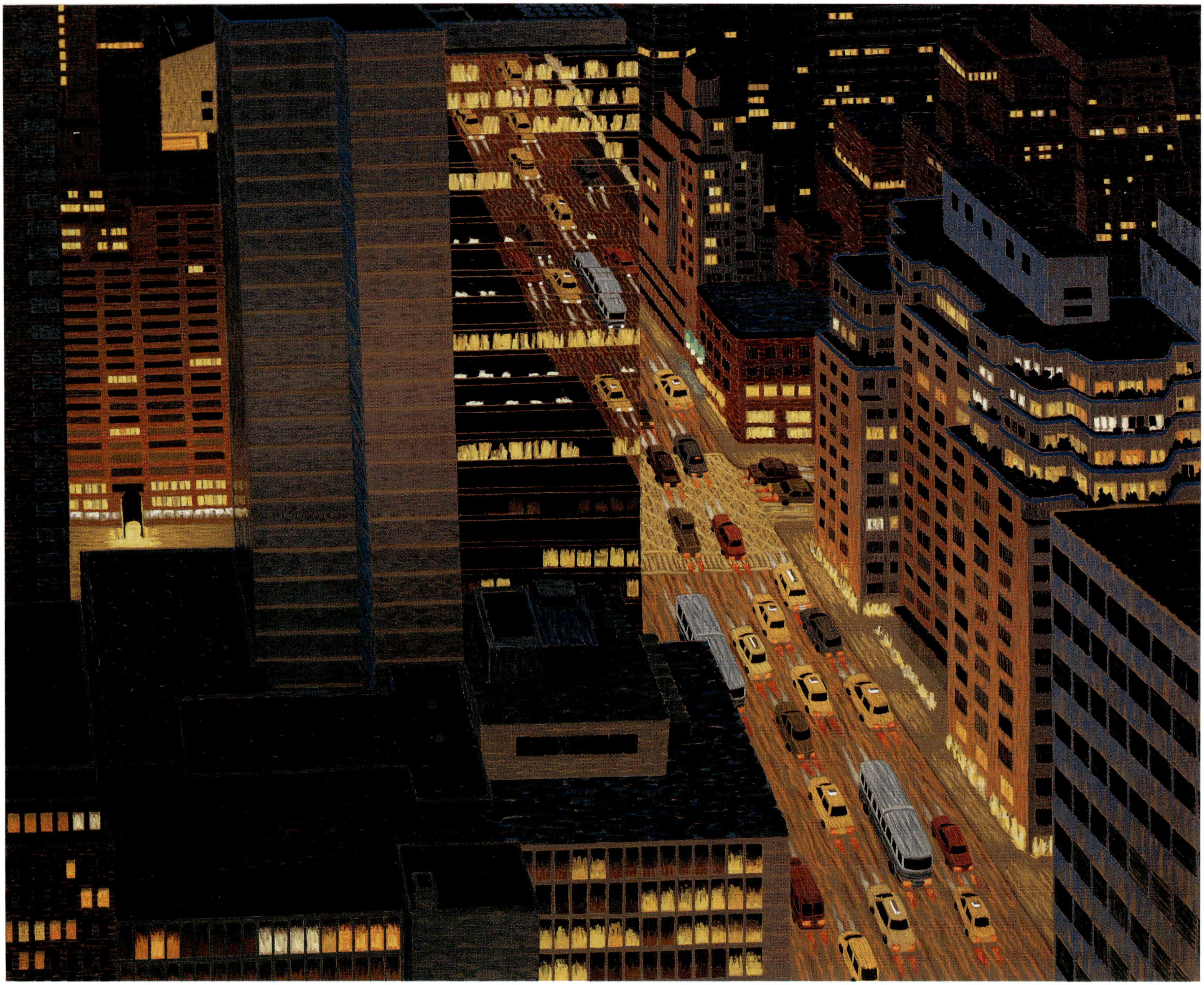

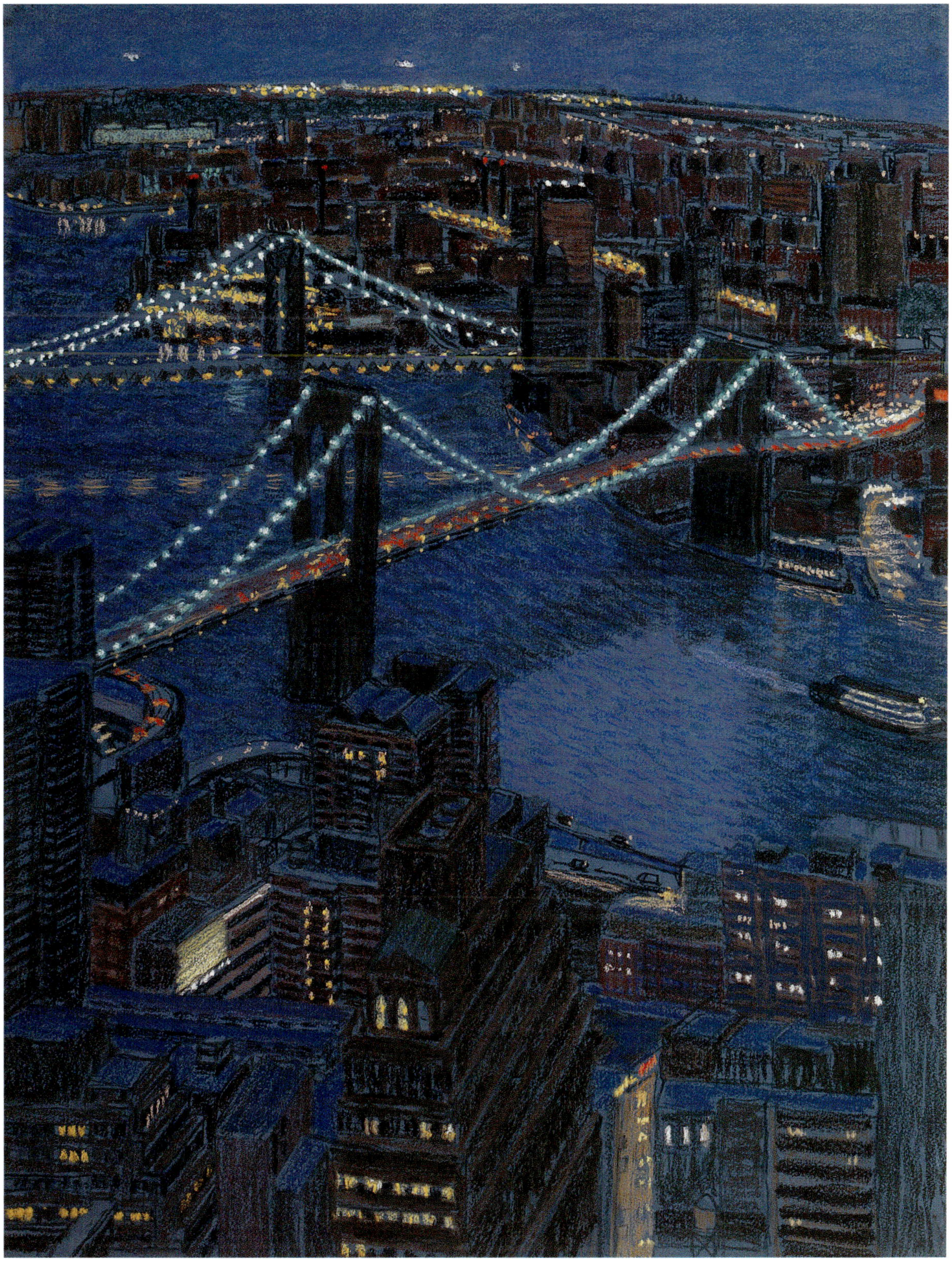

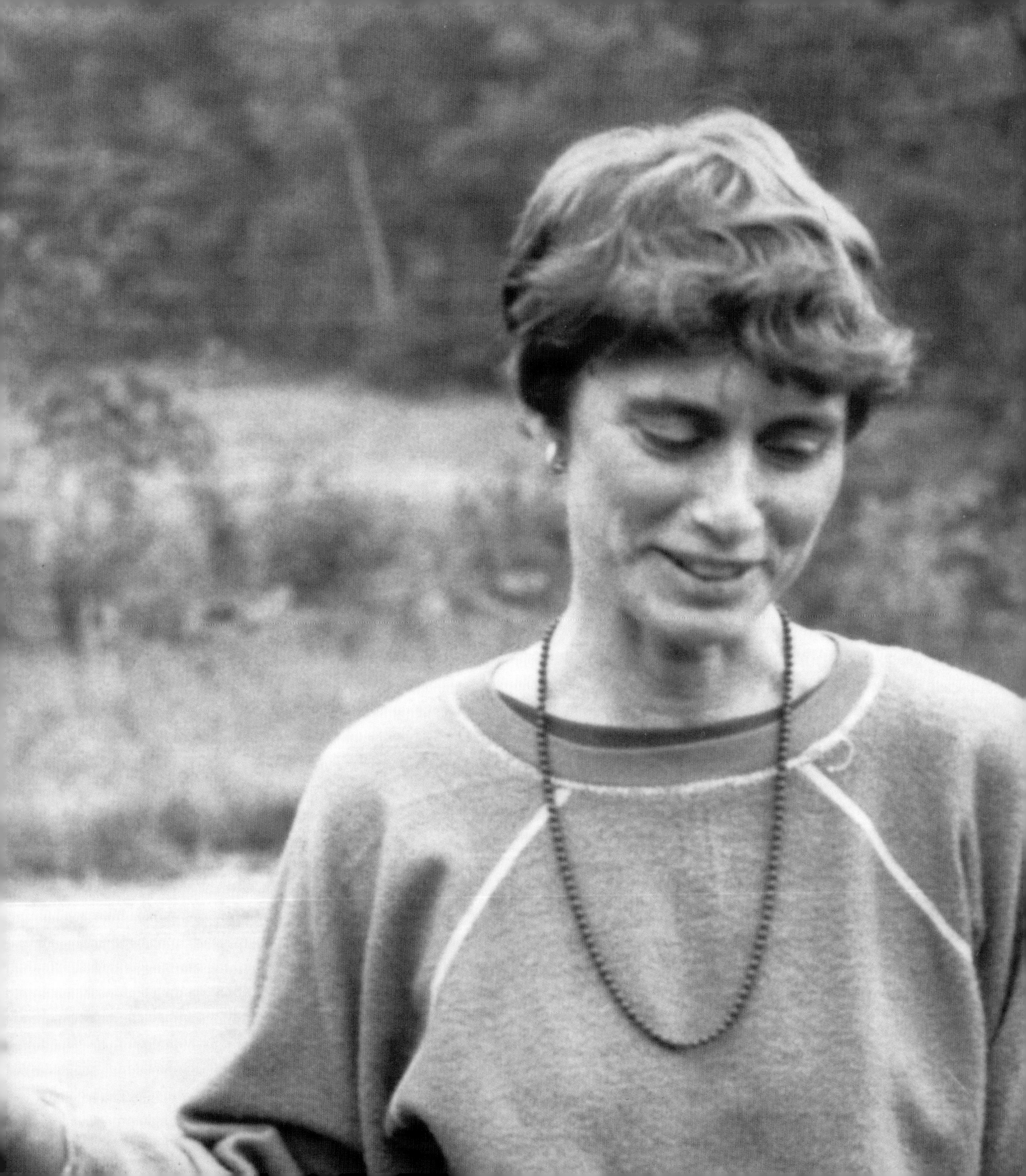

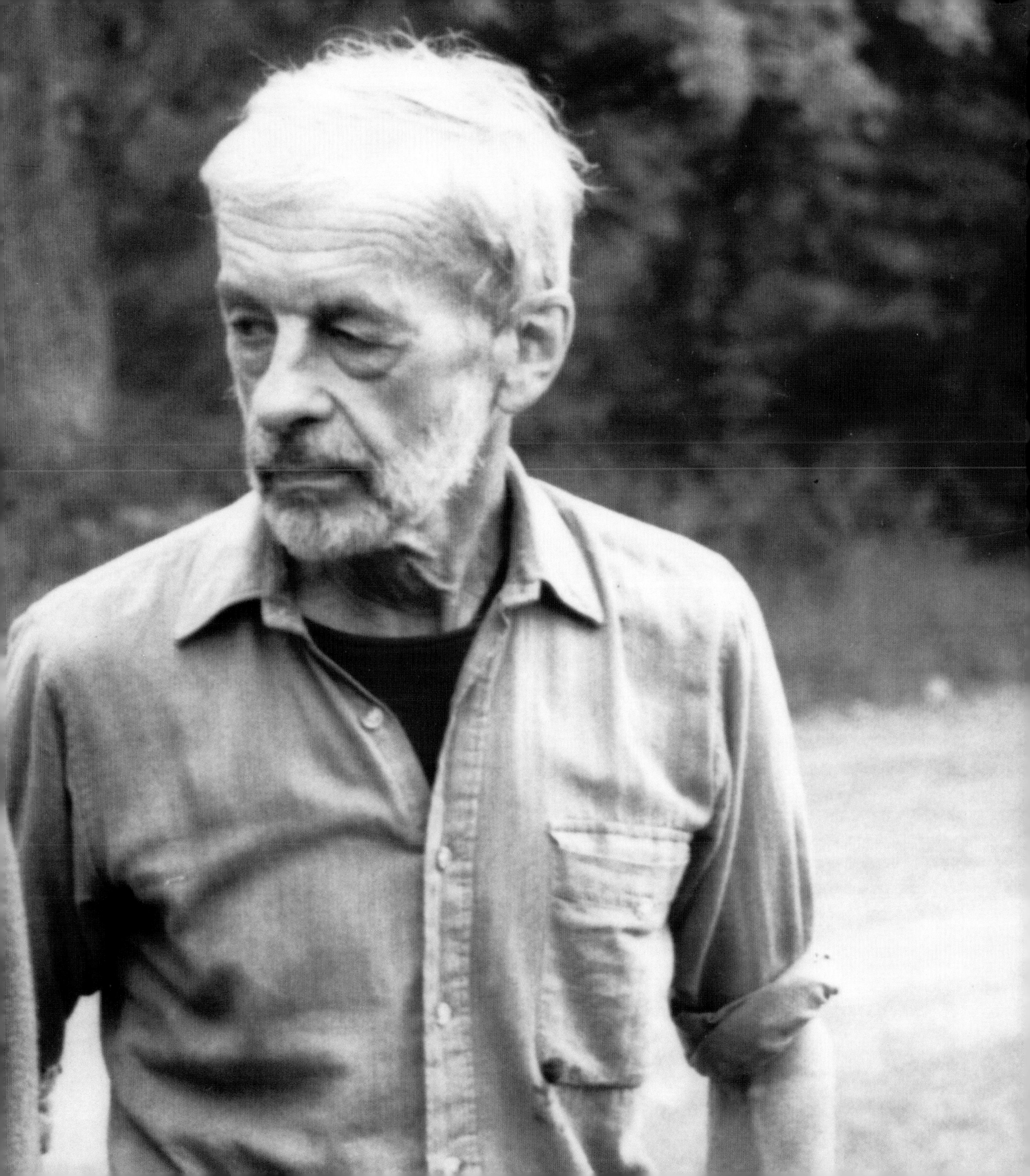

PREVIOUS PAGES
Yvonne Jacquette and Rudy Burckhardt in Searsmont, Maine, 1984
Photograph by Vincent Katz

BELOW
Rudy Burckhardt filming *Rubble Dance,* Queens, New York, 1991
Photograph by Yvonne Jacquette

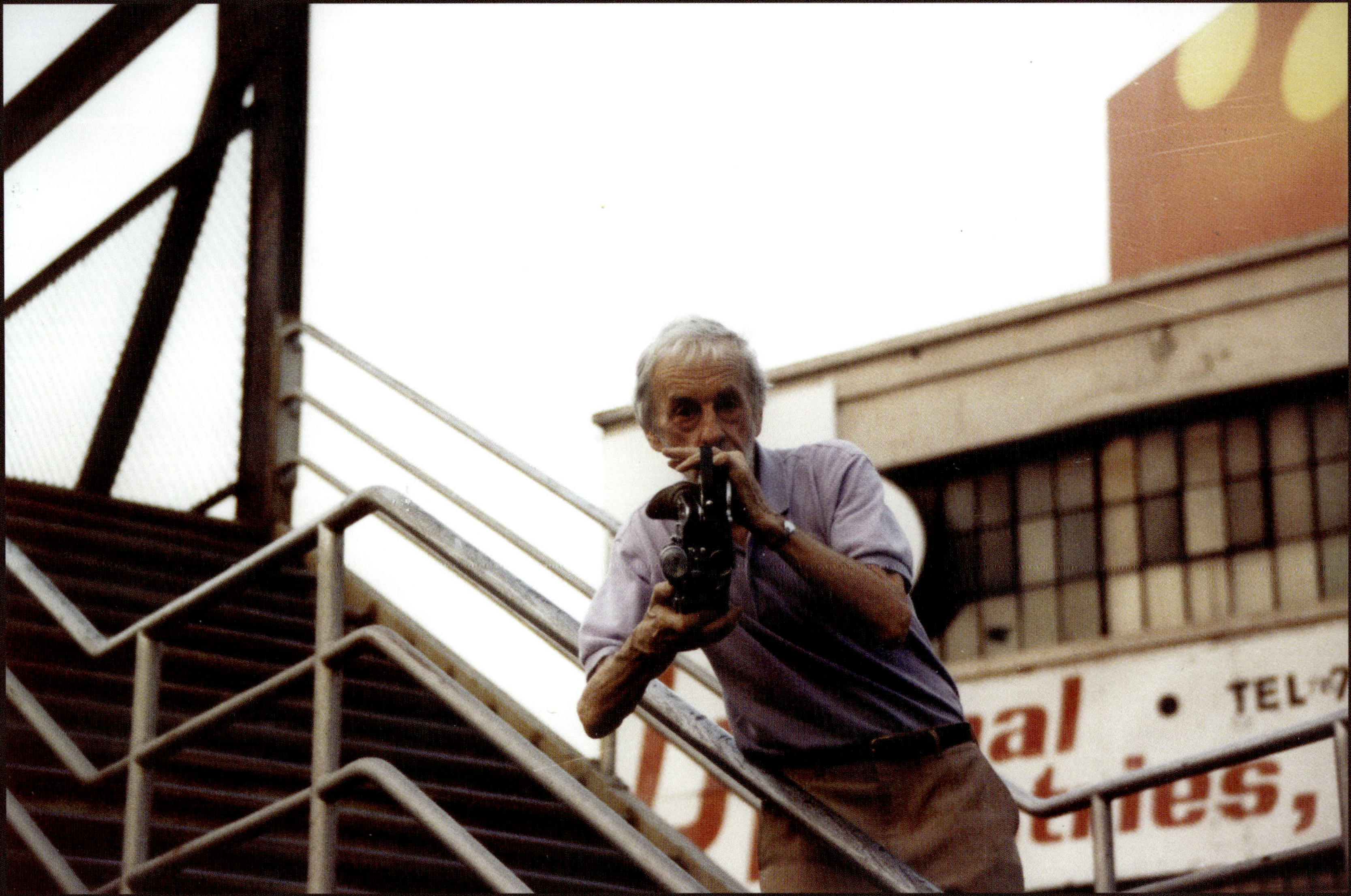

Street Dance

THE NEW YORK PHOTOGRAPHS OF RUDY BURCKHARDT

VINCENT KATZ

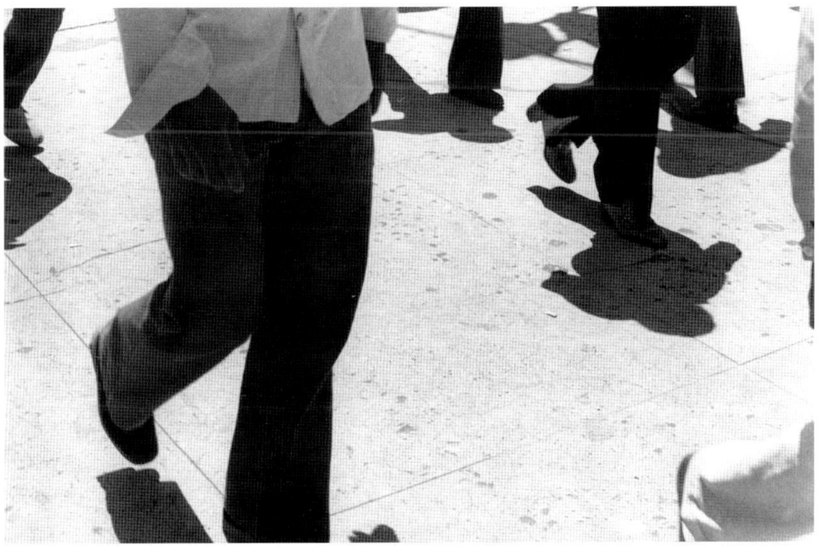

1 ABOVE
Rudy Burckhardt
Untitled, c. 1978
Gelatin silver print
6 5/8 x 9 3/4 inches
Courtesy the Estate of Rudy Burckhardt and Tibor de Nagy Gallery, New York

There are several Puerto
Ricans on the avenue today, which
makes it beautiful and warm.
—Frank O'Hara[1]

I was right there with the camera, in the crowd.
—Rudy Burckhardt[2]

Photography, as has been pointed out, resides in a different realm from painting.[3] The European tradition of painting and the modern capabilities of photography were intertwined in Rudy Burckhardt's life and art in ways that differentiated him from most other photographers of his time. Although many photographers studied painting and were friends with painters, Burckhardt saw and composed as a painter. He also thought and worked like a poet, living in a world somewhat apart from the professional worlds most photographers trafficked in.

The Basel-born artist, who moved to New York in 1935 and lived there until his death in 1999, was aware of the dichotomy posed by photography. Writing of the education he received as a youth, Burckhardt noted, "I had good grades, except for drawing and singing, and when I wanted to make pictures of what I saw around me, I turned to photography, where the lens of the camera does the drawing for you, instead of your own clumsy hand."[4] Two things are striking about this statement: one, that Burckhardt, while still a teenager, had the clear ambition to make pictures in some serious way, and two, that he forewent traditional modes of picture-making (drawing, painting, sculpting) in favor of something much more modern.[5]

Born in 1914 to a family on the right side of the Rhine (his grandfather had been a general and a judge, and his father ran a silk ribbon business), Burckhardt spent most of his life trying to escape the aristocratic confines of his upbringing in the city he later characterized as "lonely

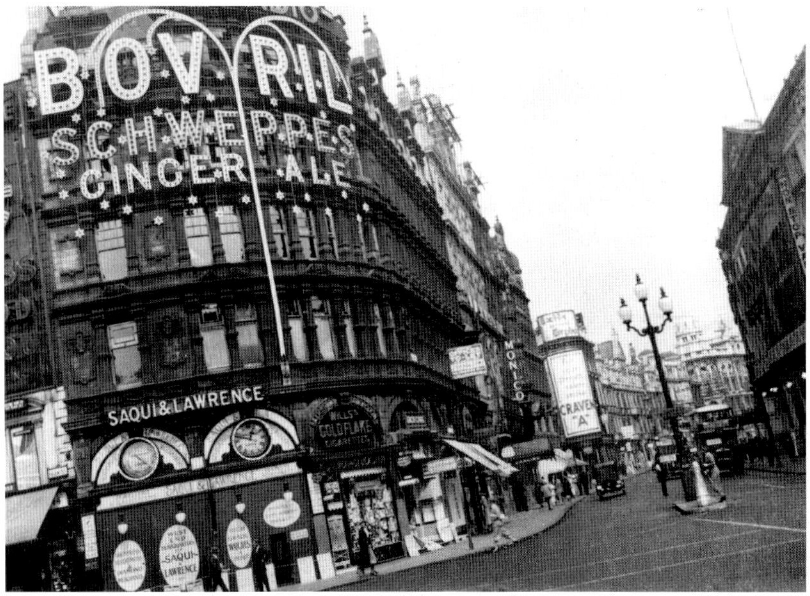

2 ABOVE
Rudy Burckhardt
Piccadilly, London, 1933
Gelatin silver print
6 x 8 inches
Courtesy the Estate of Rudy Burckhardt and Tibor de Nagy Gallery, New York

and empty and proper and clean."[6] He soaked in the Greek and Latin literature he read in school and must have been exposed to classical art as well (the famous art historian of the Renaissance, Jacob Burckhardt, was a relative).

Until 1934, when he was 20, Burckhardt does not seem to have been aware of the major movements in modern art—Cubism, Futurism, Dadaism, Surrealism—let alone Purism, with one of whose adherents, Amedée Ozenfant, he would later study painting in New York. He had access to a camera but does not seem to have known of such photographers as Stieglitz and Steichen, who had for some time been staking out a place for photography as an art form of comparable stature to painting. Instead, fueled by ancient poetry, Burckhardt would wander the streets of Basel, taking photographs. I believe it is safe to say that until he left Basel to study medicine in London in 1933, he had not been exposed to modern art.

He soon dropped out of medical school, preferring to wander London's streets, photographing with a 9 x 12 centimeter German camera. Although he did take a slightly askew photograph of Piccadilly Circus [figure 2], most of his images are of anonymous, dreary side streets or bridges, similar in tone to his early photographs of Basel. In contrast to images by other photographers of this era, Burckhardt's photographs of London do not call out for social change, despite their bleakness. They register their melancholy subjects almost casually, setting a neutral observational tone that would be characteristic of much of Burckhardt's city work. However, they are not unpassionate or uninvolved. On the contrary, Burckhardt's photographs are notable for being humanistic and sympathetic portraits of their subjects—people particularly, although the same can be said of his portraits of locales. By neutral, rather, I mean something close to noncritical. He presents people in visual terms, as individuals defined by their appearance, rather than as examples of fixed social types.

A year after his London stay, in 1934, Burckhardt was able to wander around Paris, foregrounding people in his city compositions for the first time. "In Switzerland," Burckhardt observed, "when somebody wanted to be an artist, they went to Paris, which was about four hours away by train. I went to Paris, and I liked it a lot, but I didn't want to live there. It seemed not far enough away from Basel."[7] At that time, he was not going to the Louvre or the city's other museums or art galleries. Using a hand-held Leica 35-millimeter camera, which had just

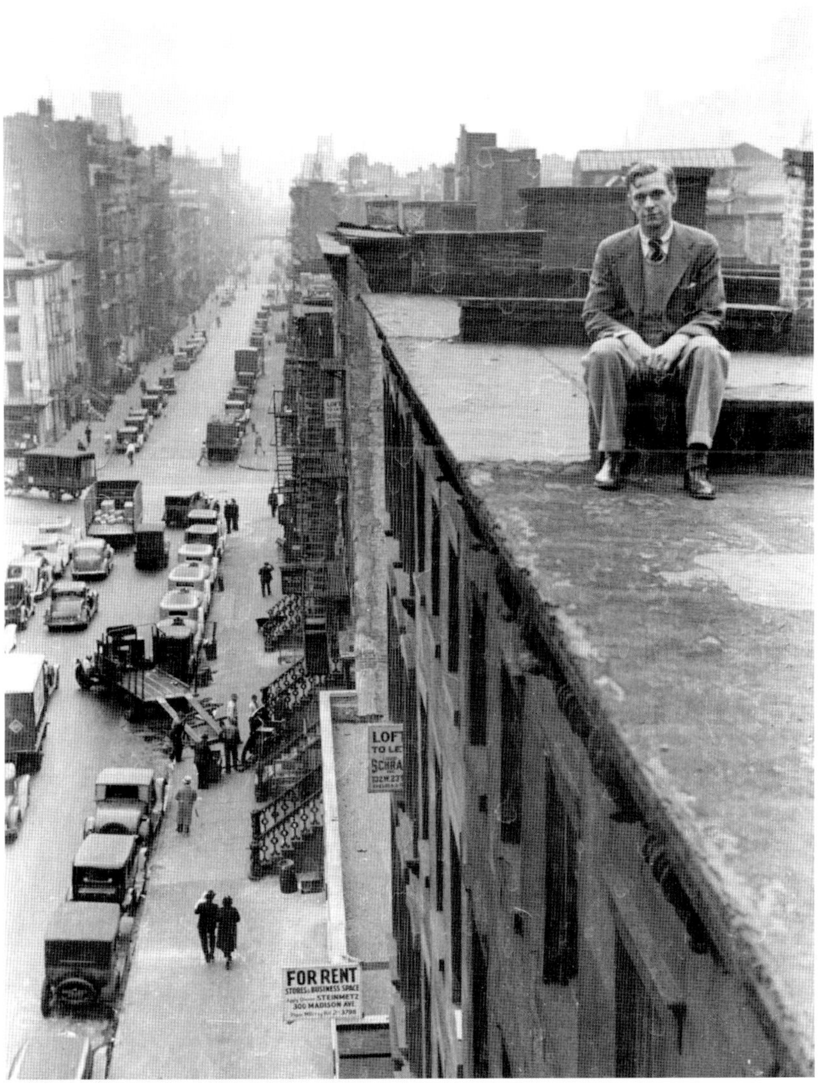

3 ABOVE
Rudy Burckhardt
Edwin Denby on West 21st Street, 1937
Gelatin silver print
8 13/16 x 6 1/2 inches
Courtesy the Estate of Rudy Burckhardt and Tibor de Nagy Gallery, New York

come on the market, Burckhardt photographed people at leisure, milling about. "I was mostly just wandering around," he observed, "and I went to these fairs that were in the middle of the boulevard."[8]

Certainly, the catalytic event for Burckhardt was his encounter in 1934 with Edwin Denby, an American poet later to become known as one of the most perceptive dance critics of his age, and at that time a dancer himself. Denby, needing a passport photo, looked up Burckhardt on a friend's advice, and the two were never separated for long after that, until Denby's death in 1983. Denby took Burckhardt to the wrong side of the Rhine, "Kleinbasel" as it was known, and embarrassed his young friend (Denby was 11 years Burckhardt's elder) by demonstrating a ballet step on a Basel street. With Denby, Burckhardt's interest in art was kindled. In 1935, they went to Paris together, where Burckhardt saw a Picasso exhibition of women with mirrors, which first opened his mind to the possibilities of modern image-making. Three years later, he would be making photographs influenced by Mondrian's rectangular compositions and minimal spaces.

The same year, 1935, Denby returned to New York, inviting Burckhardt to join him. Denby, who had enjoyed several years in Europe, associating with such figures as Jean Cocteau and Kurt Weill, decided it was time to move back [figure 3]. He encouraged Burckhardt to leave his provincial surroundings to move to the city that was quickly becoming an alternative intellectual capital, with its heady mix of European expatriates and, soon, refugees, as well as those Americans also drawn to it. Having come into an inheritance, Burckhardt took the opportunity to flee, leaving behind Basel, Switzerland, and Old Europe for the frontier of the new Metropolis.

Burckhardt's memory late in life of those early days in New York was that the scale of the city was something for which he was not prepared. "When I arrived in New York in 1935," he remembered, "I was amazed at the difference in scale between the people and the buildings. They have no relation in scale. In Europe, at that time, there were no high buildings at all, and people had a relation to the size of their buildings, the only exception being the cathedral."[9] For two years, Burckhardt was not able to imagine how to photograph New York.

Although he did not photograph until 1937, he jumped into filmmaking earlier. Obtaining a second-hand 16-millimeter Victor camera with a one-inch lens, Burckhardt began confidently. His first film,

4 TOP
Rudy Burckhardt
Film still from *The Climate of New York,* 1948
Courtesy the Estate of Rudy Burckhardt

5 BOTTOM
Rudy Burckhardt
Queens [Self Portrait with Neighborhood Boy], 1940
Gelatin silver print
7 x 4 ¾ inches
Courtesy the Estate of Rudy Burckhardt and Tibor de Nagy Gallery, New York

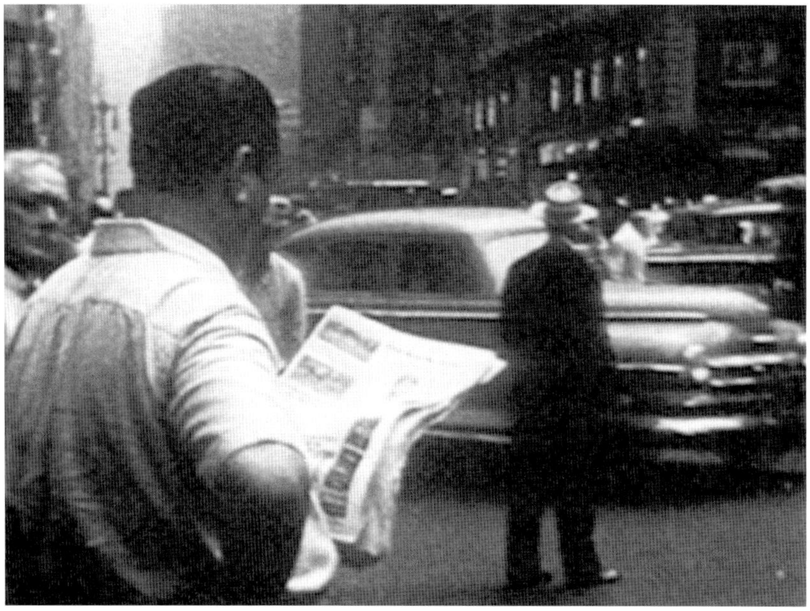

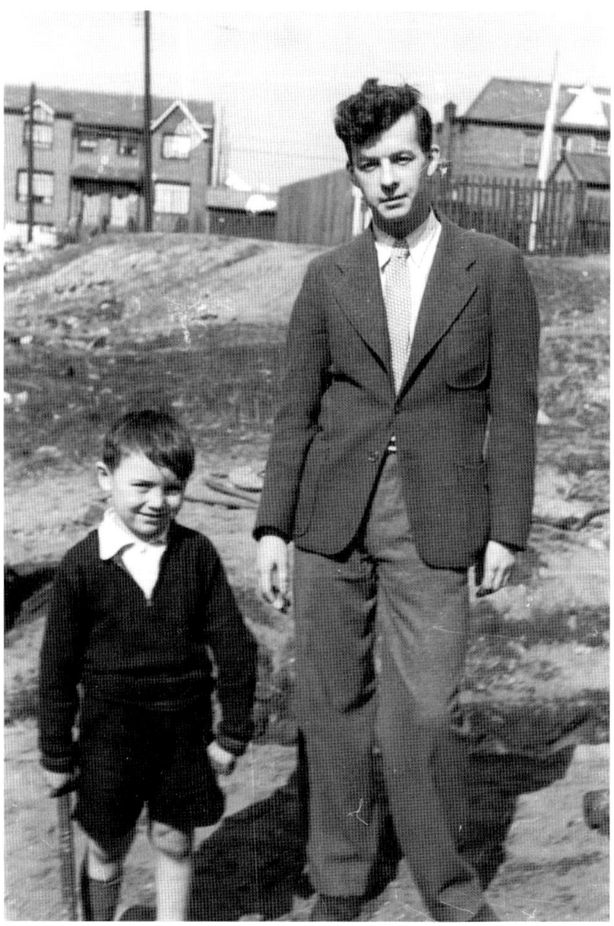

145 West 21 (1936), was a light comedy, starring Denby and composer Aaron Copland, with cameos by Virgil Thomson and Paul Bowles. He also made a film with Joseph Cotten and Virginia Welles (wife of Orson). Film would become a major part of Burckhardt's artistic output. His 101 16-millimeter films represent a significant contribution to American art filmmaking, for which Burckhardt was accorded the recognition of a 1987 film retrospective at the Museum of Modern Art in New York.[10] His films, many of which document parts of New York, often bend and create genres, including story films, travel films, diary films, and film-poems (those that use audio recordings or subtitles of poems by contemporary poets and those in which the form of filmmaking becomes poetic in itself).

Filming made-up stories with friends seemed possible, when photographing the city did not. This tells us something about Burckhardt's attitude to the city and to art-making. He wanted to give himself the time to be able to absorb the scalar difference, to feel it as part of lived existence. His restraint tells us something else. In the same way that his choice in Basel of the camera over the pencil indicated a strong desire to make pictures, so in New York the decision to wait until he could understand the city's scale indicated a serious ambition to be able to portray New York appropriately, not haphazardly.

When he did begin to take photographs, using a view camera and a tripod, it was to focus on details of architecture—edges of buildings, borders where the decoration of one entry ended and another began, meetings between façades and sidewalks, standpipes and other sidewalk hardware. When he first photographed London, people were barely visible, yet their presence was implied; similarly in these first New York pictures, there is a great implication of scale in their stripped down images. Knowing what New York buildings look like, one is likely to extrapolate from a façade fragment the immense extent of that façade and what lies behind it.

Shortly after he made his first New York photographs of architectural fragments, Burckhardt began to take a similar approach to human subjects. Often pointing his camera down at an angle, he would capture only parts of people passing—their legs, their feet, their hips, their arms, and the clothing and footwear covering those body parts [figure 7]. Another approach was to stand at the edge of the sidewalk near the gutter and to photograph towards shop fronts, capturing people as they walked past. These were the first New York photographs

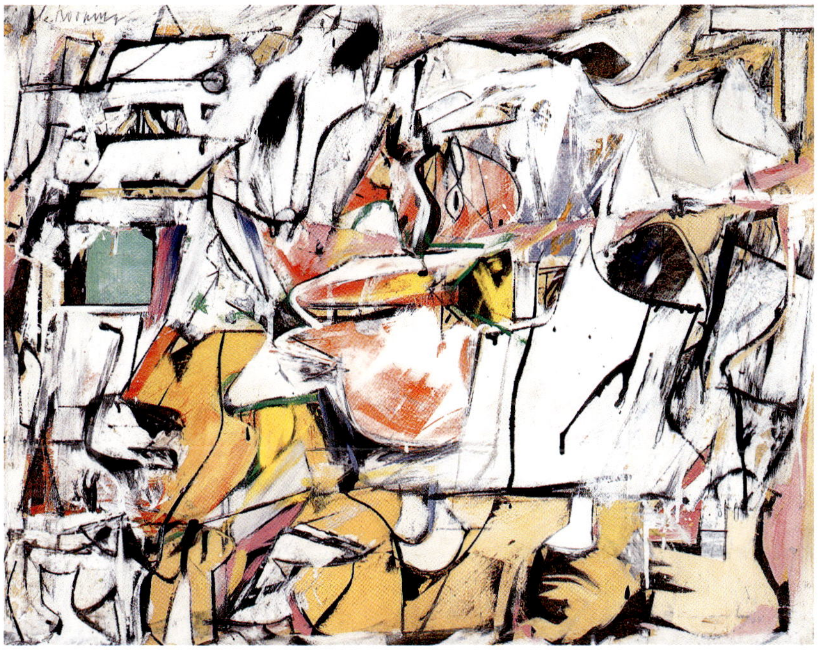

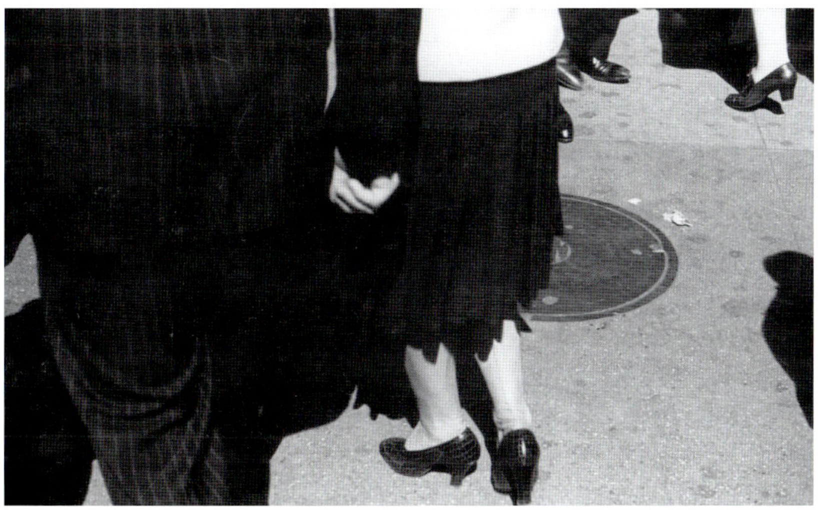

6 TOP
Willem de Kooning (1904–1997)
Asheville, 1948
Oil and enamel on cardboard
25 9/16 x 31 7/8 inches
Acquired 1952, The Phillips Collection, Washington, DC

7 BOTTOM
Rudy Burckhardt
Sidewalk, 1939
Gelatin silver print
7 1/2 x 9 7/8 inches
Courtesy the Estate of Rudy Burckhardt and Tibor de Nagy Gallery, New York

in which Burckhardt allowed himself to look up and to try to see entire human figures through the camera. In both shooting down toward the plane of the sidewalk and shooting the action between an observer and a shop front a sidewalk's width away, Burckhardt showed a quickly learned awareness of a basic structural element of the modern picture—a shallow picture plane. His early New York photographs demonstrate an understanding of Cubism as well as an exploration of compressed space similar to that already being undertaken by his painter friends Willem de Kooning and Arshile Gorky.[11]

There is a deep interconnection between Burckhardt's films and his photographs [figure 4]. Burckhardt created mesmerizing senses of movement, of lightness—lightness of foot, but also lightness of color and of mood. Both the fragmentary views of bodies on sidewalks and the scenes of people in motion in front of stores have an undeniably cinematic quality to them. For Burckhardt, photographing and filming partook of similar processes: "I started film very early. I was filming the same things I was photographing. There was no great difference, really. I went out in the street, and I was watching how people move, making up their own choreography."[12] By the end of 1939, Burckhardt had made a body of photographs that, on their own, should have earned him an important place in the history of photography.

While he was later central in many ways to the New York art world, photographing artists for the journal *ARTnews,* collaborating with them on films, associating with them, viewing their exhibitions, it would be a long time before his photography would become known outside of that world. Even as his films became known by the underground film community in the 1960s, partly through the support of Jonas Mekas of Anthology Film Archives, his photographs were still not accorded significance within the photographic canon. This rankled Burckhardt, and he later spoke out in an interview in defense of these early works: "I'd like to talk about these photographs, the first ones I took in New York. They're totally everyday-like. Sometimes I had like x-ray vision, and I could take six or seven that were interesting in one day. They are original, because at that time most people did social-conscious photographs. They used to say, 'You have to take photographs showing how people live on the Lower East Side. You have to live with them to understand them, and then you can get their soul.' What I did, I went midtown where people totally anonymously pass each other, and they just walk around. They don't look at each other, and they just seem to avoid

8 TOP
Edward Steichen (1879–1973)
The Flatiron, 1904, printed 1909
Gum bichromate over platinum print
18 13/16 x 15 1/8 inches
The Metropolitan Museum of Art,
Alfred Stieglitz Collection, 1933 (33.43.39)

9 BOTTOM
Walker Evans (1903–1975)
Untitled [People Posing in Window and On Stoop of Clapboard House, Ossining, New York], 1930–32
Film negative, 7 x 5 inches
The Metropolitan Museum of Art,
Walker Evans Archive, 1994 (1994.255.93)

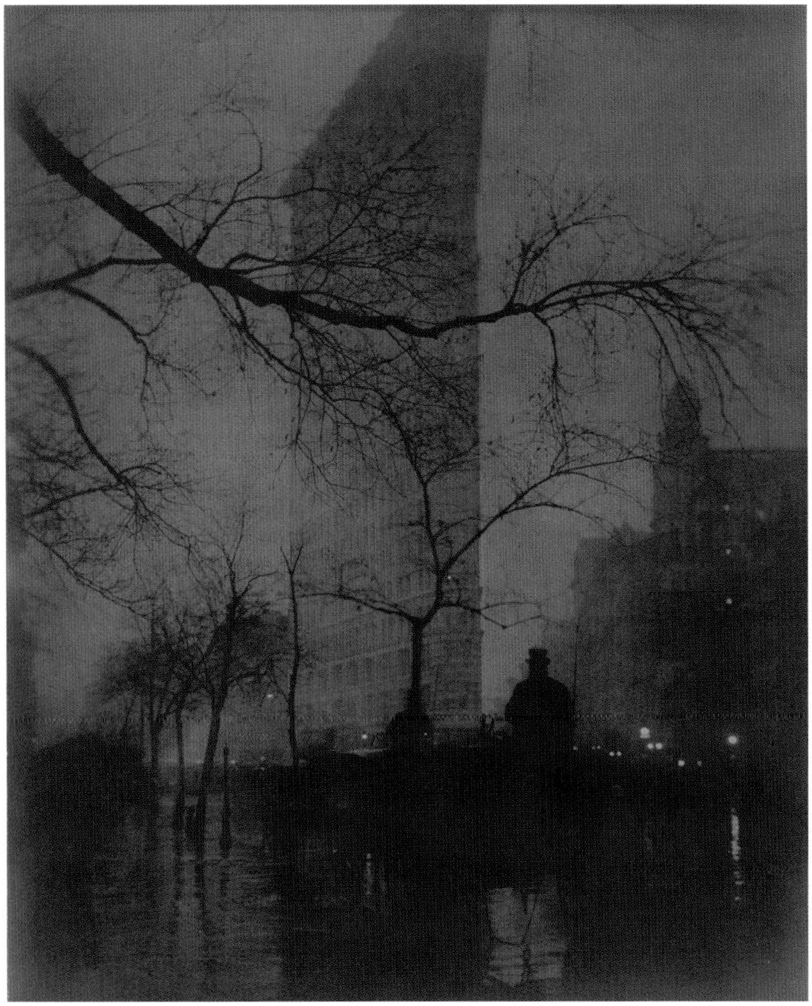

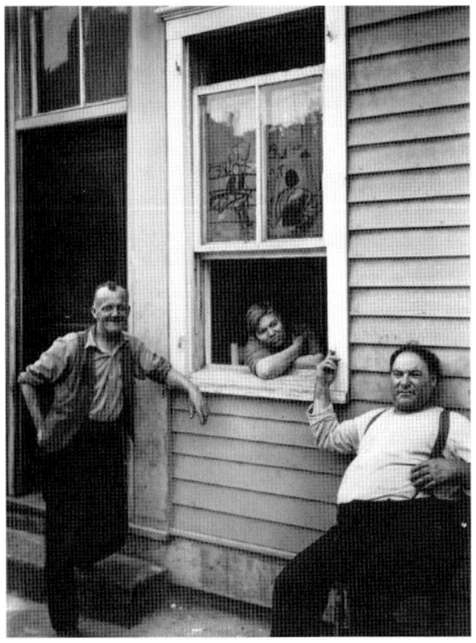

collision. Much later, Merce Cunningham said that he was trying to choreograph the way people move in the street, and his dancers used to move by each other, never looked at each other, never touched each other. It was very abstract, like the way these people [in my late 1930s photographs] move around."[13] An argument can be made that the factors that made Burckhardt's photography hard for 1930s audiences to understand—its lack of a social conscience, its detached, elated attitude towards its subjects, and its willful fragmentation of subject matter—are precisely the elements that would find resonance in the later work of artists as diverse as Cunningham and the contemporary photographer Jack Pierson.

Burckhardt's arrival in New York paralleled the earlier arrivals of two other photographers who had spent time in Europe, Berenice Abbott and Walker Evans. Burckhardt, like Abbott and Evans, pursued an unaffected portrayal of the city, in opposition to the atmospheric one favored by Stieglitz and Steichen [figure 8]. Evans was, like Burckhardt, a sensitive youth, but he was more tuned in to modern developments. A fan of Ezra Pound and James Joyce, Evans had gone to Paris in 1926, at the age of 23. He spent a year, frequenting Sylvia Beach's famous Shakespeare & Company bookstore. After returning to New York in 1927, Evans gradually turned to photography, partially with the encouragement of an enterprising friend, Lincoln Kirstein, who included him in a photography exhibition at Harvard and published his work in his magazine, *Hound & Horn*. By 1938, three years after Burckhardt's arrival in New York, and at the same time he was beginning to photograph the city, Evans had an exhibition at the Museum of Modern Art and published *American Photographs*, destined to become widely influential and to establish Evans as a major voice in the visual culture of the United States.

Berenice Abbott was another American photographer who did a stint in Paris; unlike Evans, she stayed for eight years during the 1920s, becoming Man Ray's assistant and eventually taking over part of his portrait clientele. With help from the art dealer Julien Levy, she also bought Eugène Atget's photographic archive when he died and then worked to bring the photographs of that master of a dying Paris to light. On her return to New York, Abbott resolved to document a New York she thought would soon change. The Museum of the City of New York was instrumental in supporting this project, serving as her institutional sponsor and giving her solo exhibitions in 1934 and 1937. In 1939, her book, *Changing New York: Photographs by Berenice Abbott*, was

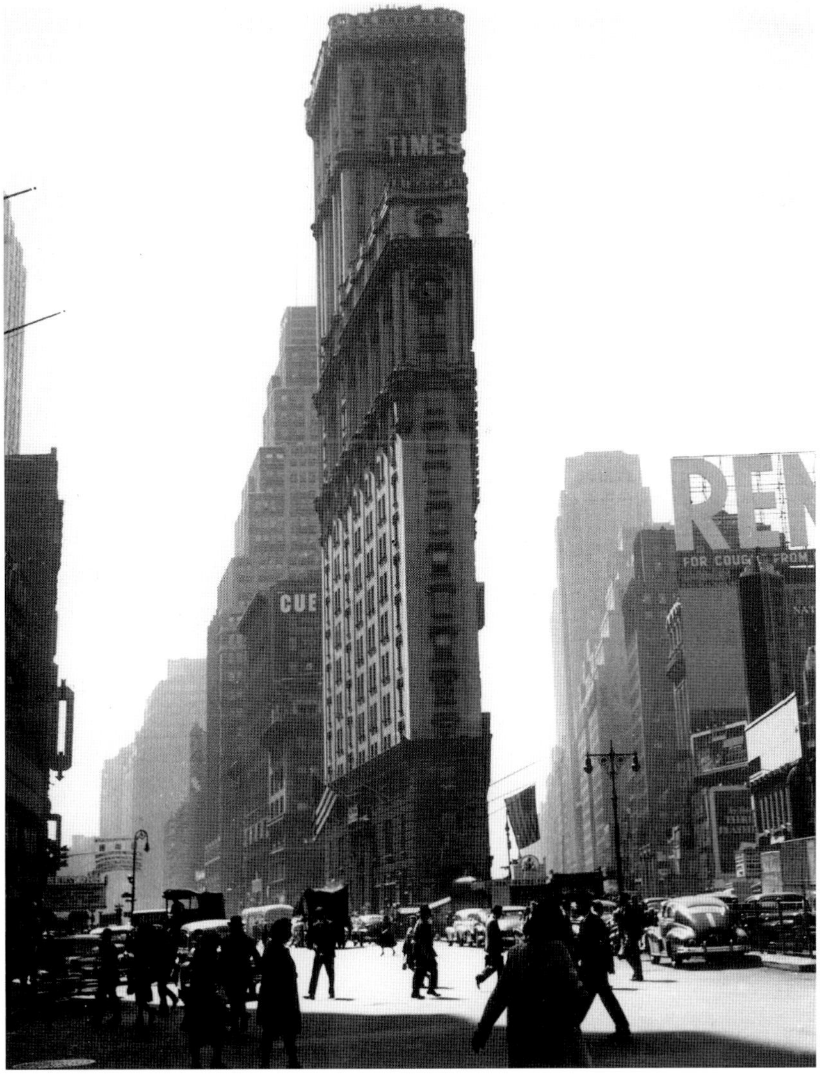

10 ABOVE
Rudy Burckhardt
Times Building, 1947
[see plate 69]

published. Abbott's method, as described by Audrey McMahon, was more controlled and time-consuming than Burckhardt's: "Amid traffic, haste, vibration, crowds, confusion, she has set up her 8 x 10 camera, leveled it off with a tiny carpenter's spirit level, composed the image on the ground glass, focused it, calculated exposure, and taken the picture."[14]

Evans had a big ambition, as did Abbott, though they worked differently. Abbott's greatest work may be her Paris portraits; her pictures of New York give us much useful information, but they often do not convey much feeling about the city's inhabitants. Her aerial shots use buildings as modernist compositional elements; in general, in her street photography, she was more interested in buildings than in people. Evans was closer to Burckhardt—he liked to go to the wrong side of the tracks—but his photographs are intended to shock or at least surprise [figure 9]. While his images were perhaps not created with the same intention of drawing attention to social ills as, say, Lewis Hine's or Dorothea Lange's, still Evans did want to make provocative pictures of little-seen sides of American life. He wanted to expose unseen American things, and that is what made him an important influence on a later generation. Robert Frank, in particular, in his 1958 publication, *The Americans,* picked up where Evans left off in *American Photographs,* updating Evans' vision of a misunderstood, disturbing America. Since Burckhardt's best images are not disturbing or haunting, like Evans' or Frank's, and since they are not dramatic, like Abbott's, they have often been overlooked [figure 10, plate 69]. Although his photographs are not unsettling, neither are they "precious," the criticism leveled at them by Evans himself. Rather, their energy emanates from Burckhardt's painterly approach to photography.

Burckhardt painted throughout his life, and he became deeply involved in looking at painting. It is in painting that one finds the key to his approach to photography. Edwin Denby believed that Rudy Burckhardt's photographs were the only ones he knew with visual interest all over.[15] He may have been thinking of de Kooning, whom he greatly admired, when he said that. Indeed, every part of a de Kooning painting like *Asheville,* 1948, is occupied by active visual energy [figure 6]. Similarly, a Burckhardt photograph such as *34th Street and Broadway,* c. 1947 [figure 11], shows not only the movement evinced in the pedestrians and cars crossing the busy intersection at Herald Square, but also impeccable composition, within which every part of the photograph is activated. The pedestrians form a band covering

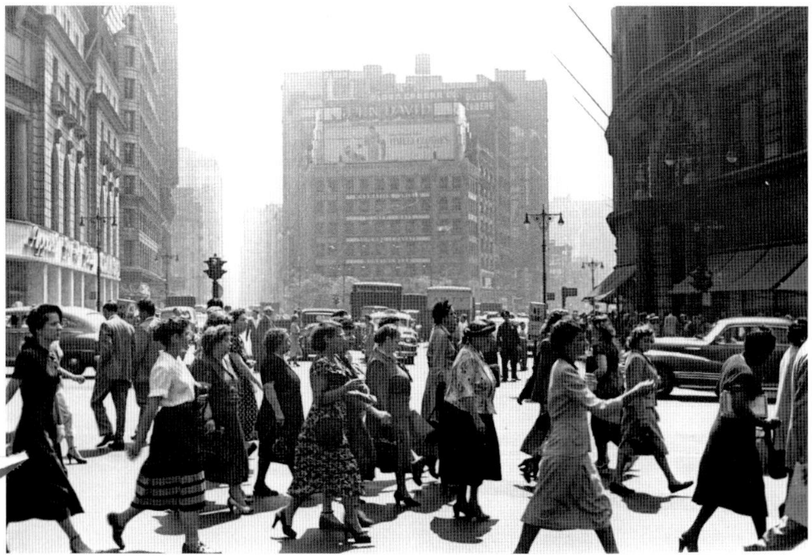

11 ABOVE
Rudy Burckhardt
34th Street and Broadway, c. 1947
Gelatin silver print
7 ⅛ x 9 ⅞ inches
Courtesy the Estate of Rudy Burckhardt and Tibor de Nagy Gallery, New York

the lower third of the image, while above a classically balanced array of three banks of buildings, left, center, and right, completes the structure. Even the negative space of the sky and street canyons surrounding the middle building is carefully proportioned, and the three building groups complement one another visually—they vary in terms of tone and detail, and their differences counterbalance their similarity in size within the picture.

Yet, all this is merely the setting. Seduced by the harmoniousness of the composition, the eye begins scanning the picture for details. As in most of Burckhardt's street photographs of people, there is an almost endless supply, beginning with the central subject, a frieze of women walking across 34th Street at the intersection of Broadway and Sixth Avenue. One can observe their clothing, their shoes, some with high heels, some without, which create a rhythmic pattern in the center of the picture, highlighted by the figures' shadows on the street beneath them. A woman near the middle is wearing a flowery summer dress with short sleeves, handbag draped in the crook of her elbow. A woman near the right edge is wearing a lightweight, light-colored, skirt suit, while one stepping into the frame at left is wearing a dark dress and hat. Each woman has her own particular way of walking, counterpointed by the two men in business suits walking away from them at the left rear.

Looking into the background, one sees that the composition holds yet another tripartite configuration: one that goes into depth, the sides being nearer the viewer than the center, which is nearer than the distances created by avenues framing the center block. The eye is led ever deeper, finding decorative motifs in the designs of street lights and lamps, signs, a more distant range of people crossing on the other side of 34th Street, the cars and trucks waiting there at the light, boxy signs that say "NO TURNS," and then one notices a policeman back there, his cap and badge recognizable. There is all this and more—the "Amity" truck and the sign for "John David Timely Clothes" on a high billboard.

The found phrases in Burckhardt's photographs highlight his sensitivity to language. In this photograph, one could argue, the words indicate that he, and by extension the viewer, is in the right place at the right time, and therefore "no turns" are necessary. Everyone in this scene is behaving civilly to one another, a first step towards "amity." The clothes in Burckhardt's vision are "timely" in the sense of giving

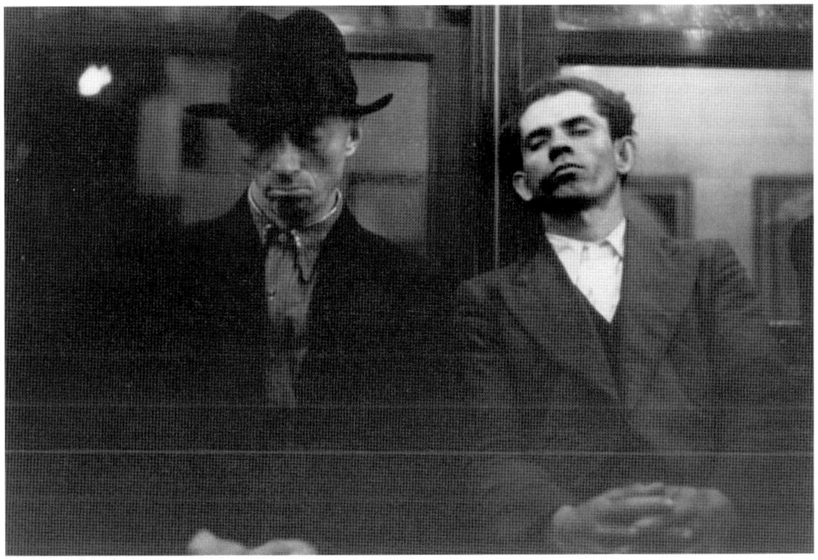

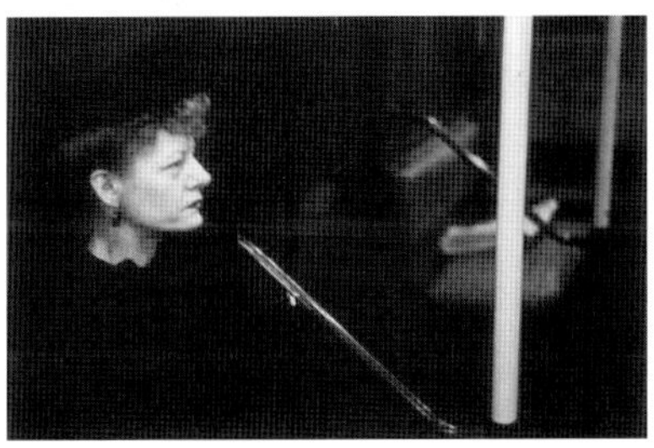

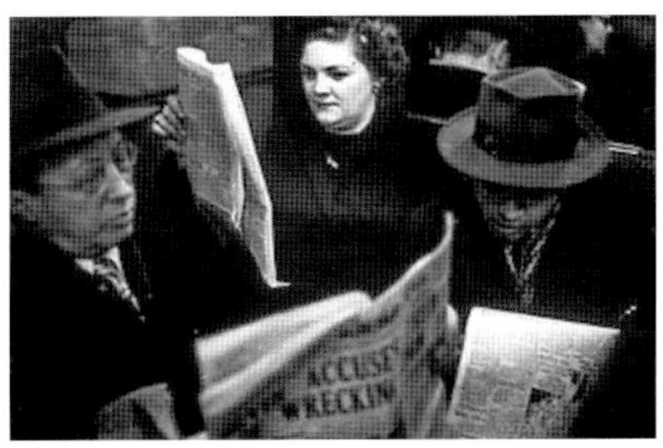

12 TOP
Walker Evans (1903–1975)
New York [Two Men Asleep in Subway Car], 1938
Gelatin silver print
4 13/16 x 7 1/4 inches
The Metropolitan Museum of Art,
Ford Motor Company Collection, Gift of Ford Motor Company and John C. Waddell, 1987 (1987.1100.472)
© Walker Evans Archive, The Metropolitan Museum of Art

13 BOTTOM LEFT
Rudy Burckhardt
Subway VI, 1947
Gelatin silver print
6 3/4 x 9 1/4 inches
Colby College Museum of Art,
Gift of the Alex Katz Foundation, 2006.040

14 BOTTOM RIGHT
Rudy Burckhardt
Subway V, 1947
Gelatin silver print
7 1/8 x 9 5/8 inches
Courtesy the Estate of Rudy Burckhardt and Tibor de Nagy Gallery, New York

evidence of their era and in the deeper sense of contributing to a propitious moment. This sense of being in the right place at the right time in New York's Midtown is original to Burckhardt and would later be adapted to become the central contribution of the poetics of mid-century's great poet of the city, Frank O'Hara.[16]

The witty use of language, compositional verve, all-over interest, and sense of propitiousness are elements that recur over and over in Burckhardt's street photographs from the 1930s and 40s: "The detail is accidental, but you do have the feeling that it is a decisive moment. Things happen in a split second, and you do have the feeling that it's the right split second." The "decisive moment," Henri Cartier-Bresson's contribution to photographic discourse, was appreciated by Burckhardt, yet Burckhardt's moments, while decisive in the formal sense, achieve unexpectedly intimate expressions, a result of his ability to introduce himself into the situation, whether in an artist's studio, a foreign country, or on the streets of New York.

"At the same time," his statement continues, "I never used a hidden camera. I never did that. I was right there with the camera, in the crowd. I was never doing peep-hole photography."[17] This may have been a dig at Evans, who did devise a way of hiding a camera under his coat to do his famous series of passengers in the New York subways from 1938–41 [figure 12]. Burckhardt did his own subway series in 1947, and the results are quite different. For one thing, there is the occasional person aware that Burckhardt is taking the photograph, but more than that (as he had developed a way of moving in and taking a photograph in the moment just before the subject was aware of it), Burckhardt's subway photographs, like his sidewalk photographs, are exquisitely composed. Part of the difference is that Evans' subway images were often cropped later, in the studio, giving his series a repetitive quality, while Burckhardt's show more compositional variety. Evans' tend to be straight on (he would often sit opposite a subject), while Burckhardt's present a range of angles, proximity to the subjects, combinations of figures, and relationships between figures and subway car fixtures [figures 13 and 14].

After spending the years 1941–44 in Trinidad as a troop photographer, Burckhardt returned to New York at the height of its post-war euphoria. It was during the next few years that he created the photographs that have become most strongly identified with him. The expansiveness of his images of these public places in New York—Herald Sqaure,

15 TOP
Rudy Burckhardt
Flatiron Building, Summer, 1947
[see plate 67]

16 BOTTOM
Berenice Abbott (1898–1991)
Flatiron Building, Madison Square, 1938
Gelatin silver print
10 x 8 inches
Museum of the City of New York, Museum purchase with funds from the Mrs. Elon Hooker Acquisition Fund, 40.140.105

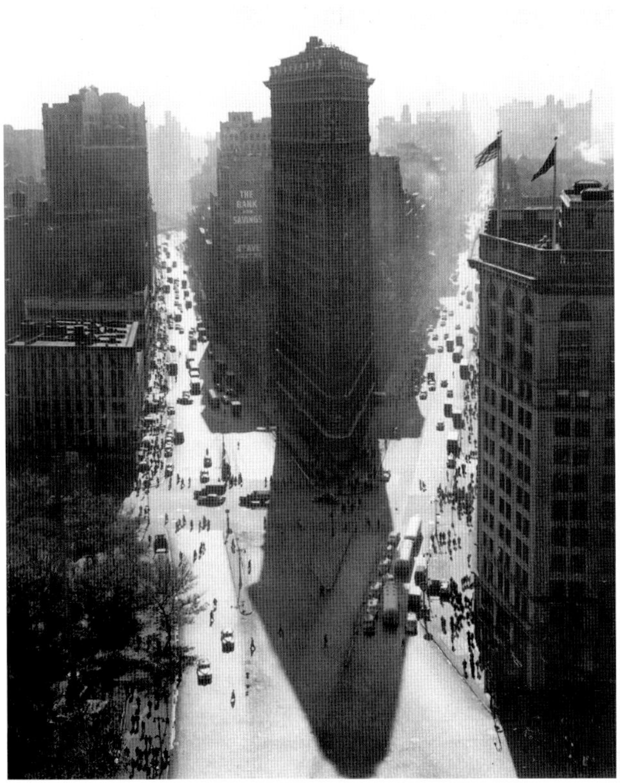

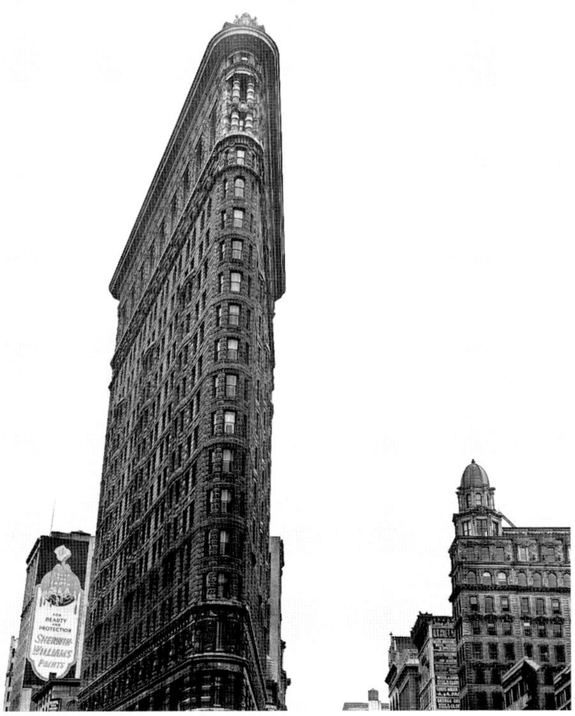

Times Square, Astor Place, Madison Square—does not, however, have to do with any national mood of self-congratulatory release. Just as his photographs of the 1930s do not give evidence of the Depression or, on the other hand, romanticize images of glamorous celebrity, but rather create compositions from the movements and details of average New Yorkers walking in midtown, so now, almost ten years later, his post-war photographs present a view of a capital city that is, at least in theory, democratic, but whose vision is more one of the city as a natural phenomenon than something novel or surreal.

In *Flatiron Building, Summer*, 1947 [figure 15, plate 67], as in *34th Street and Broadway,* c. 1947, a strong formal composition draws the eye into the photograph, leading it down the two avenues that flow past the angled sides of the Flatiron Building in the center. The most arresting feature of this photograph is the huge, down-turned shadow of the Flatiron, which occupies the bottom half of the center of the photograph, ending precisely where the frame ends and creating other angled forms of light on its sides. Beyond its suave interplay of large-scale forms, the entire picture has a deeper motivation, which is to serve as a setting for the daily activities of a group of individuals—citizens or visitors, but at this moment, participants in the life of the city. The same applies to *Astor Place,* 1947 [plate 66], where the view is from lower down and more personal detail is observable, and *Times Building*, 1947 [figure 10, plate 69], the first photograph in which Burckhardt was able to include pedestrians in the same frame with a tall building. Burckhardt's account of photographing the Flatiron Building illuminates his whole approach to photography: "This is a well-known picture I took one day. By accident, I got on top of this building when the shadow was about the same size as the building. They had elevator men; there were no automatic elevators. I'd ask for the top floor, pretending I had some business there. I'd look for an exit sign, and if I was lucky, I'd find an exit door and get up on a roof with these wonderful, completely unexpected, views. I think I just took one shot that day. This was taken on a 2 ¼ by 2 ¼ camera, not a Leica 35-millimeter. It is a square format camera. You had 12 photos on the roll, and I didn't take many of them."[18] His custom not to take many photos, while not using a tripod, came more from clarity of vision than a desire to be economical.

Berenice Abbott photographed the Flatiron Building from street level and also from above but preferred the street level view [figure 16]. She wrote, "There is no doubt in my mind that this building looks better

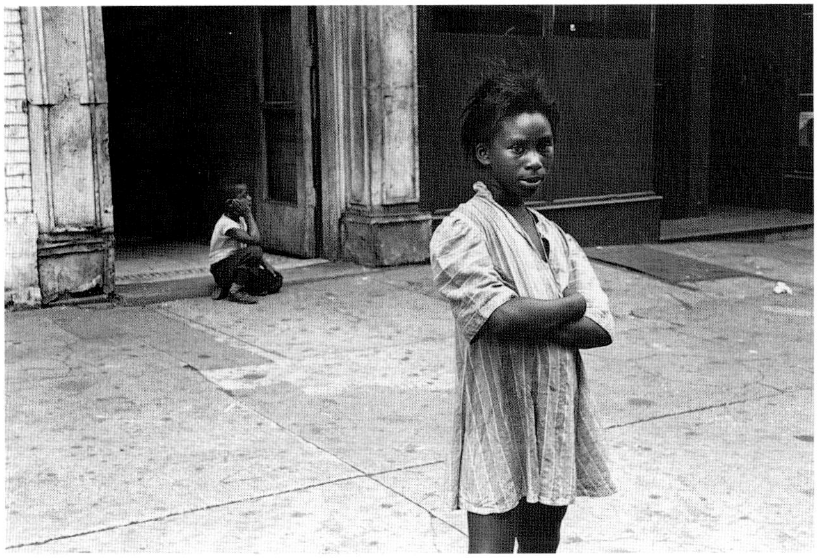

17 ABOVE
Helen Levitt (born 1913)
New York, c. 1940
Gelatin silver print
7 1/4 x 10 1/2 inches
Photography Collection, Miriam and Ira D. Wallach Division of Art, Prints and Photographs, The New York Public Library, Astor, Lenox and Tilden Foundations

from street level, and I was careful in picking the precise location to set my camera."[19] The photograph she took shows the building as though uprooted from its context; it becomes an artifact rather than an anchoring structural presence in a vast public space, as in Burckhardt's interpretation [figure 15].

Unlike Abbott, who carefully planned her views of the city and often did several exposures in order to be sure to get one she liked, Burckhardt was more interested in capturing the right mood, something to do with the air. He rarely photographed in inclement weather, wanting to depict people and scenes at their airiest. The tonal aspect of Burckhardt's New York photography becomes clear in his aerial views, including a series he did of rooftops, some of which he titled *Chelseascape* [plate 61]. Scanning one of these photographs, one finds a highly sensitive range of tones, from dark blacks to ever lighter shades of grey. Clearly, Burckhardt's decades of looking at painting affected how he saw the city, which in turn enabled him to make photographs of it with increased tonal depth.

The city photographers closest to Burckhardt in attitude to subject are Garry Winogrand and Helen Levitt. Levitt's photographs of children on sidewalks share with Burckhardt's an interest in urban architectural detail, possibly inherited from Evans, and a sense of the sidewalk as a social space. Her figures tend to be more isolated than Burckhardt's, and, as opposed to being part of the incessant movement of life he captures, are often forlornly paused in a quiet setting [figure 17]. Burckhardt's images possess surprising tonal richness; his prints, however, do not always live up to that richness. Burckhardt's living in the moment, his aloofness from serious expectations, gave him great powers as a photographer but could have a negative effect when it came to making prints and taking care of his archive. Working more in the realm of the idea, Burckhardt could be careless with his negatives, which could end up scratched, and also with his choices of paper. This attitude, it can be argued, is part of his bohemian appeal and gives his prints an unpretentious quality that separates them from the world of professional photography, which is done for hire and upholds established technical standards. It also helps to explain why he was sometimes not considered serious by serious photographers. In Helen Levitt's prints of Harlem children, there is an evenness to the darker tonalities that one occasionally finds lacking in Burckhardt's more superficial printing.

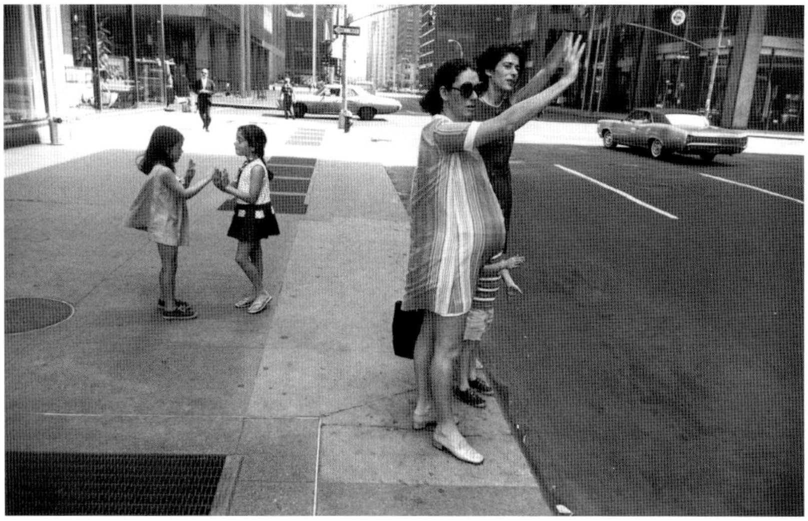

18 ABOVE
Garry Winogrand (1928–1984)
New York, 1968
Gelatin silver print
11 x 14 inches

Courtesy Fraenkel Gallery, San Francisco

Winogrand shared with Burckhardt a love of fast-moving sidewalk action, of stylish women moving with self-assurance through Midtown. His depictions of people, though, including women, tended toward the freakish, aligning him more with Diane Arbus and Frank than with Burckhardt's more welcoming view of humanity. While Winogrand could be frankly admiring of female beauty, making statements like, "Women are better than men; not only have they survived, they do prevail," he still isolated them in space, highlighting the awkwardness of their dress and their surroundings. The awkwardness was partly the result of the wide-angle lens he liked to use, which spread out the edges of the image, giving it an unreal quality.

The only Winogrand in his DEP Editions portfolio that has the mood of a Burckhardt—*New York*, 1968—pairs the carefree yet meaningful playing of two girls with the careful, calm diligence of their mothers on a sun-dappled Avenue of the Americas [figure 18]. The picture is grainy, its taken-on-the-spot quality rendered with the same sense of movement as in a Burckhardt. It is not a pristine picture technically. Compositionally, though, it is precise, the central adult duo standing on the dividing line between safety and danger, echoed by the child duo and two cars that seem to circle their island of safety. Winogrand's characteristic use of a wide-angle lens, however, flattens that view out, rendering it less immediate than in Burckhardt's more constricted lens.

In addition to mastering the central locations of New York City, Burckhardt maintained a parallel, and different, trend in his work until the end of his life, a trend that began in his earliest photographs, that of an explorer of the city, who wanders far to discover spaces ordinarily unnoticed or not commented on by their inhabitants. In New York, Burckhardt developed a special fondness for Astoria, Queens. It was there that he took, in 1940, the photographs that made up the artist's book *An Afternoon In Astoria*, a facsimile of which was published in 2002 by the Museum of Modern Art.[20] One photograph from that group is titled *A View From Astoria* [figure 19, plate 51]. In it, one sees in the distance Manhattan's skyline, punctuated by silhouettes of the Empire State and Chrysler buildings, while in the foreground one sees a railroad yard with a boxcar, a roadster pulled up to it, an engine in the distance, and three station houses straddling the tracks. In Burckhardt's photograph, these nondescript, workaday structures obscure most of the famous skyline, while the top and bottom of the image are dominated by expanses of sky and beat-up tiled ground. This

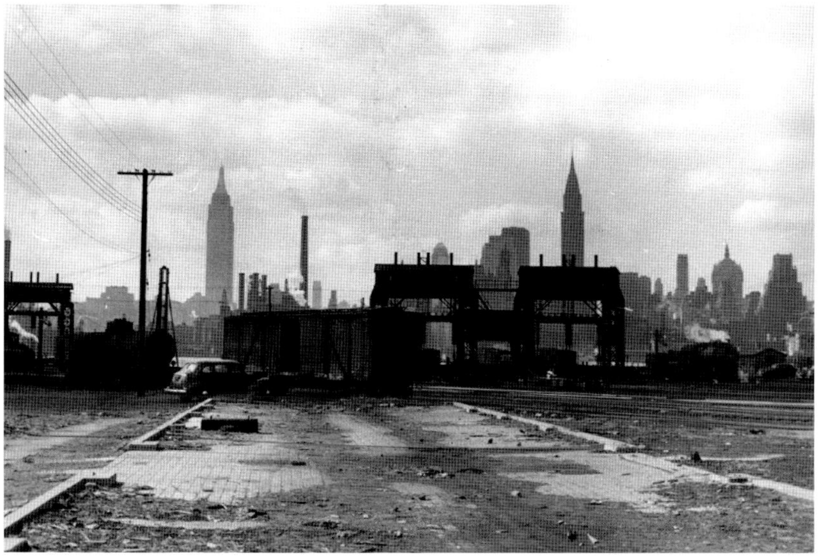

19 ABOVE
Rudy Burckhardt
A View from Astoria, 1940
[see plate 51]

picture has a particular meaning to it—obscuring the famous by the mundane, the expected by the unexpected—but it also has a formal beauty that one finds in many other Burckhardt photographs of Queens, of the canyons formed in Manhattan by jagged shapes of sky visible on streets between tall buildings, and in more meditative images of sidewalks, fire hydrants, manholes, and street crossings.

In his later years, Burckhardt devoted much time to filmmaking, painting, and occasionally to writing. There were periods, such as the 1960s, during which he did not photograph as prolifically as he once had. Collaboration became more and more important to him. As new generations of poets, painters, and dancers would come to New York, Burckhardt would befriend many of them, often inviting them to work on films together. Through the years, he made films with writers John Ashbery, Joe Brainard, Jim Carroll, Clark Coolidge, William Corbett, Larry Fagin, Elisabeth Fox, Kenneth Koch, Rochelle Kraut, Phillip Lopate, Alice Notley, Frank O'Hara, Ron Padgett, Bob Rosenthal, Harris Schiff, Peter Schjeldahl, Daniel Shapiro, David Shapiro, Christopher Sweet, Anne Waldman, Arnold Weinstein, Trevor Winkfield, and Bill Zavatsky, dancers Yoshiko Chuma and the School of Hard Knocks, Grazia Della Terza, William Dunas, Douglas Dunn and Dancers, Dana Reitz, and Paul Taylor Company, musicians Alvin Curran, Elliott Carter, Bill Cole, Ron Kuivila, and Christian Marclay, and visual artists Joseph Cornell, Elaine de Kooning, Rackstraw Downes, Jane Freilicher, Red Grooms, Mimi Gross, Alex Katz, Fairfield Porter, Larry Rivers, Charles Simmonds, and Neil Welliver, not to mention his first wife, Edith Schloss, his second, Yvonne Jacquette (both painters), and his sons, Jacob and Tom (filmmaker and painter respectively). Edwin Denby participated in many, as writer or actor or both. The influence all these people had on one another was surely mutual, but it is clear that Burckhardt influenced many of them. To quote just one, Denby wrote, "Daily life is wonderfully full of things to see. Not only people's movements, but the objects around them . . . the ornaments architects make around windows and doors, the peculiar ways buildings end in the air, the water tanks, the fantastic differences in their street facades on the first floor . . . As for myself, I wouldn't have seen such things if I hadn't seen them first in the photographs of Rudolph Burckhardt."[21]

When Burckhardt did begin to photograph extensively again, which he did from the early 1970s to his death in 1999, he often returned to themes and ideas that had interested him earlier with different

20 TOP
Sally Stein (born 1949)
New York Subway, 1977
Gelatin silver print
Museum of the City of New York, gift made possible through the Creative Artists Service Program, 82.179.2
Courtesy of the photographer

21 BOTTOM
Rudy Burckhardt
Joe DiMaggio, 1975
Gelatin silver print
7 ¾ x 9 ½ inches
Courtesy of the Alex Katz Foundation

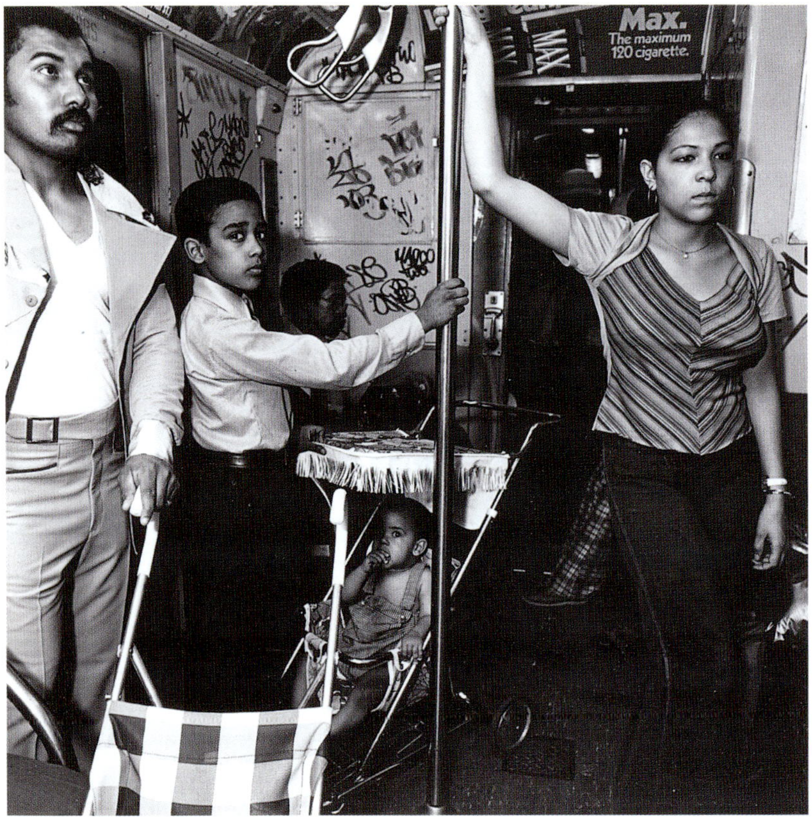

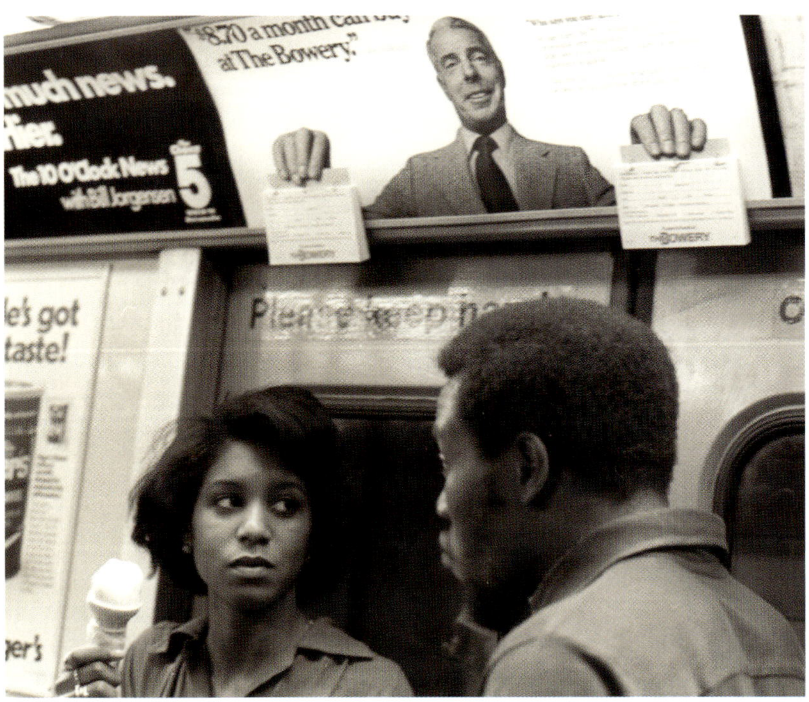

emphases in terms of focus, composition, and physical relation to his subjects. His photographs of reflections of the Flatiron Building, taken in the 1970s, have an elegiac quality to them, as though Burckhardt were seeing an image of primal importance to him reduced or codified [plates 70-72]. The surrounding plaza is stripped away, the building itself is gone; only the reflection remains, its reflected beauty hauntingly tangible. A series of photographs of shadows of street lamps and figures cast on sidewalks is similarly reduced [plates 85-87]. Burckhardt had used shadows within larger compositions in a painterly way from his early days. In the 1970s, he limited his compositions to the shadows themselves plus the feet and ankles directly connected to those shadows. The compositional expertise he long exercised achieved new clarity in photographs such as *V-Back*, 1985 [plate 78], which calls to mind a Renaissance altarpiece in the equipoise of its three turning figures, and *Untitled*, c. 1985 [plate 74], in which each element of the picture is perfectly weighted, and, as Edwin Denby observed, there is visual interest throughout.

It is informative to compare Burckhardt's later subway photographs to those of other photographers. To take one example, Sally Stein used flash to take photographs in the New York subway in 1977, and the resulting pictures provide information about the time, but the flash clearly alerted her subjects to her presence, so that they are posed by the time the exposure is made [figure 20]. More significantly, the lighting of the subway car is drastically modified. Burckhardt's avoidance of flash correlates with other nonintrusive habits: he rarely used a tripod; the vast majority of his work is hand held; as mentioned earlier, he never did hidden-camera photography; he took few exposures of a given subject; and he did little cropping.

His subway photograph *Joe DiMaggio*, 1975 [figure 21] is an excellent example of his later work. Burckhardt has zeroed in on a young couple standing near the closed subway doors. She is looking at him with skepticism or disbelief; he purses his lips as he prepares his response. The details are exquisite, particularly the still-fresh ice-cream cone in her hand, bought on a warm day, symbolizing her freshness, but also the drily humorous inclusion of the former baseball star looming over them, a fading relic that may call to mind Burckhardt's "Coca Cola Goddess" of Astor Place [plate 66] in another era, DiMaggio's era.

What is particularly striking about this, and many of Burckhardt's later photographs of people, is the way he has managed to approxi-

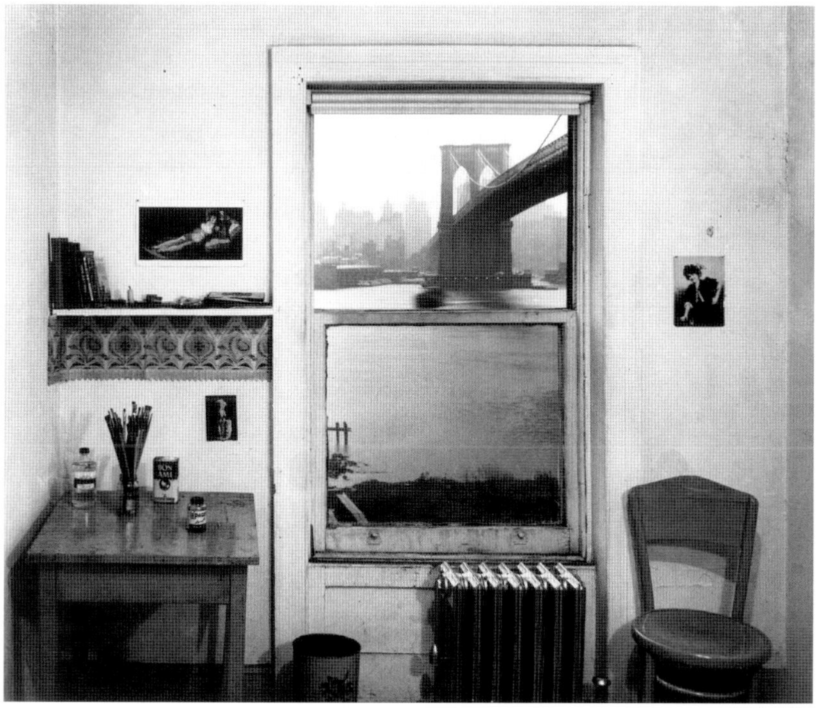

22 ABOVE
Rudy Burckhardt
A View from Brooklyn II, 1953
Gelatin silver print
9 x 10 ½ inches
Courtesy the Estate of Rudy Burckhardt and Tibor de Nagy Gallery, New York

mate himself to them, to insinuate himself into their discussion, without, apparently, being noticed. He made himself one of the crowd, a quiet observer providing a service to the city. He did not see freakishness, and he does not ask viewers of his photographs to see it. He did not see social ills, although he knew they existed. Rather, he noted appearances and presented people, places, and things in a sympathetic light, not idealized by long exposures or mutated by flash but close to how it was. As the complexion of the city changed, Burckhardt was glad to follow those changes. He always felt drawn to people of the African diaspora, whether it was in Haiti, where he lived for nine months, in the American South, or in New York City. His late photographs contain many remarkable portraits of people of color, encountered in public spaces.

In summarizing Burckhardt's achievement as a photographer, one can make the following conclusions. The works that are less original are those that try to show some element of commercial reality, such as newsstands or signage, on its own. The still lifes that he photographed in the mid-1940s, using found materials, seem like exercises; one can sense that Burckhardt was not particularly interested in these objects. He found ways to energize such subject matter, by combining it with walking people (in the case of signage) or with spectacular views of Manhattan and the Brooklyn Bridge through his studio window (in the case of the still lifes) [figure 22]. The aspects of his photography that are most original include his early minimalist, Mondrian-like aesthetic; his downward-focused fragments on sidewalks; his ability to keep visual interest in all parts of a composition; and his sensitivity to texture and to tonal variation, particularly in the lighter areas. This tonal lightness conveys a psychological lightness, which, Phillip Lopate has written, comparing Burckhardt to Evans, is "more playful and tender, less melodramatic, more true to the spirit of the everyday."[22] One could add that Burckhardt's ability to see things as they are and picture them as timeless, as in the poetry of O'Hara and James Schuyler, written decades later, often opens into an appreciation of humanity unparalleled in other street photographers.

The critic Robert Storr characterized Burckhardt's work as "nonjudgmental," saying, "he saw things you wouldn't see, because he wasn't driving at social documentation. He wasn't driving at a particular psychological read, although there's lots of psychology in his pictures. He wasn't anticipating or determining or ruling on what would make a good photograph—he was looking. His decisive moments tended

23 TOP
Jack Pierson (born 1960)
From the 6th Floor, 243 West 42nd Street, 1992
Type "C" print
30 x 30 inches
Edition of 10
Courtesy of the photographer and
Cheim & Read, New York

24 BOTTOM LEFT
Rudy Burckhardt
Film still from *Square Times,* 1967
Courtesy the Estate of Rudy Burckhardt

25 BOTTOM RIGHT
Wolfgang Tillmans (born 1968)
Paula, typewriter, looking, 1994
C-print
Dimensions variable
© Wolfgang Tillmans, courtesy
Andrea Rosen Gallery, New York

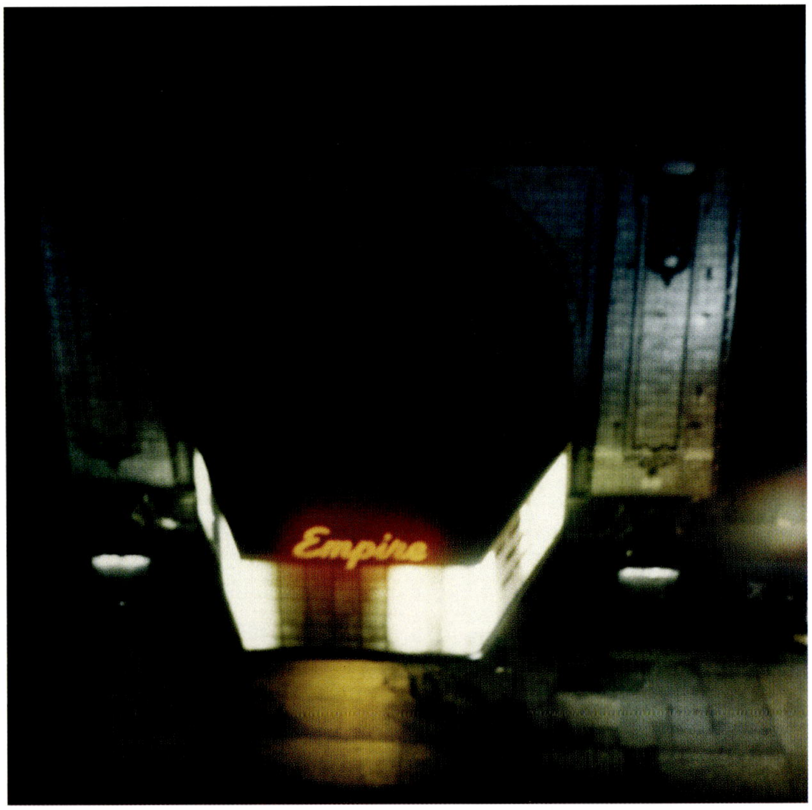

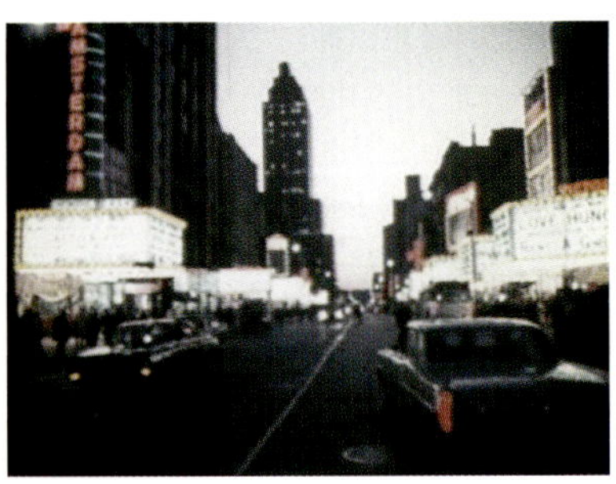

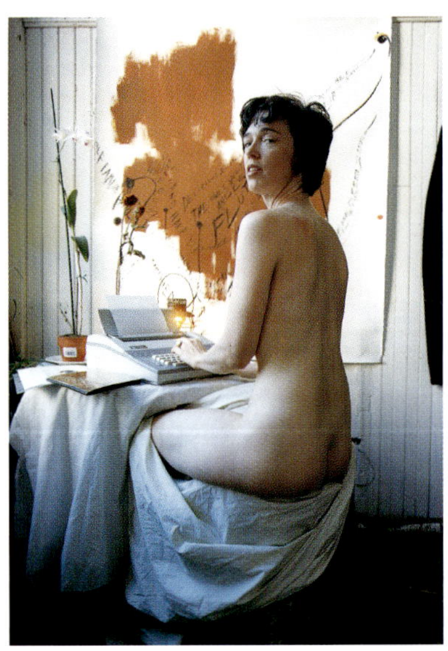

to be other people's indecisive moments."[23] The socially neutral nature of Burckhardt's work made it difficult for early photography audiences to get, but it lines it up with a lot of photography that emerged in the 1980s and 1990s. Elements of Burckhardt's work that might appeal to contemporary photographers like Nan Goldin, Jack Pierson, and Wolfgang Tillmans include Burckhardt's relaxed, informal approach to picture-making, whether that be a decision about what light to use or where to place oneself to capture a scene or the ability to let go of sharp focus if that will give the photograph a feeling of energy or motion [figures 23 and 25]. These younger photographers would also identify with Burckhardt's portrayal of the city in his films, as a context for liberated bohemian behavior. Burckhardt quietly influenced generations of artists, from Edwin Denby to Frank O'Hara and beyond. Who knows? Maybe there is a young person about to move to New York, who will one day find something in Rudy Burckhardt's photographs that we have not noticed.

1
Frank O'Hara, *Lunch Poems* (San Francisco: City Lights Books, 1964), 16.

2
Rudy Burckhardt interview in *Man in the Woods: The Art of Rudy Burckhardt*, film, by Vivien Bittencourt and Vincent Katz, Checkerboard Film Foundation, 2003.

3
Susan Sontag, *On Photography* (New York: Anchor Books Doubleday, 1989), 148, writes, "Although photography generates works that can be called art … photography is not, to begin with, an art form at all. Like language, it is a medium in which works of art (among other things) are made."

4
Rudy Burckhardt, "How I Think I Made Some Of My Photos And Paintings," *Rudy Burckhardt* (Valencia: IVAM Centre Julio González, 1998): 194. In addition to the text cited above, the IVAM catalogue contains the texts by Rudy Burckhardt, "How Did I Meet Edwin?" and "How I Think I Made Some Of My Films," and essays by Robert Storr and Vincent Katz.

5
Burckhardt studied painting and painted throughout his life, achieving some critical acclaim in later years. His way of seeing through photography informed the imagery of his paintings.

6
Interview with author, January, 1998.

7
Interview with author, January, 1998.

8
Interview with author, March, 1998.

9
Interview with author, January, 1998.

10
The film retrospective was curated by Phillip Lopate.

11
In his first New York apartment, which he shared with Denby, Burckhardt had de Kooning for a neighbor, and he would often visit the older painter's studio, occasionally buying his work.

12
Rudy Burckhardt, interview in *Man In The Woods* (see note 2).

13
Rudy Burckhardt, interview in *Man In The Woods* (see note 2).

14
Audrey McMahon, *Changing New York: Photographs by Berenice Abbott* (New York: E.P. Dutton & Company, Inc., 1939), vii.

15
Cited by Burckhardt in "How I Think I Made Some Of My Photos And Paintings," *Rudy Burckhardt* (see note 4): 194.

16
The poet and critic Frank O'Hara, a central figure in the New York School of Poetry that arose in the 1950s, favorably reviewed the poetry of Edwin Denby and participated in two Burckhardt films.

17
Rudy Burckhardt, interview in *Man In The Woods* (see note 2).

18
Interview with author, January, 1998.

19
Berenice Abbott: American Photographer (New York: McGraw-Hill Book Company, 1982), 162.

20
Rudolph Burckhardt, *An Afternoon In Astoria* (New York: The Museum of Modern Art, 2002), with an essay by Sarah Hermanson Meister.

21
Edwin Denby, "Dancers, Buildings, and People in the Streets," in *Dance Writings and Poetry* (New Haven: Yale University Press, 1998): 258.

22
Phillip Lopate, *Rudy Burckhardt* (New York: Harry N. Abrams, Inc., 2004), 14.

23
Robert Storr, interview in *Man In The Woods* (see note 2).

NOTE
Consultation with a clothing specialist, Phyllis Magidson, Curator of Costumes and Textiles, Museum of the City of New York, confirmed my suspicion that the photograph of Herald Square in figure 11 was most probably taken in the mid to late 1940s, not in 1939, as earlier supposed.

I would like to thank the following for their advice and assistance in various aspects of preparing the exhibition and catalog essay: Andrew Arnot, Henk van Assen, Carole Kitchel Bellew, Ib Bellew, Vivien Bittencourt, Melanie Bower, Amanda Bowers, Eric Brown, Sean Corcoran, Sharon Corwin, Bethany Engstrom, Andrea Henderson Fahnestock, Juan Gomez, Sarah Henry, Yvonne Jacquette, Meghan Jewett, Susan Gail Johnson, Susan Henshaw Jones, Patricia King, Abby Lepold, Phyllis Magidson, Giacomo Mirabella, Autumn Nyiri, Stephen Saitas, Angela Waldron, and Lora Urbanelli.

34
Untitled, 1937
Gelatin silver print
9 ¾ x 8 inches
Courtesy the Estate of Rudy Burckhardt and Tibor de Nagy Gallery, New York

35
Encroachment, 1938
Gelatin silver print
9 ½ x 7 ¾ inches
Collection of Eric Cohler, courtesy Tibor de Nagy Gallery, New York

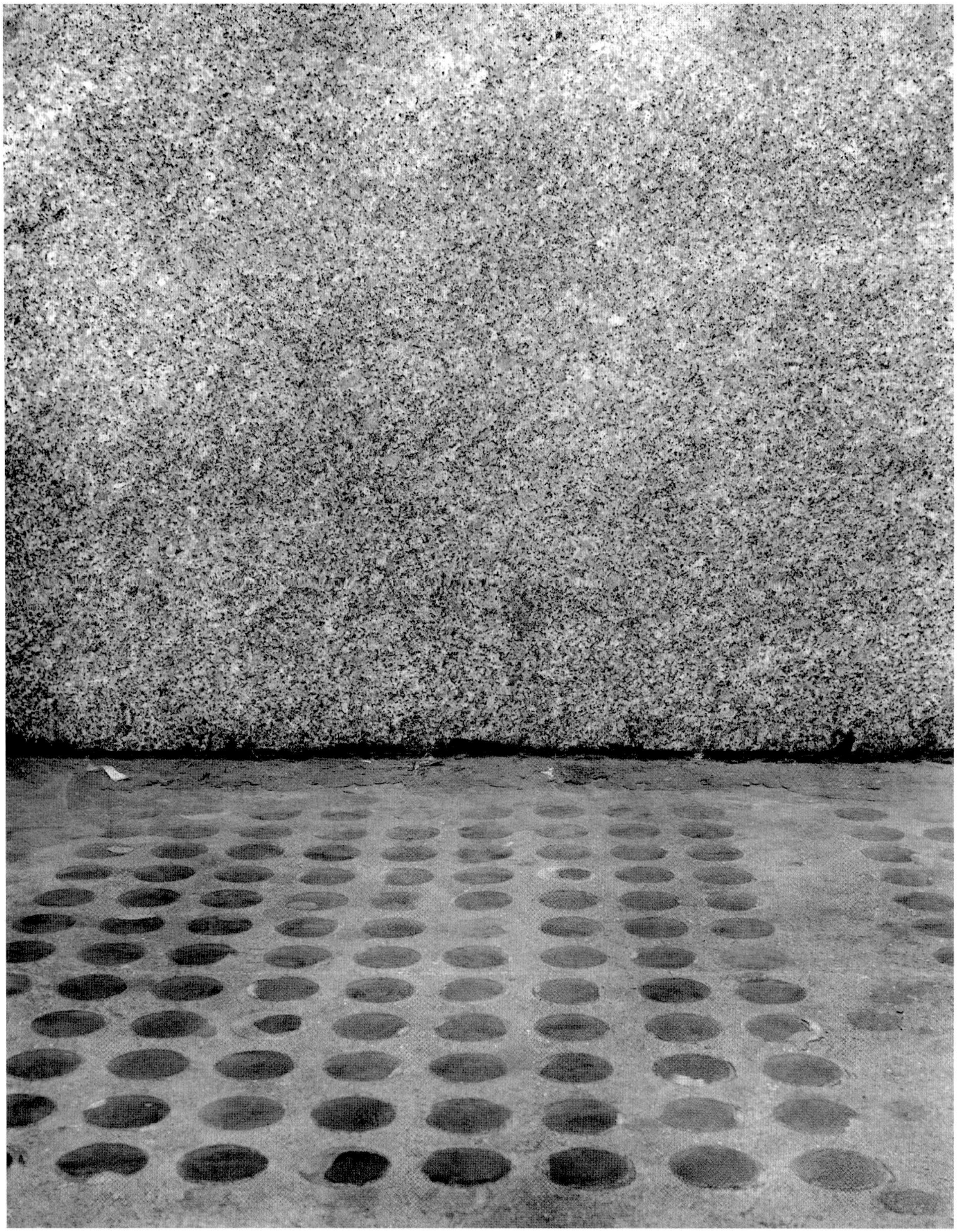

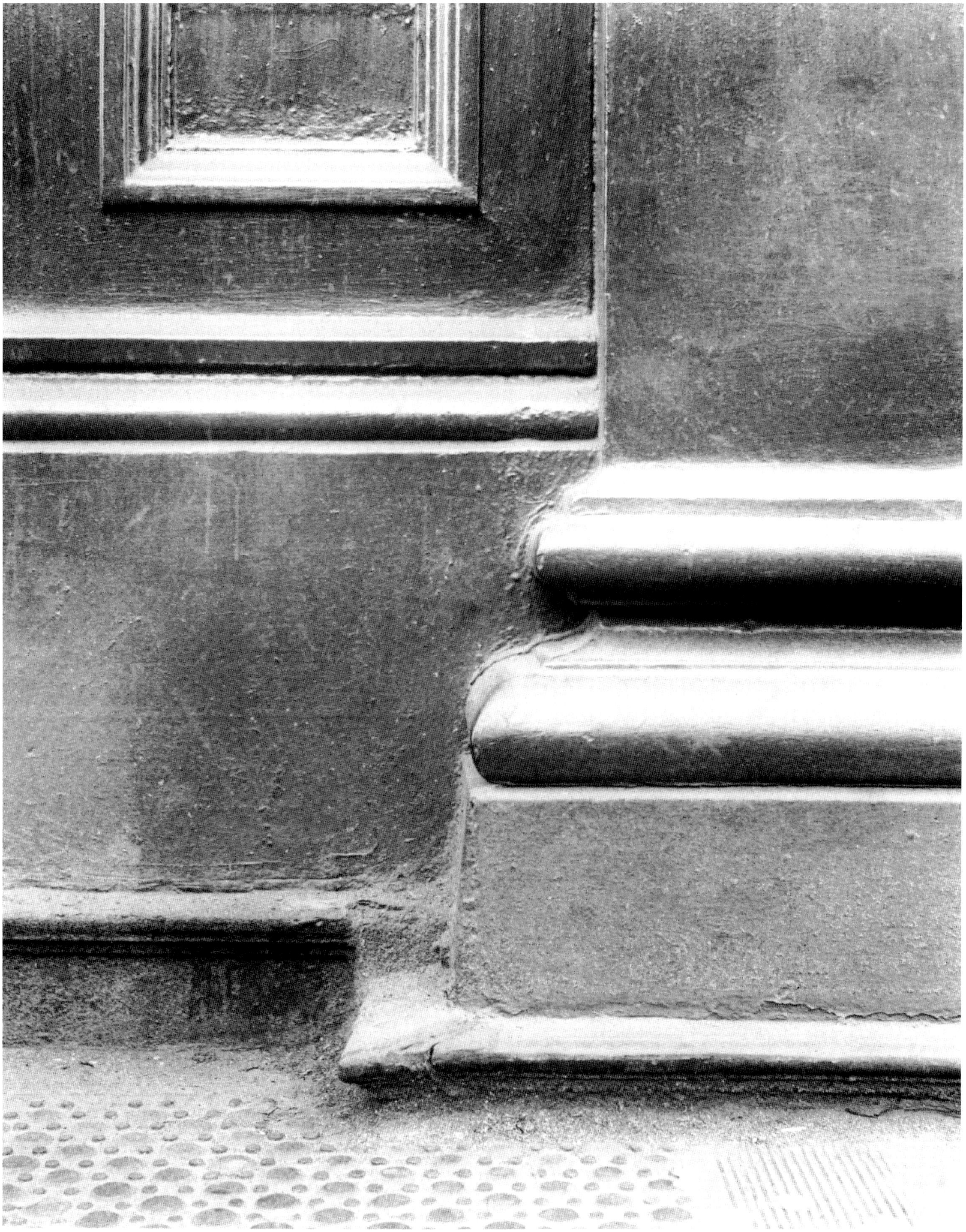

36
New York, 1939
Gelatin silver print
8 ¾ x 6 ¾ inches
Farnsworth Art Museum,
Gift of the Alex Katz Foundation,
2006; 2006:4:2

37
No Encroachment, c. 1938
Gelatin silver print
13 ½ x 9 ¾ inches
Courtesy the Estate of Rudy Burckhardt
and Tibor de Nagy Gallery, New York

38
Standpipe, c. 1937
Gelatin silver print
9 ¾ x 8 inches
Courtesy the Estate of Rudy Burckhardt
and Tibor de Nagy Gallery, New York

39
Sterling Mount Co., 1938
Gelatin silver print
11 ¾ x 9 inches
Courtesy the Estate of Rudy Burckhardt
and Tibor de Nagy Gallery, New York

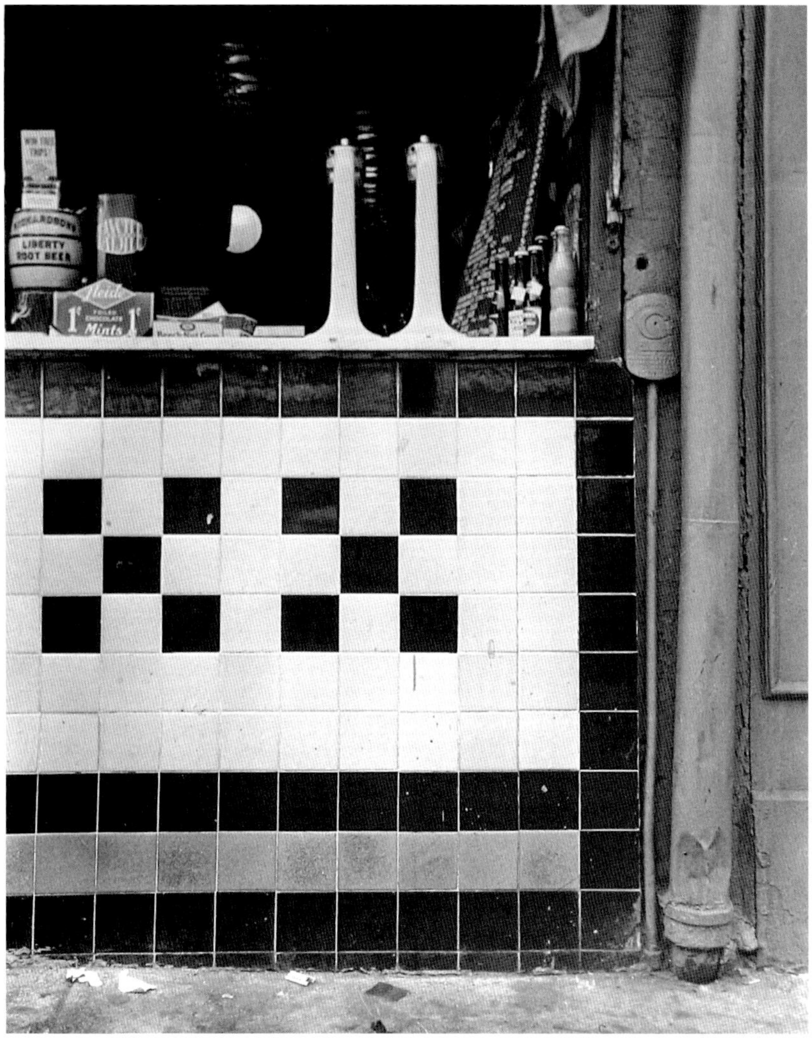

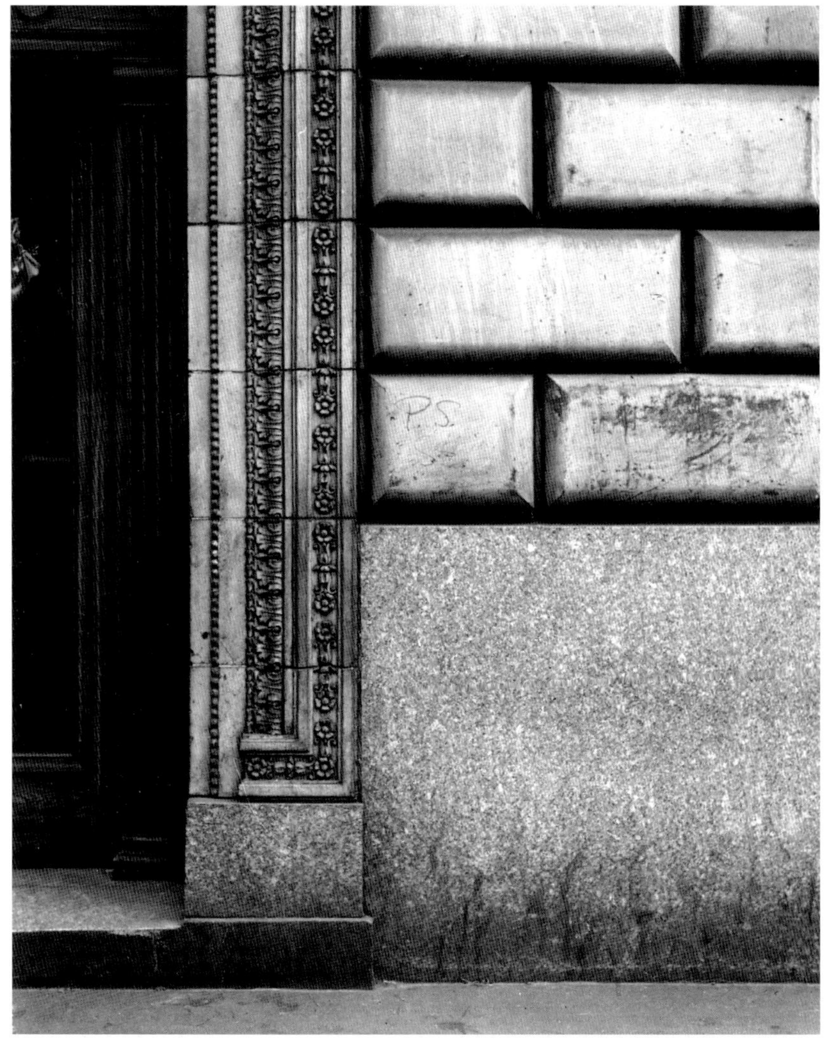

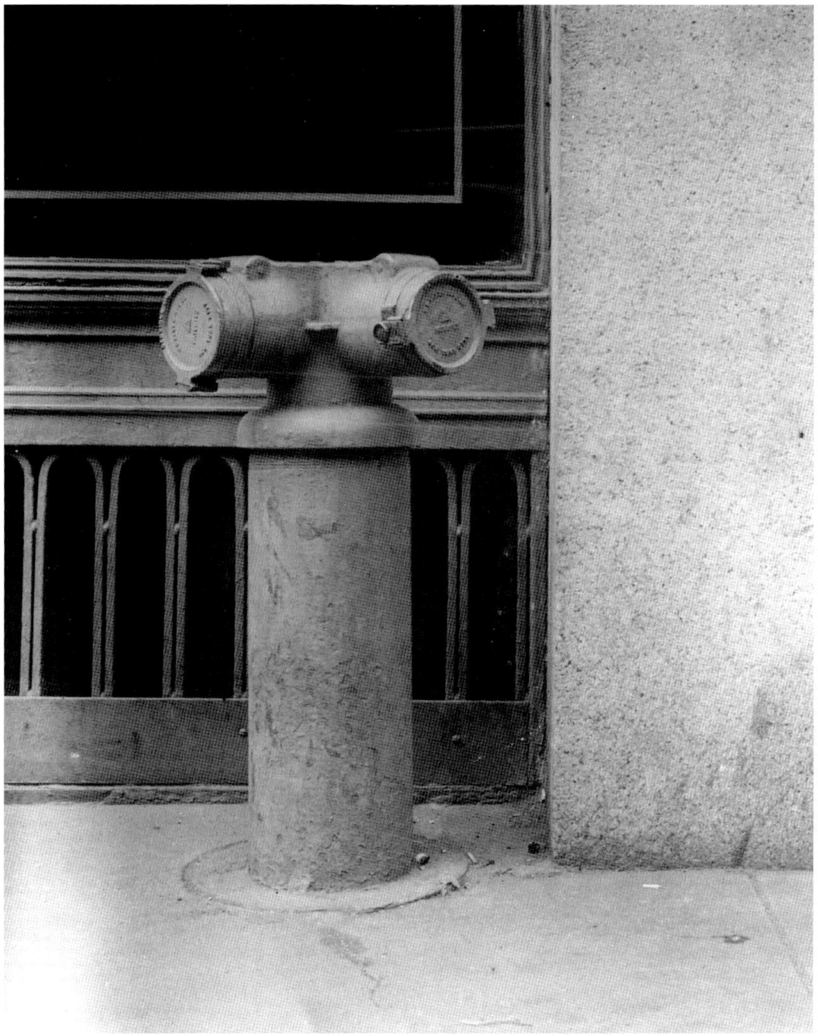

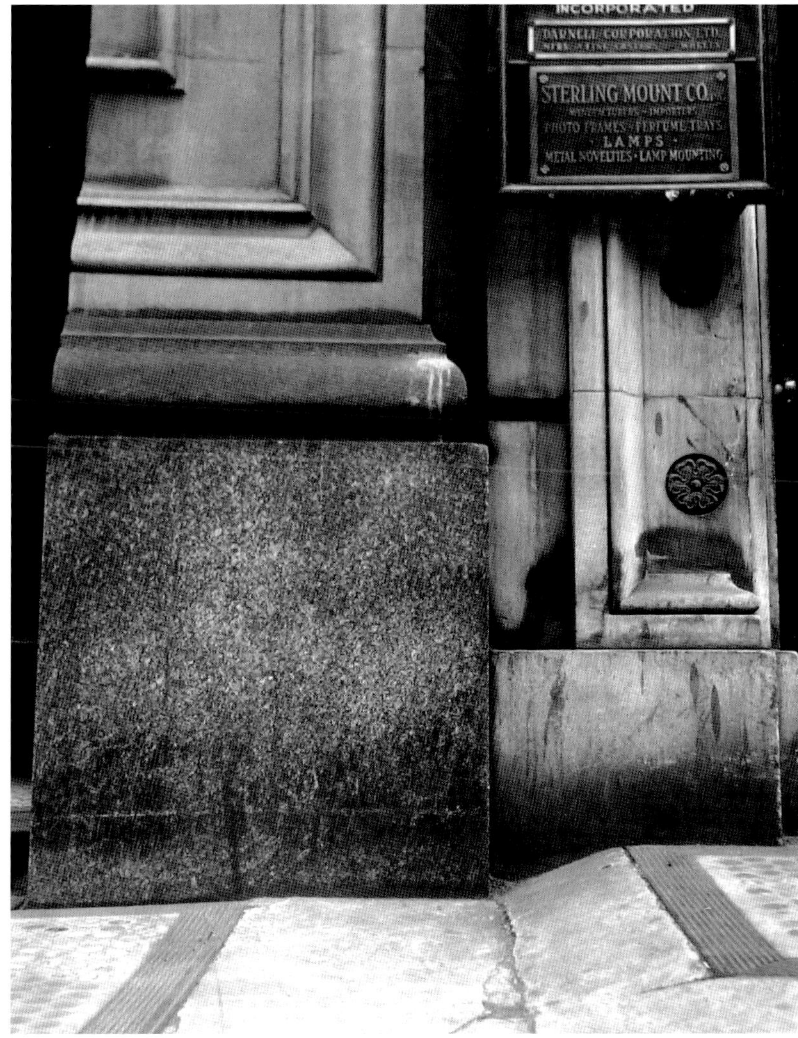
INCORPORATED
STERLING MOUNT CO.
LAMPS
METAL NOVELTIES · LAMP MOUNTING

40
Circles, 1939
Gelatin silver print
12 x 16 inches
Colby College Museum of Art,
Gift of the Alex Katz Foundation, 2006.032

41
Sidewalk XIX, 1939
Gelatin silver print
6 ¼ x 9 ⅜ inches
Colby College Museum of Art,
Gift of the Alex Katz Foundation, 2006.020

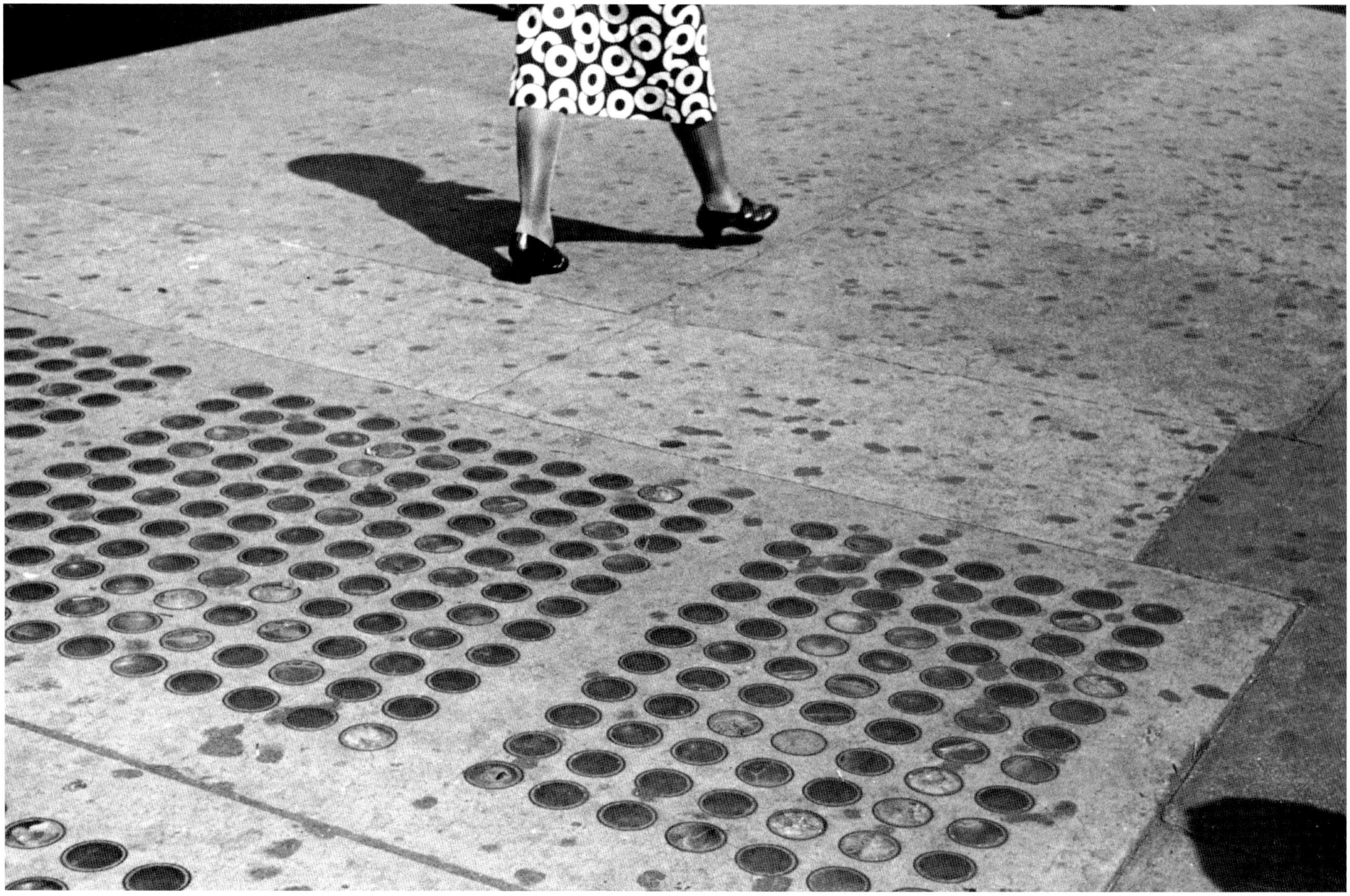

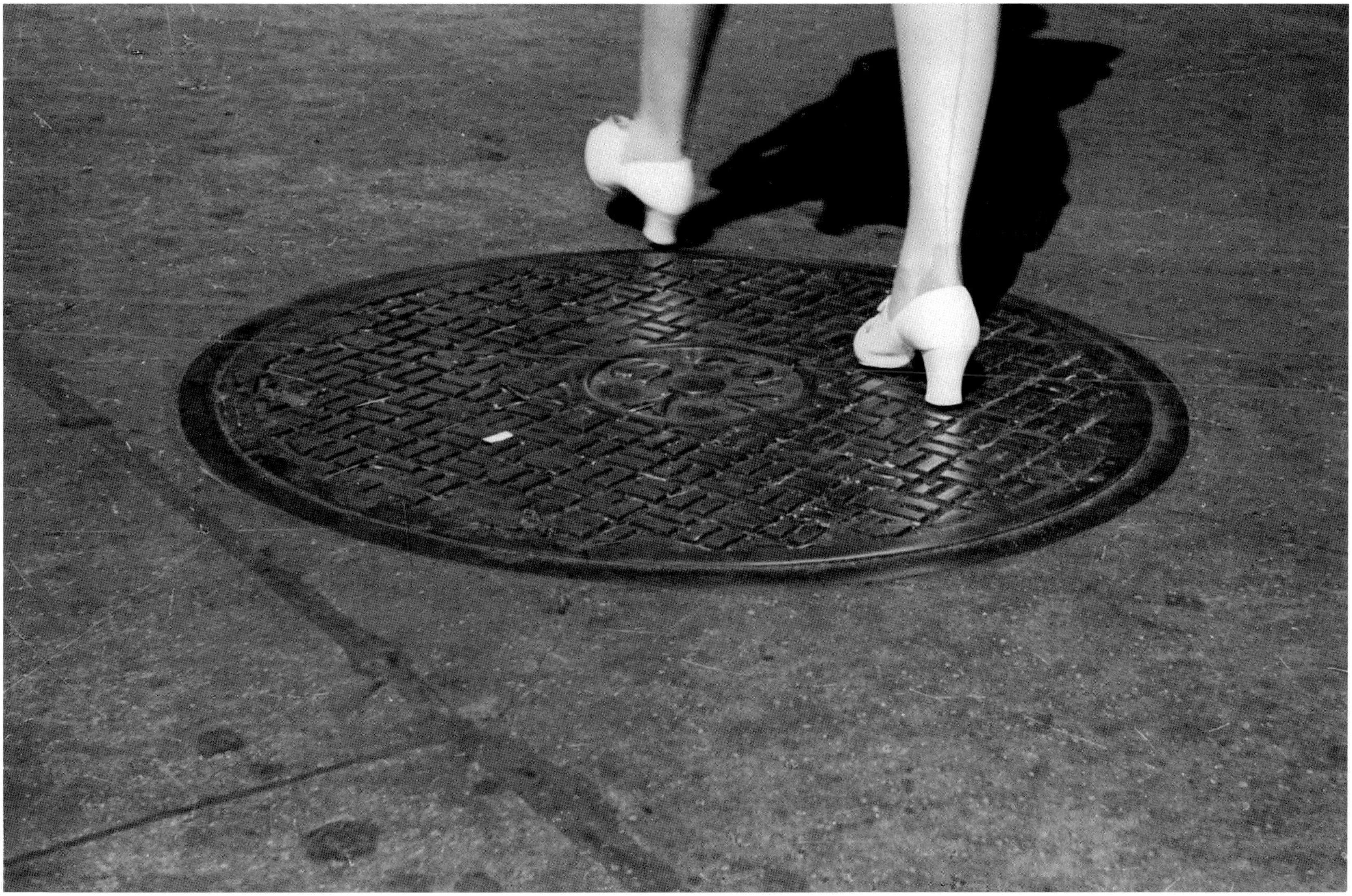

42
Sidewalk III, 1939
Gelatin silver print
8 x 10 inches
Courtesy the Estate of Rudy Burckhardt
and Tibor de Nagy Gallery, New York

43
Sidewalk IV, 1939
Gelatin silver print
7 ¼ x 9 ¼ inches
Colby College Museum of Art,
Gift of the Alex Katz Foundation, 2006.021

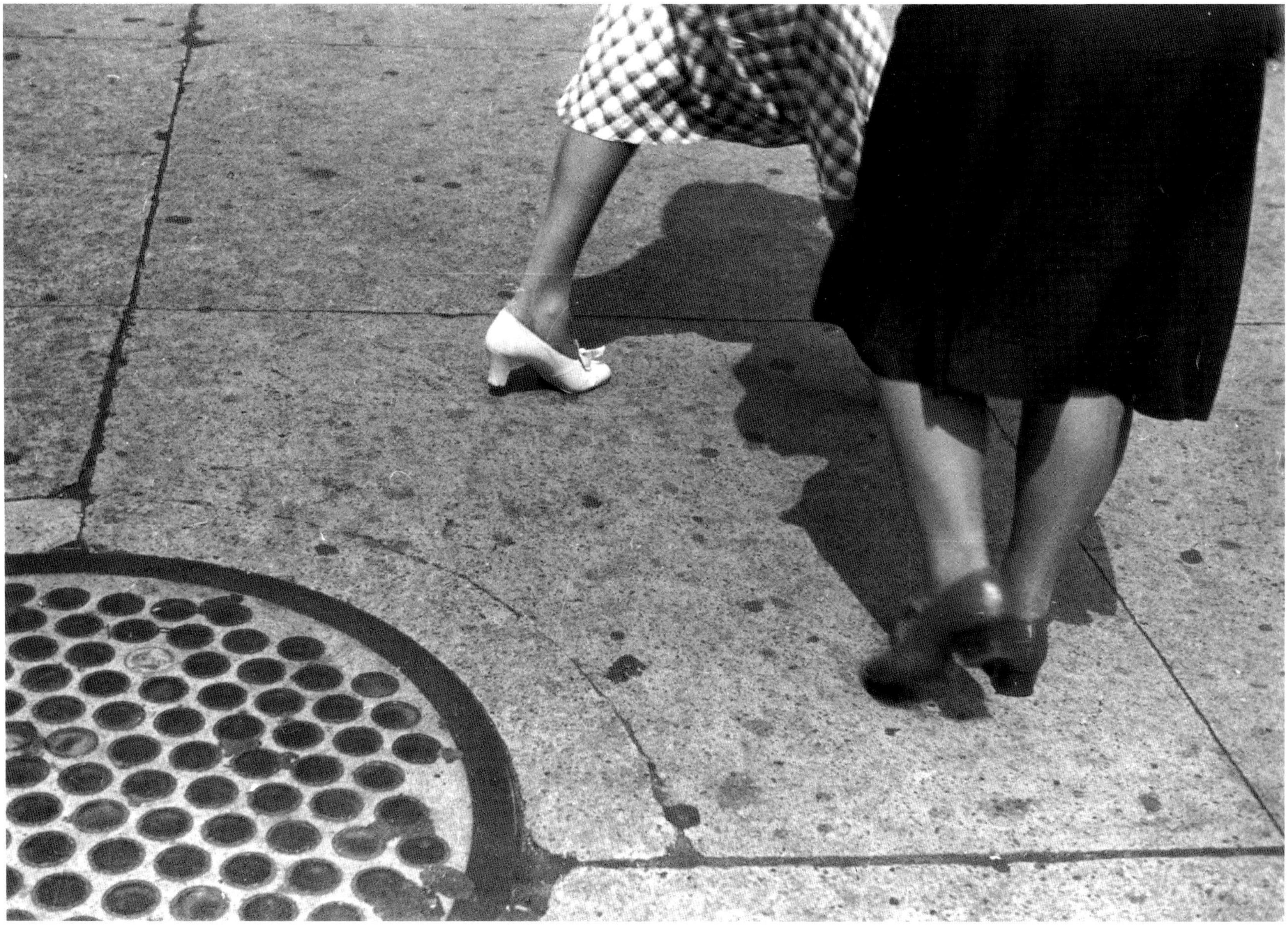

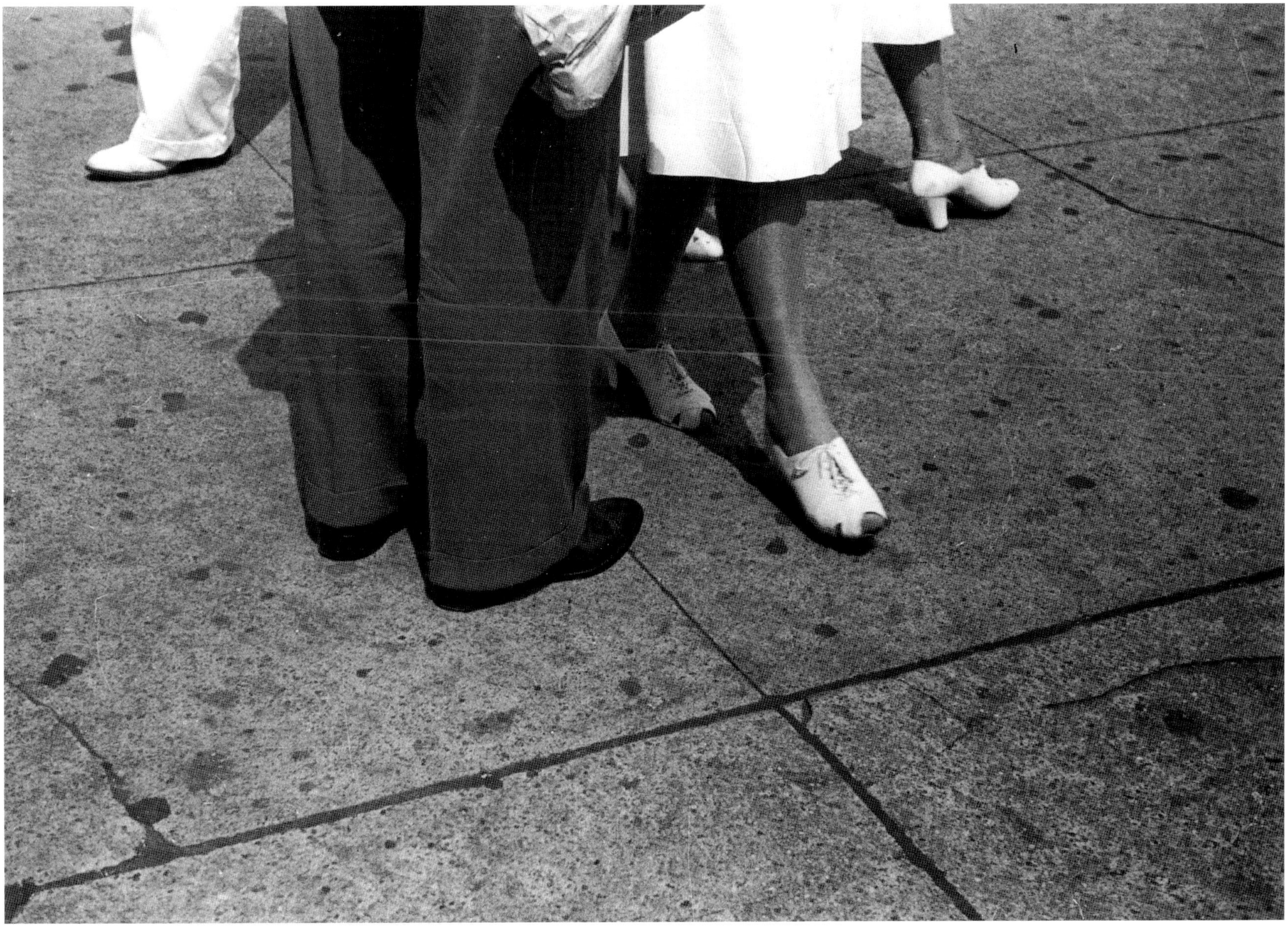

44
Malted Milk, c. 1939
Gelatin silver print
9 x 7 ¾ inches
Courtesy the Estate of Rudy Burckhardt
and Tibor de Nagy Gallery, New York

45
Lifebuoy, 1939
Gelatin silver print
10 x 7 inches
Courtesy the Estate of Rudy Burckhardt
and Tibor de Nagy Gallery, New York

46
Saks, 1939
Gelatin silver print
9 x 6 ½ inches
Colby College Museum of Art,
Gift of the Alex Katz Foundation, 2006.033

47
Shave 20 Cents, 1939
Gelatin silver print
7 ¼ x 4 ¾ inches
Courtesy the Estate of Rudy Burckhardt
and Tibor de Nagy Gallery, New York

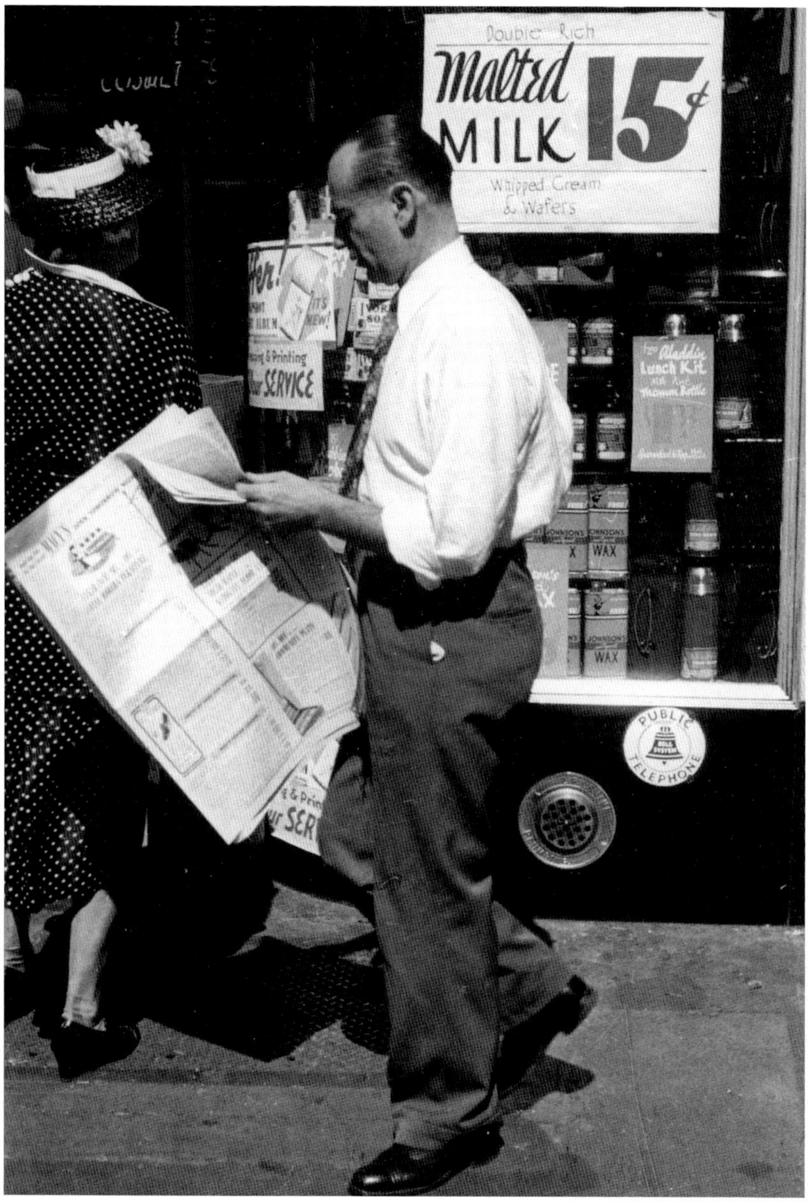

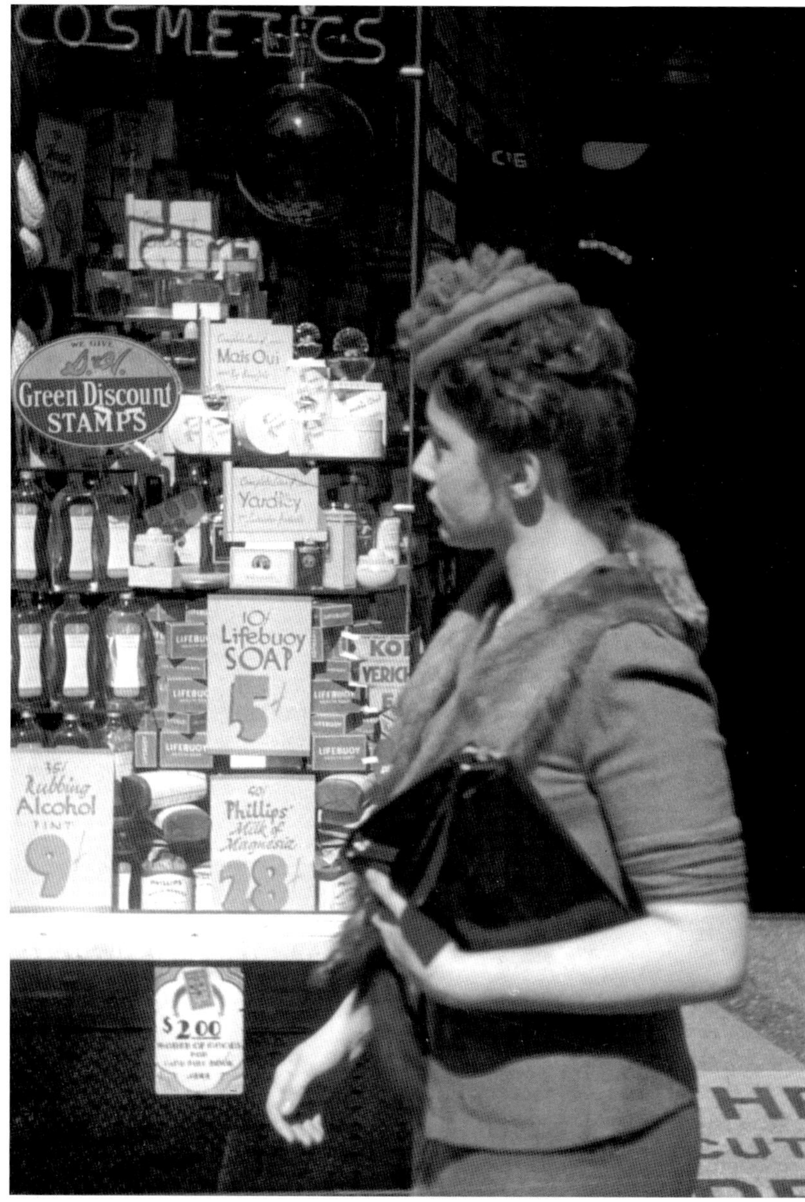

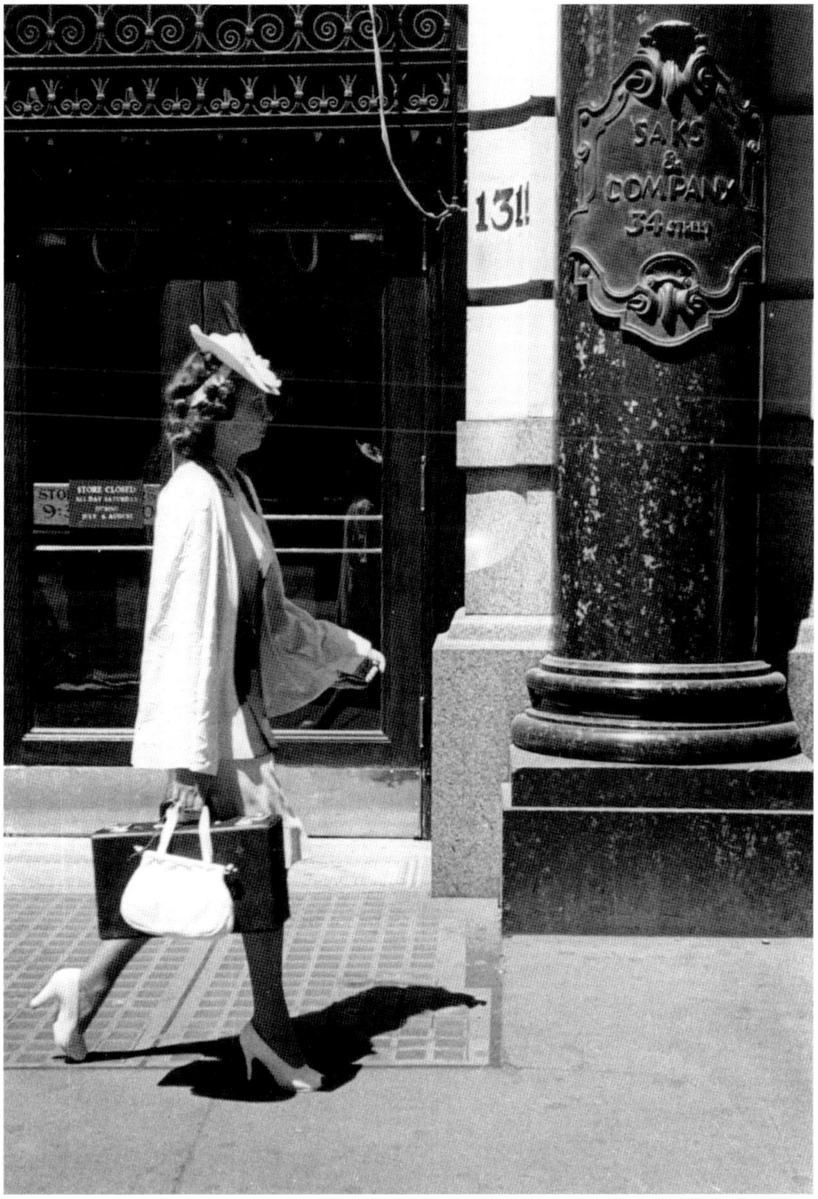
1311
SAKS
&
COMPANY

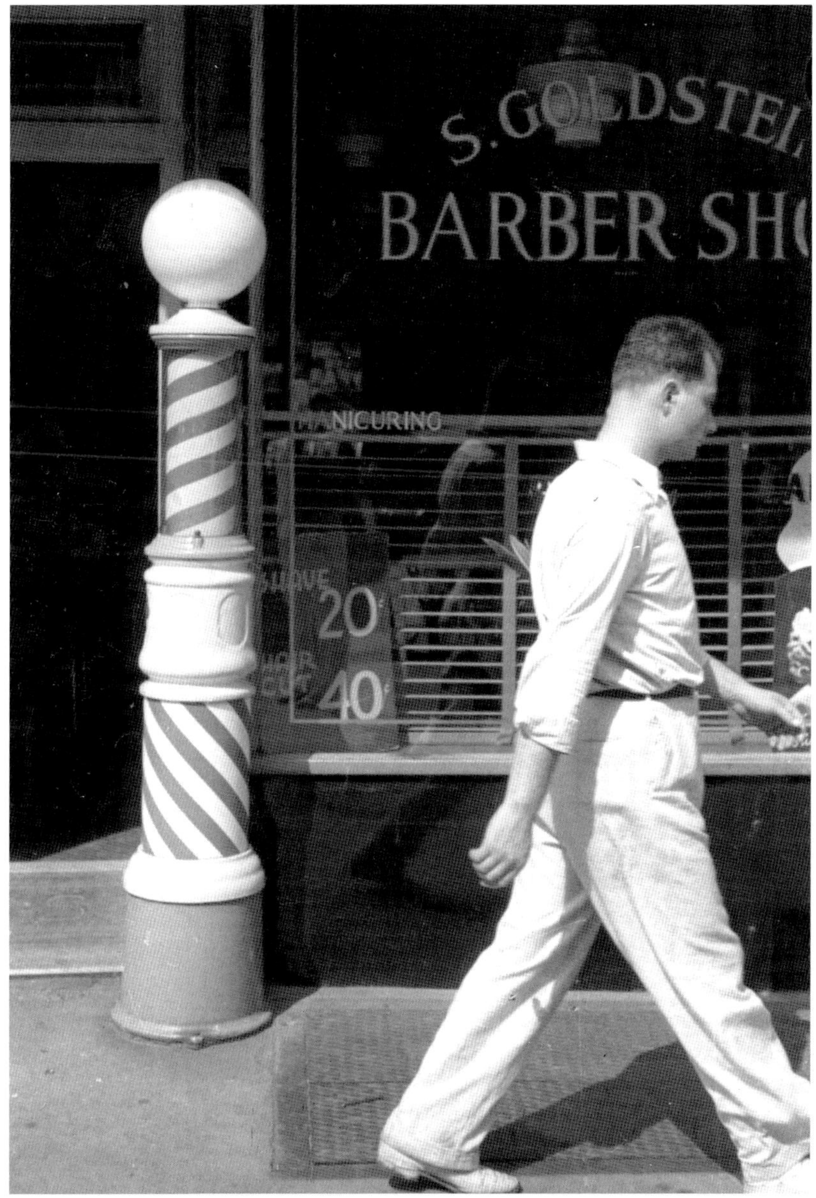
MANICURING

48
Rudley's, c. 1939
Gelatin silver print
3 ¾ x 5 ½ inches
Colby College Museum of Art,
Gift of the Alex Katz Foundation, 2006.019

49
Hot Roast Beef Sandwich 25¢, 1939
Gelatin silver print
8 x 10 inches
Colby College Museum of Art,
Gift of the Alex Katz Foundation, 2006.018

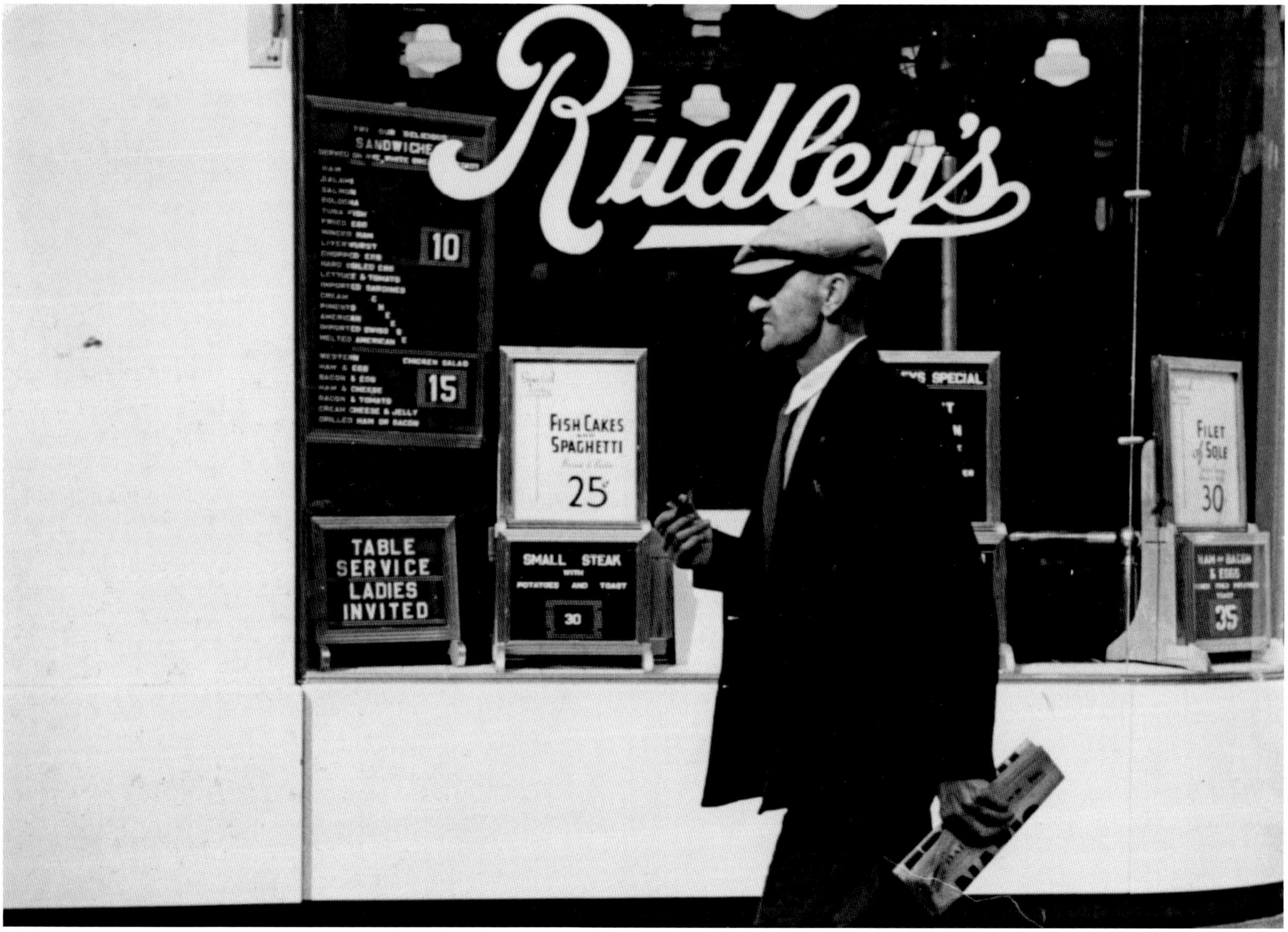

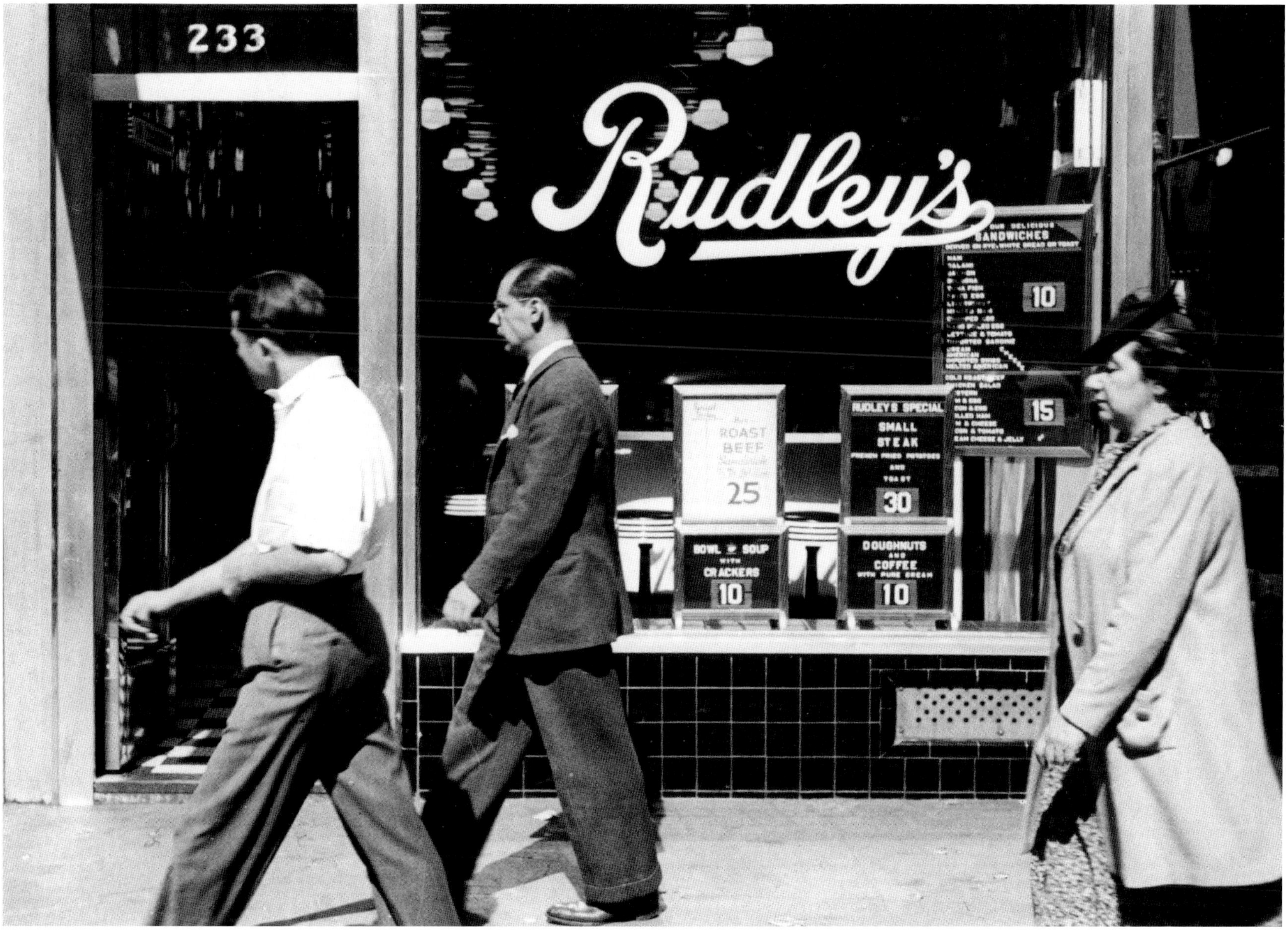
233
Rudley's
SANDWICHES
10
15
ROAST BEEF
25
RUDLEY'S SPECIAL
SMALL STEAK
30
BOWL OF SOUP
CRACKERS
10
DOUGHNUTS
COFFEE
10

50
Overpass [Astoria, Queens], 1940
Gelatin silver print
6 ⅞ x 9 ⅞ inches
Courtesy the Estate of Rudy Burckhardt
and Tibor de Nagy Gallery, New York

51
A View from Astoria, 1940
Gelatin silver print
11 x 13 ¾ inches
Farnsworth Art Museum,
Gift of Alex Katz Foundation, 2006; 2006.4.17

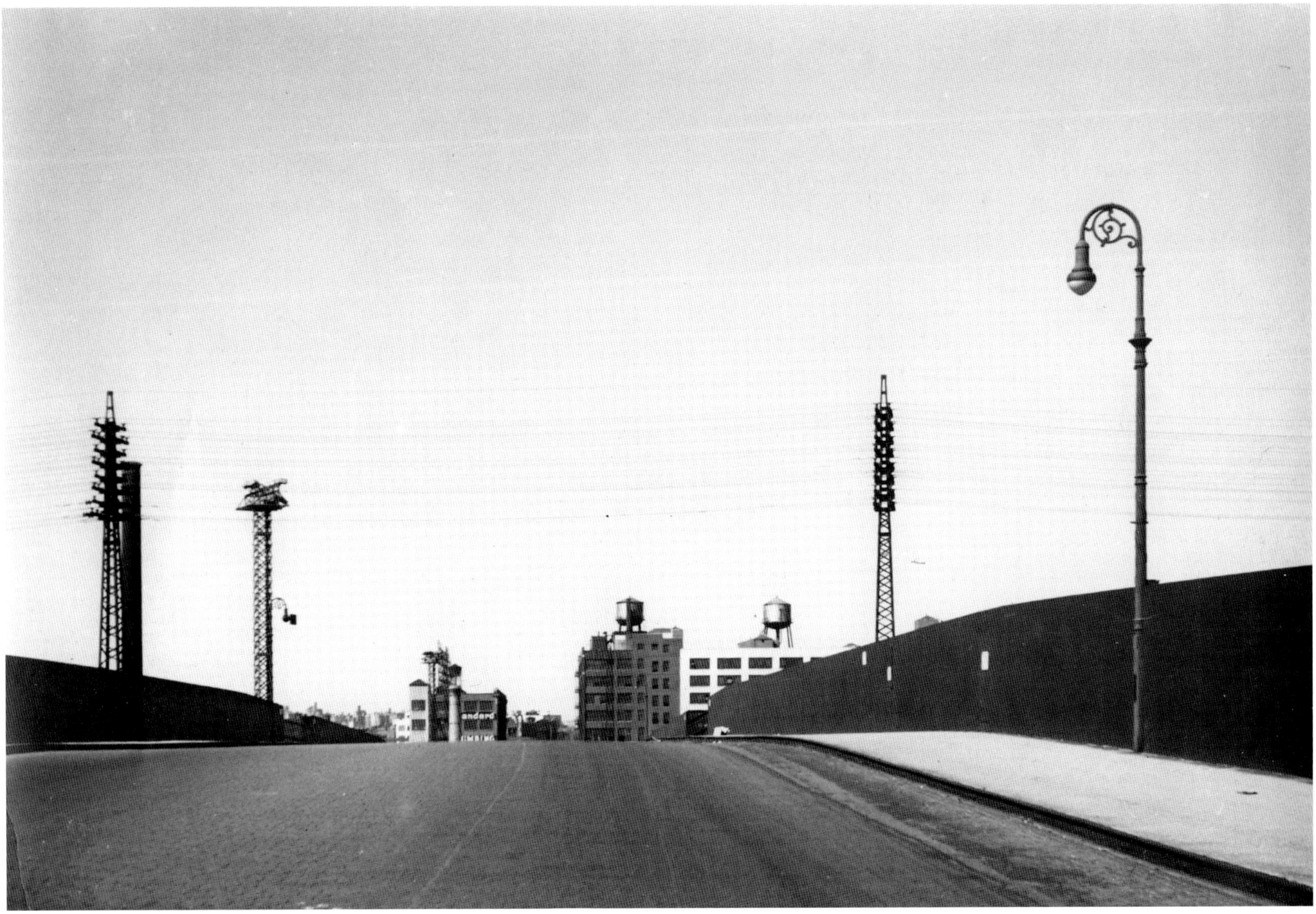

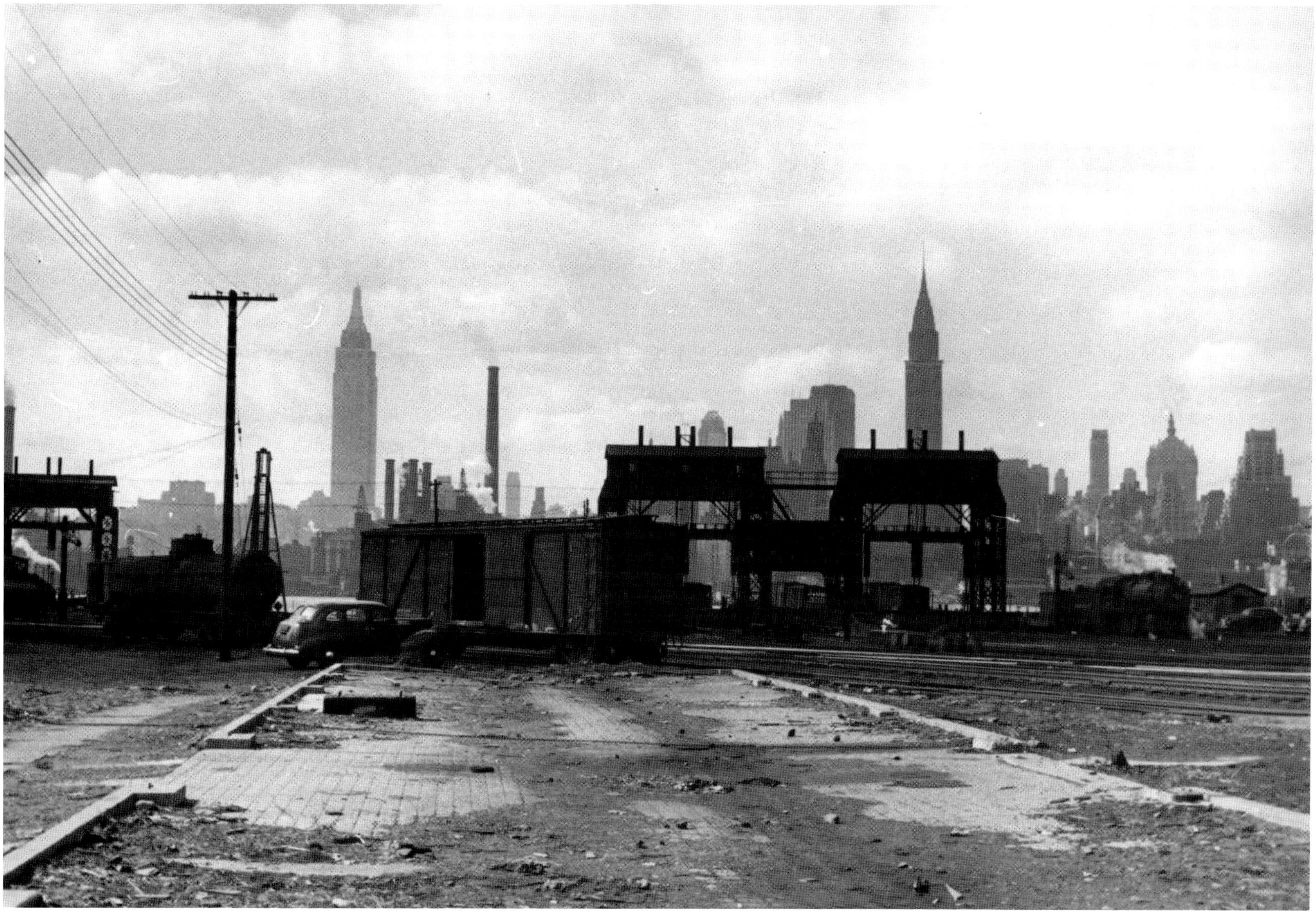

52
Chelsea Evening I, 1970
Gelatin silver print
13 ½ x 9 inches
Courtesy the Estate of Rudy Burckhardt and Tibor de Nagy Gallery, New York

53
Crossing, c. 1948
Gelatin silver print
10 x 8 inches
Courtesy the Estate of Rudy Burckhardt and Tibor de Nagy Gallery, New York

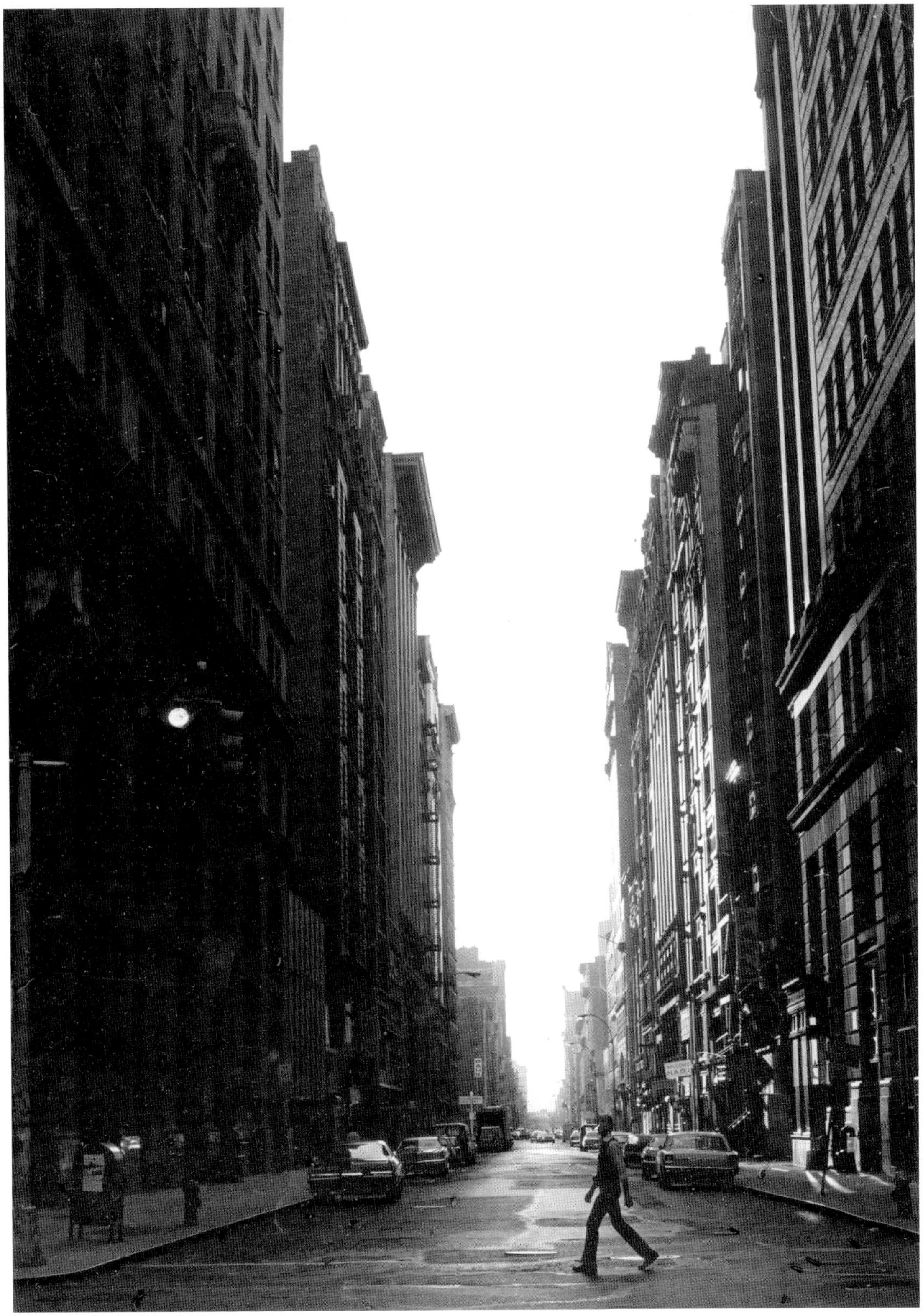

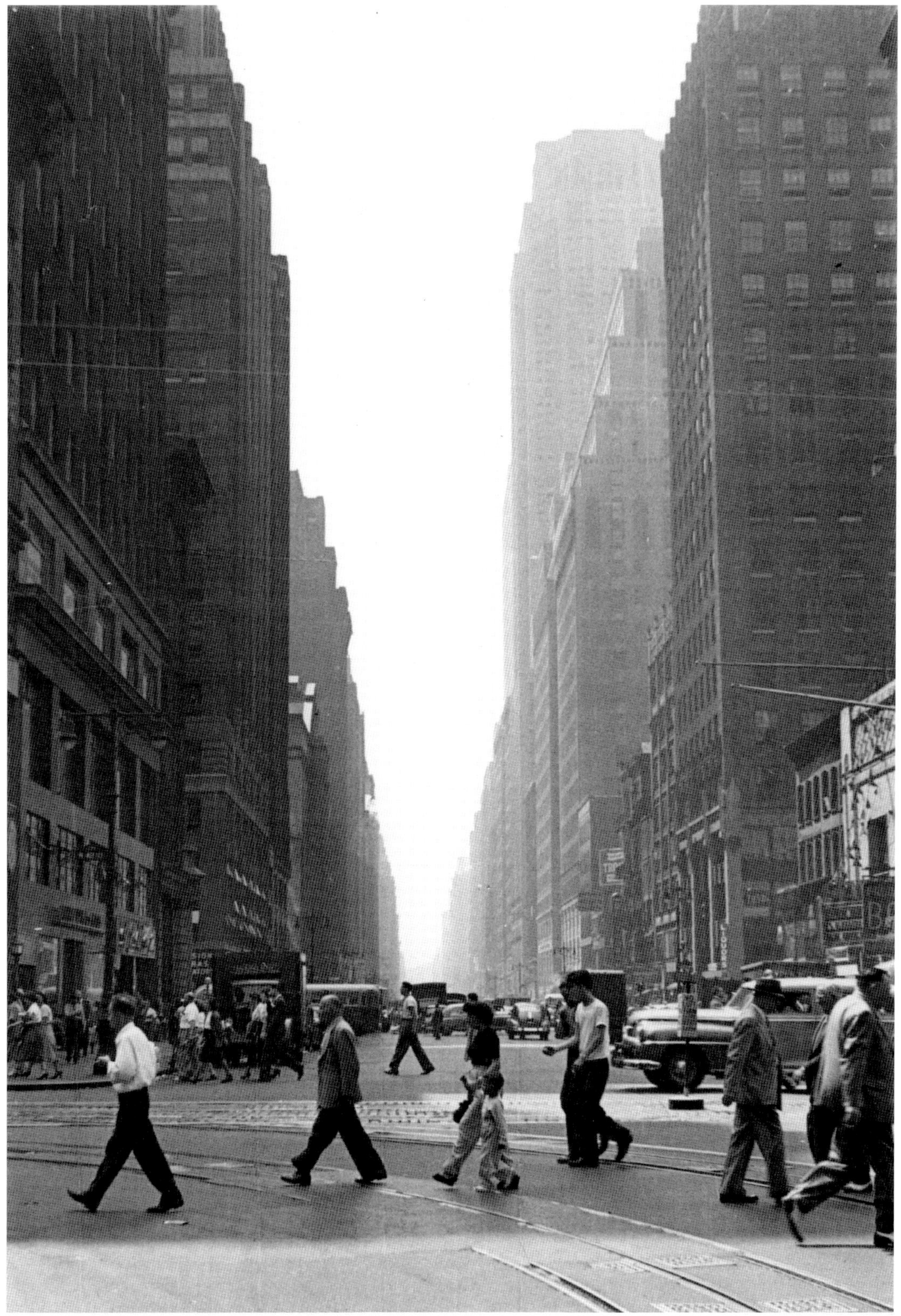

54
Subway, 1947
Gelatin silver print
5 ¼ x 8 ⅛ inches
Colby College Museum of Art,
Gift of the Alex Katz Foundation, 2006.031

55
Subway VII, 1947
Gelatin silver print
7 ⅞ x 10 inches
Colby College Museum of Art,
Gift of the Alex Katz Foundation, 2006.036

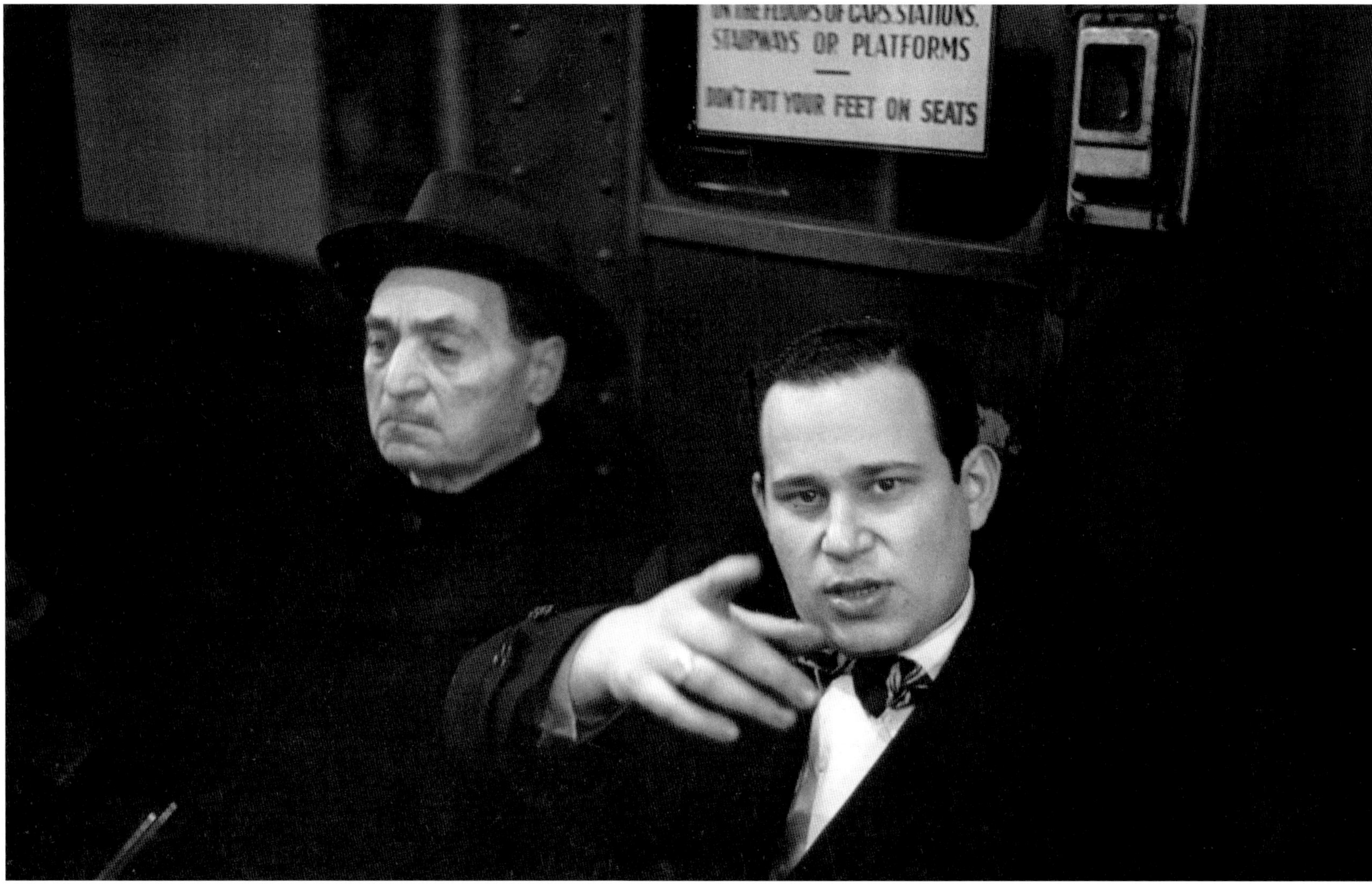

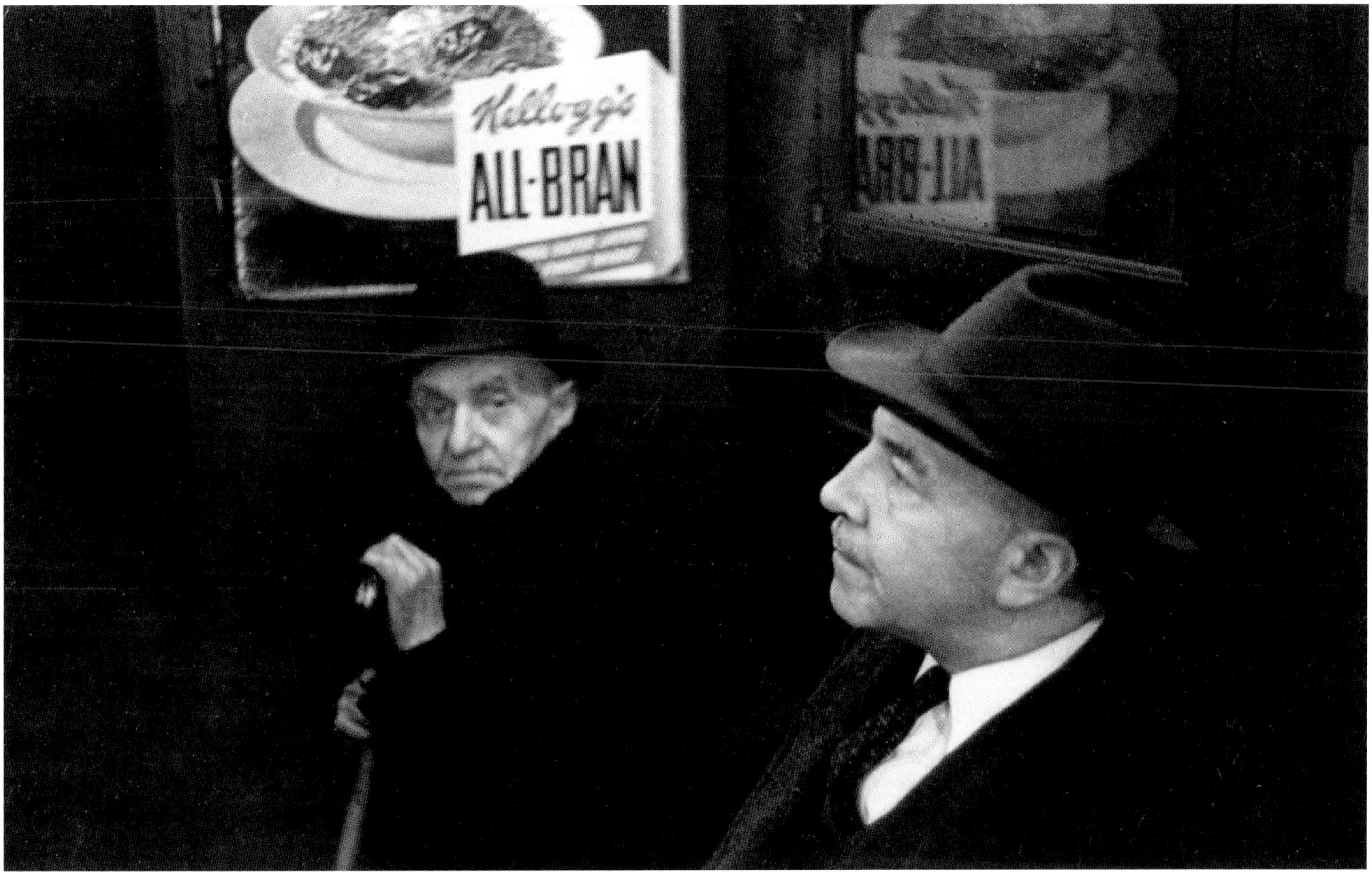
Kellogg's
ALL-BRAN

56
Subway VIII, c. 1947
Gelatin silver print
6 ½ x 8 inches
Colby College Museum of Art,
Gift of the Alex Katz Foundation, 2006.037

57
Subway I, 1947
Gelatin silver print
11 x 14 inches
Colby College Museum of Art,
Gift of the Alex Katz Foundation, 2006.039

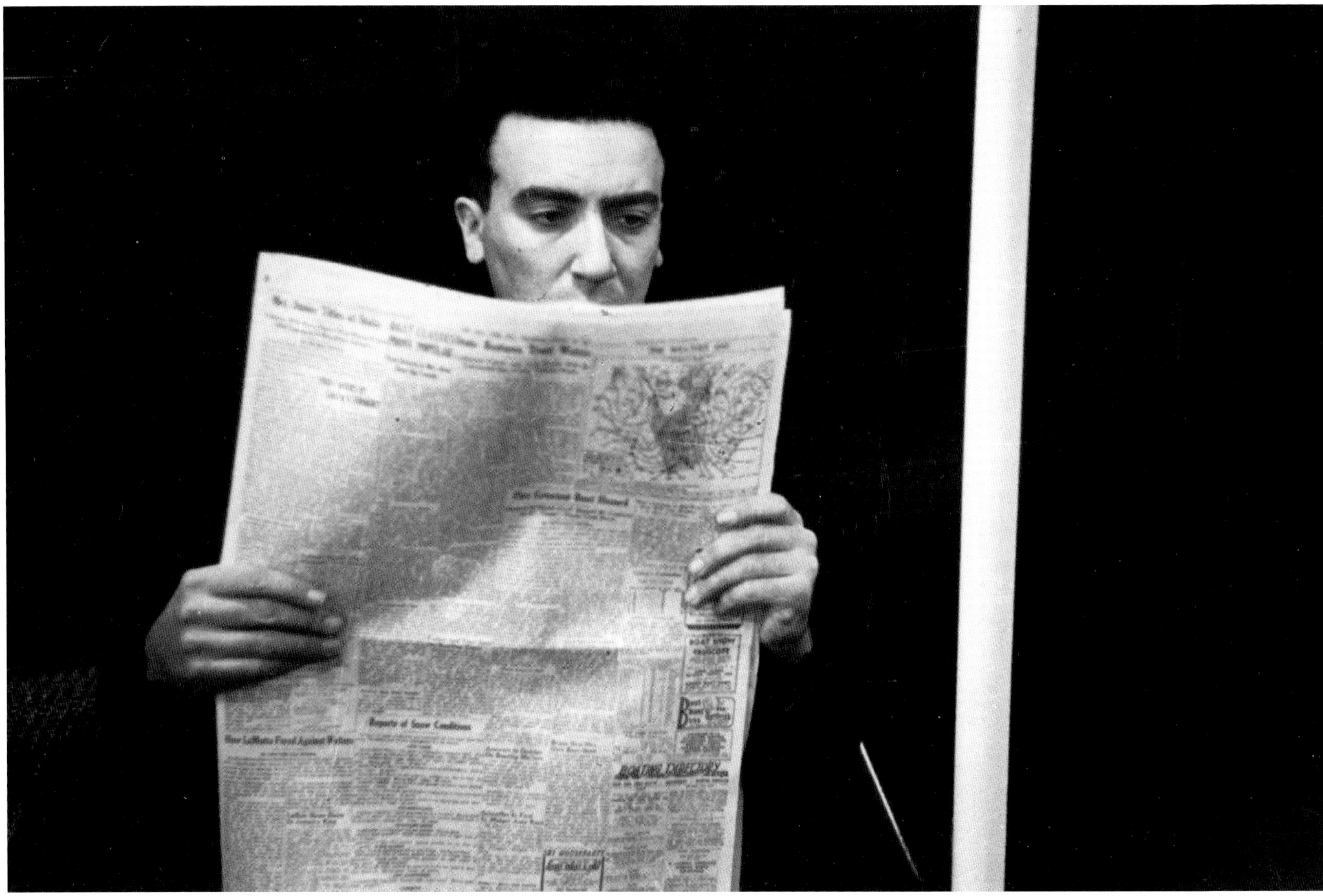

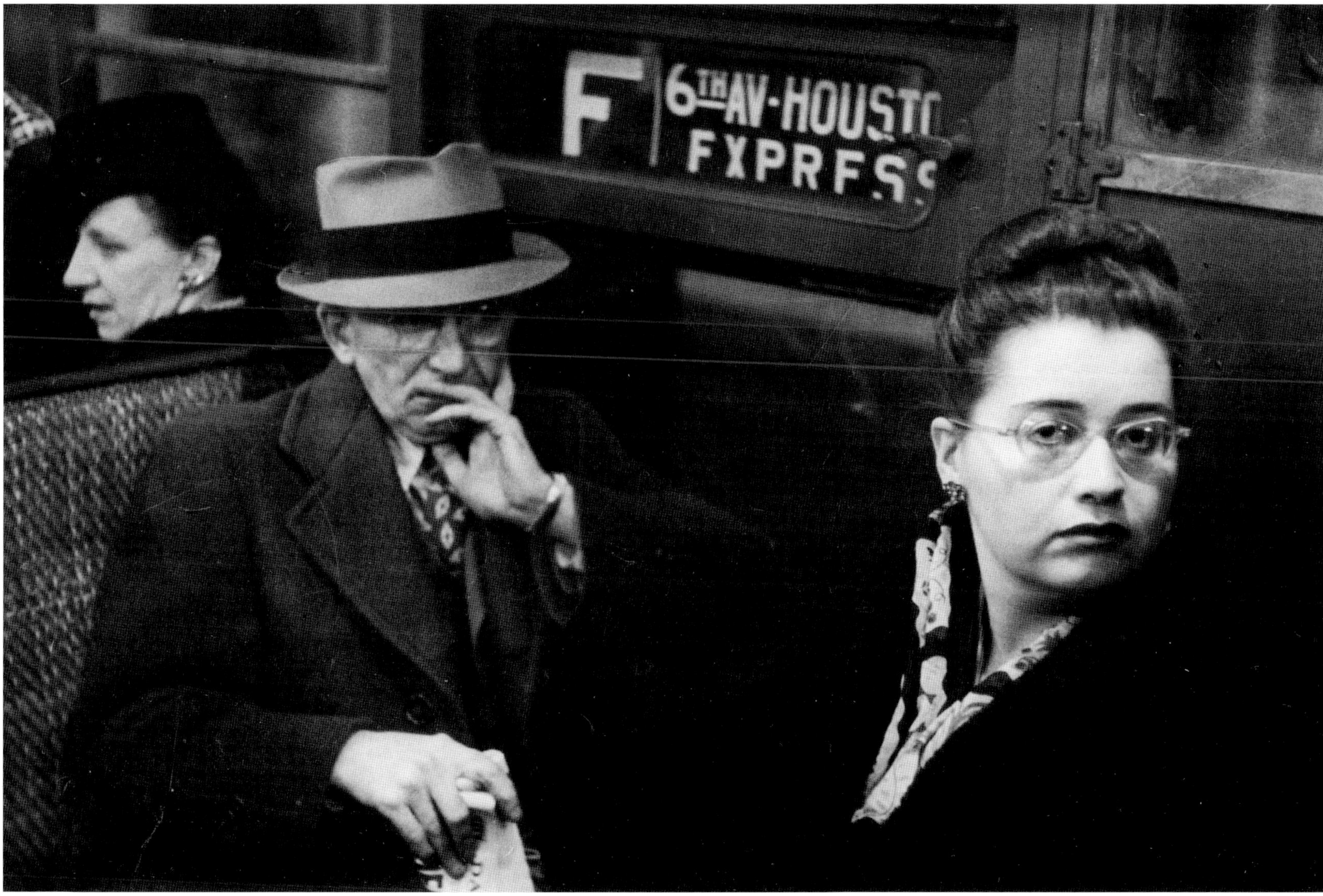
F
6TH AV-HOUSTO
EXPRESS

58
Sidewalk I, 1939
Gelatin silver print
8 x 5 ¾ inches
Courtesy the Estate of Rudy Burckhardt and Tibor de Nagy Gallery, New York

59
Sidewalk VI, 1939
Gelatin silver print
9 ¼ x 6 ⅜ inches
Colby College Museum of Art, Gift of the Alex Katz Foundation, 2006.023

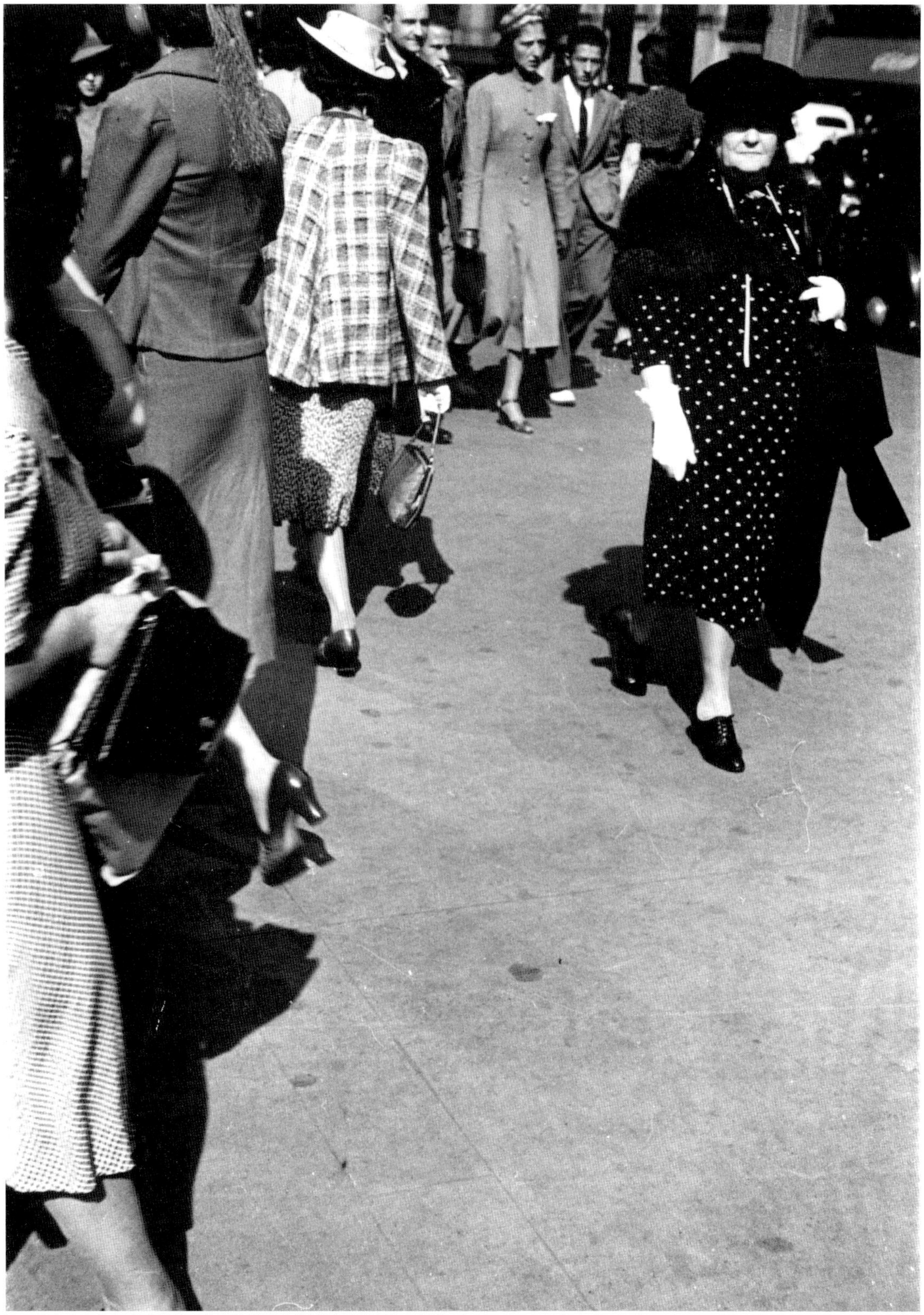

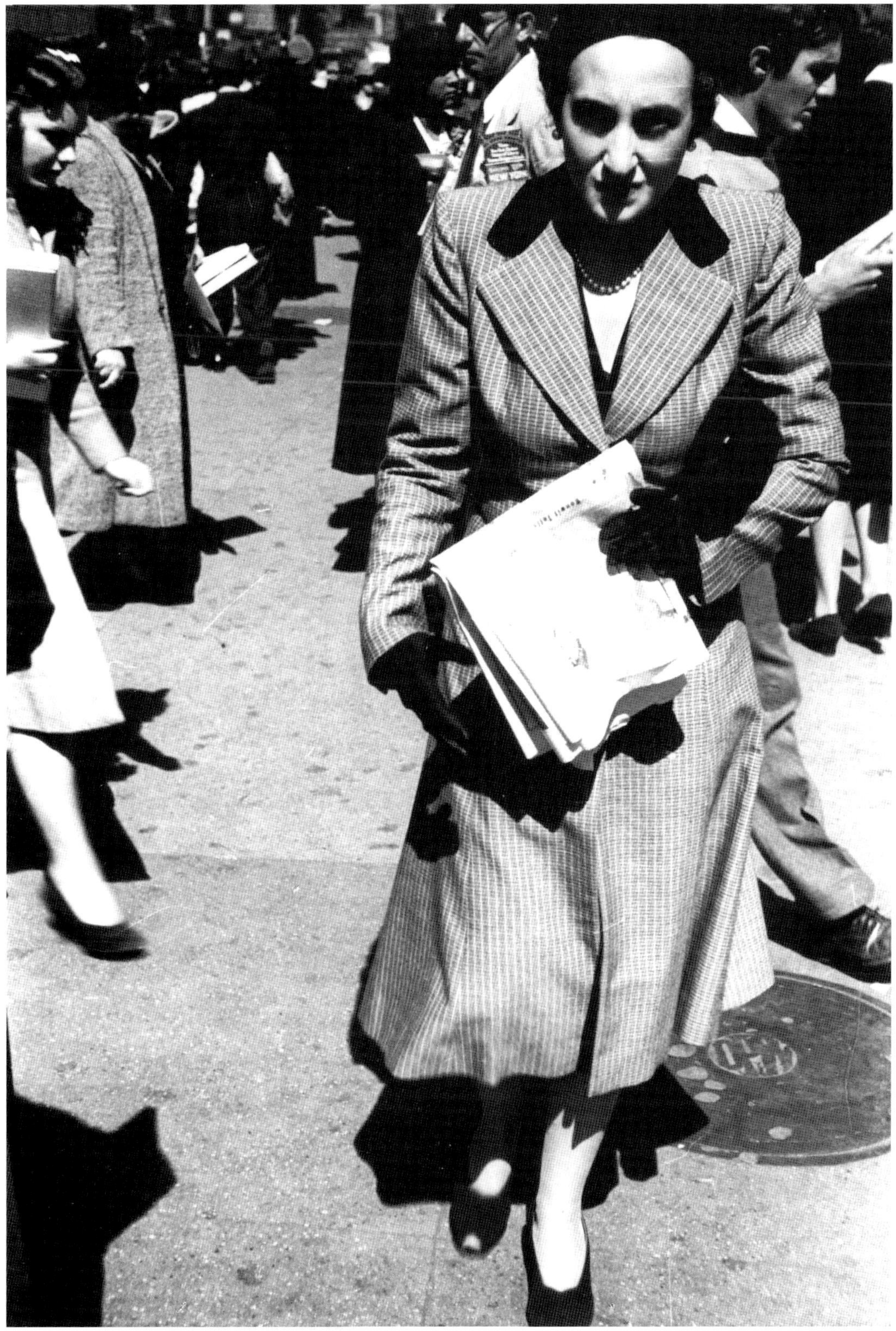

60
Brooklyn, 1940
Gelatin silver print
5 ¾ x 5 ½ inches
Collection of Eric Cohler, courtesy Tibor de Nagy Gallery, New York

61
Chelseascape III, c. 1947
Gelatin silver print
8 x 10 inches
Courtesy the Estate of Rudy Burckhardt and Tibor de Nagy Gallery, New York

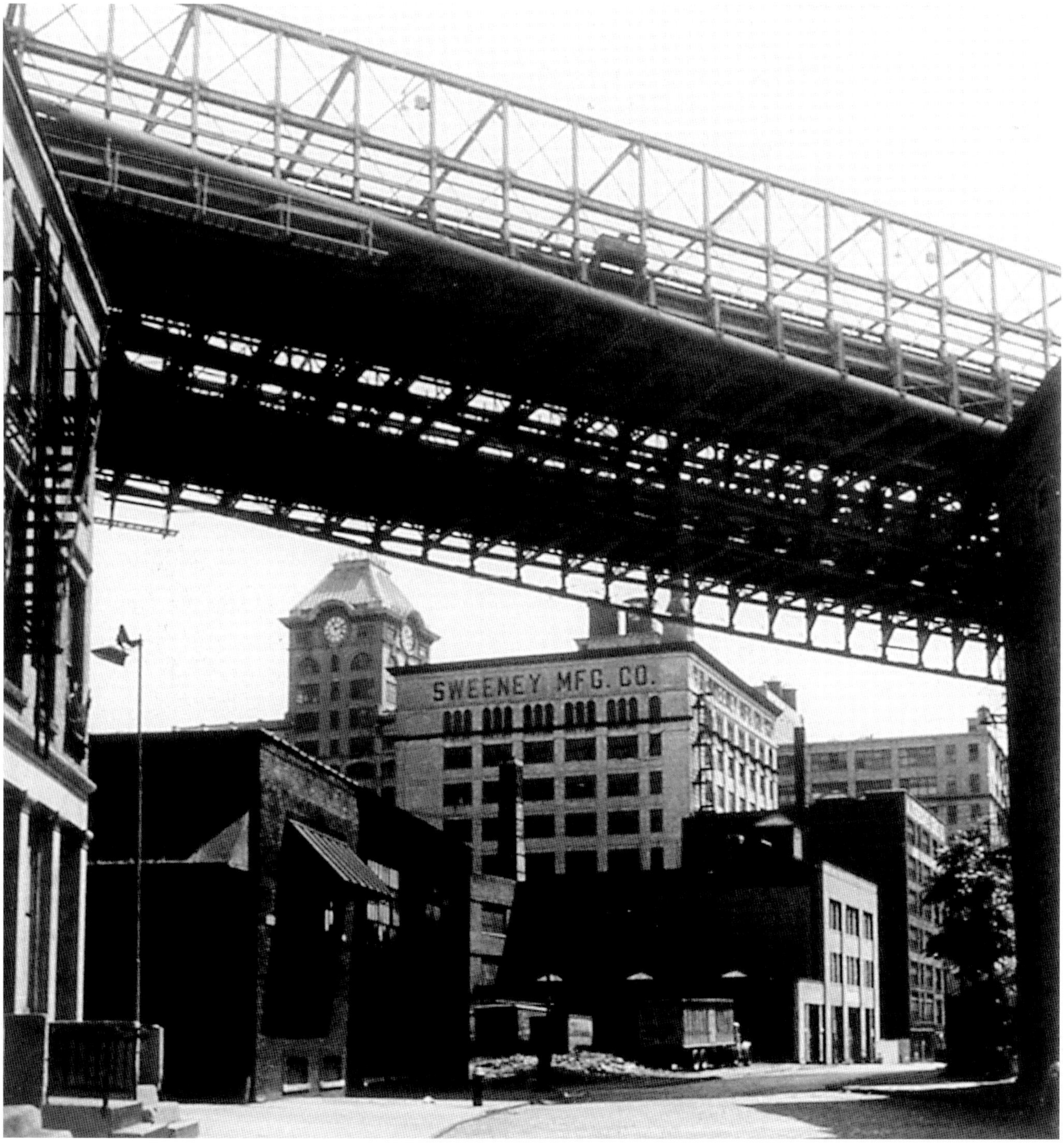

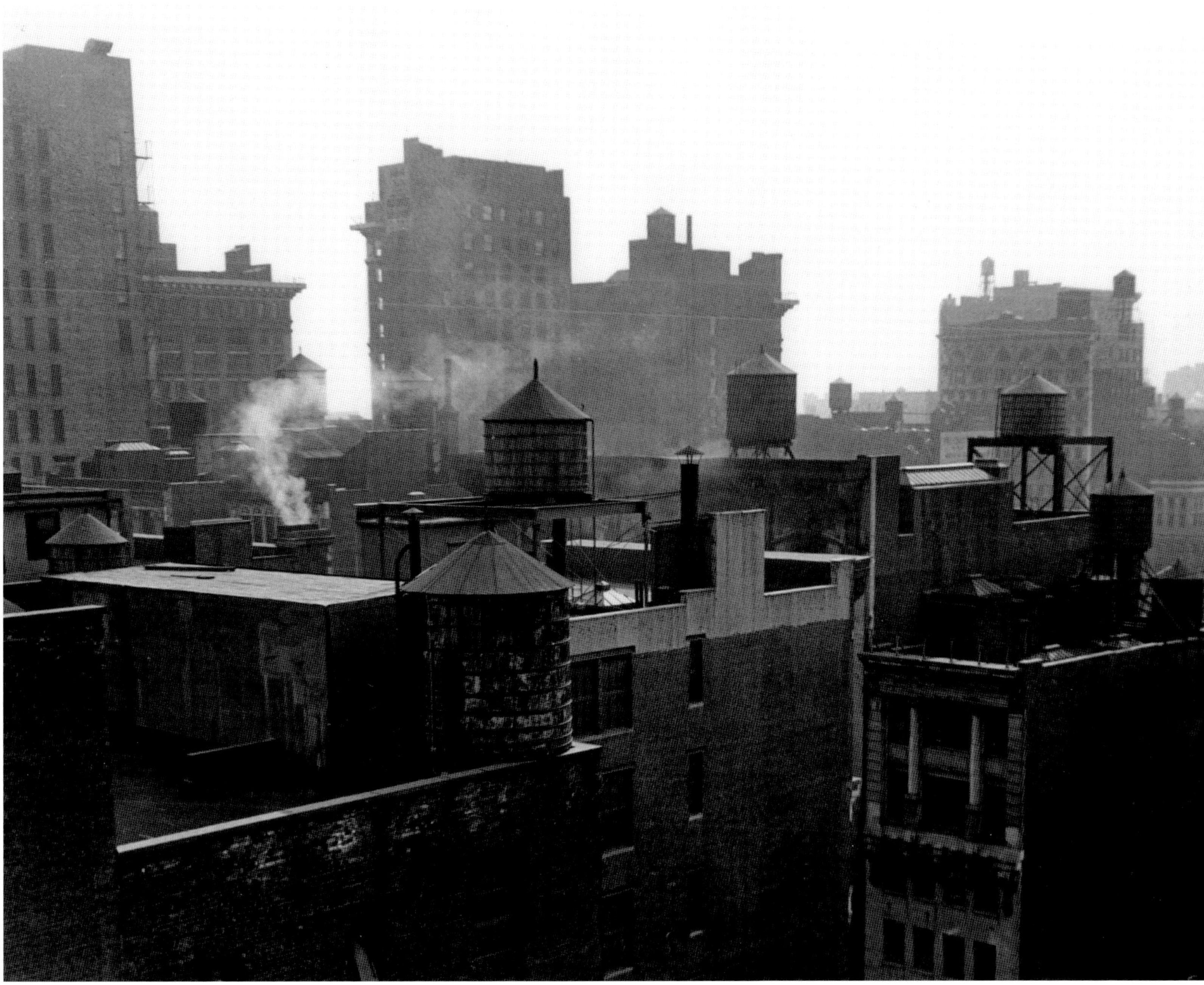

62
Queens, 1940
Gelatin silver print
7 ¾ x 8 inches
Courtesy the Estate of Rudy Burckhardt
and Tibor de Nagy Gallery, New York

63
Erie Railroad, c. 1940
Gelatin silver print
7 x 8 ½ inches
Courtesy the Estate of Rudy Burckhardt
and Tibor de Nagy Gallery, New York

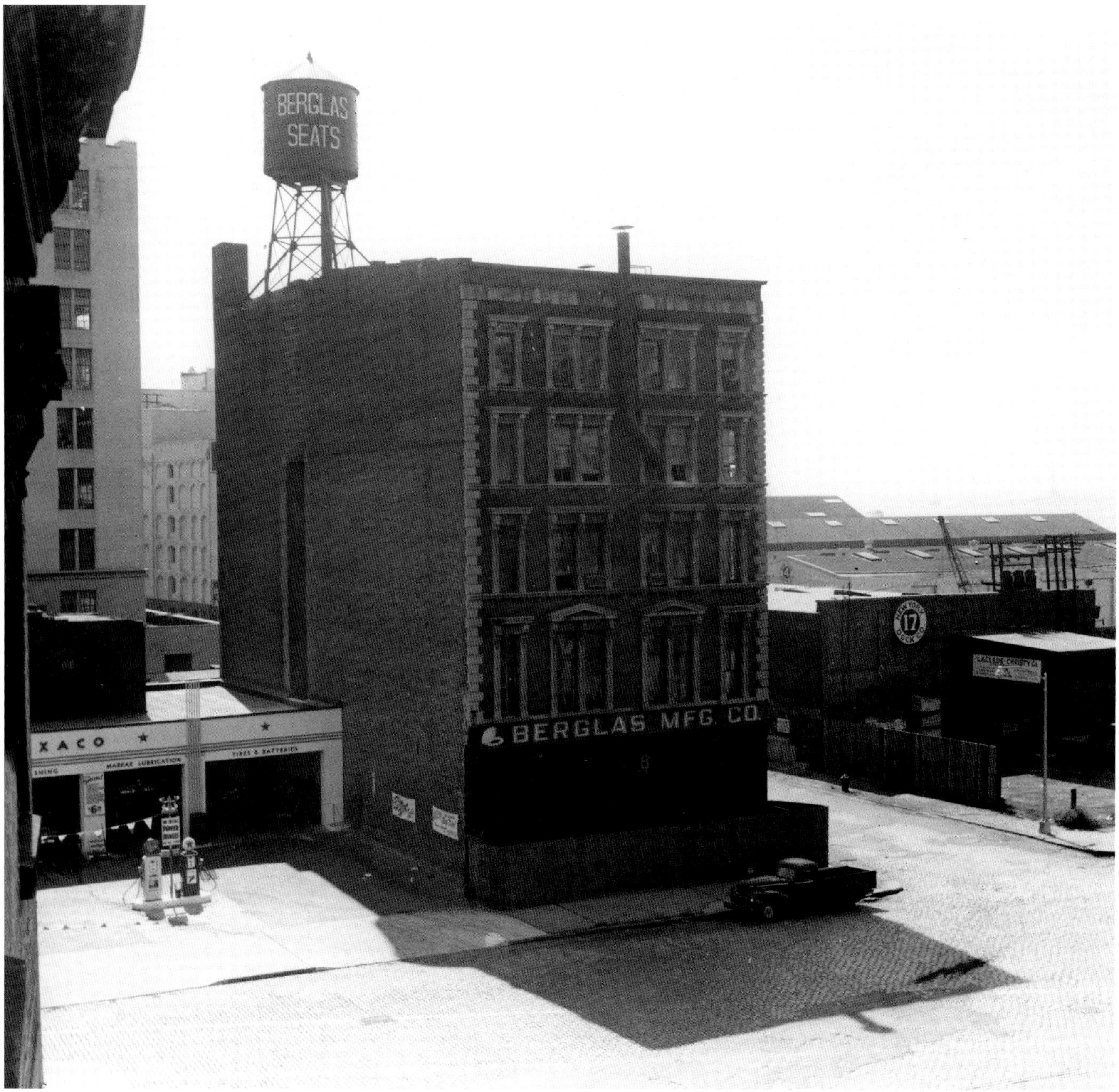

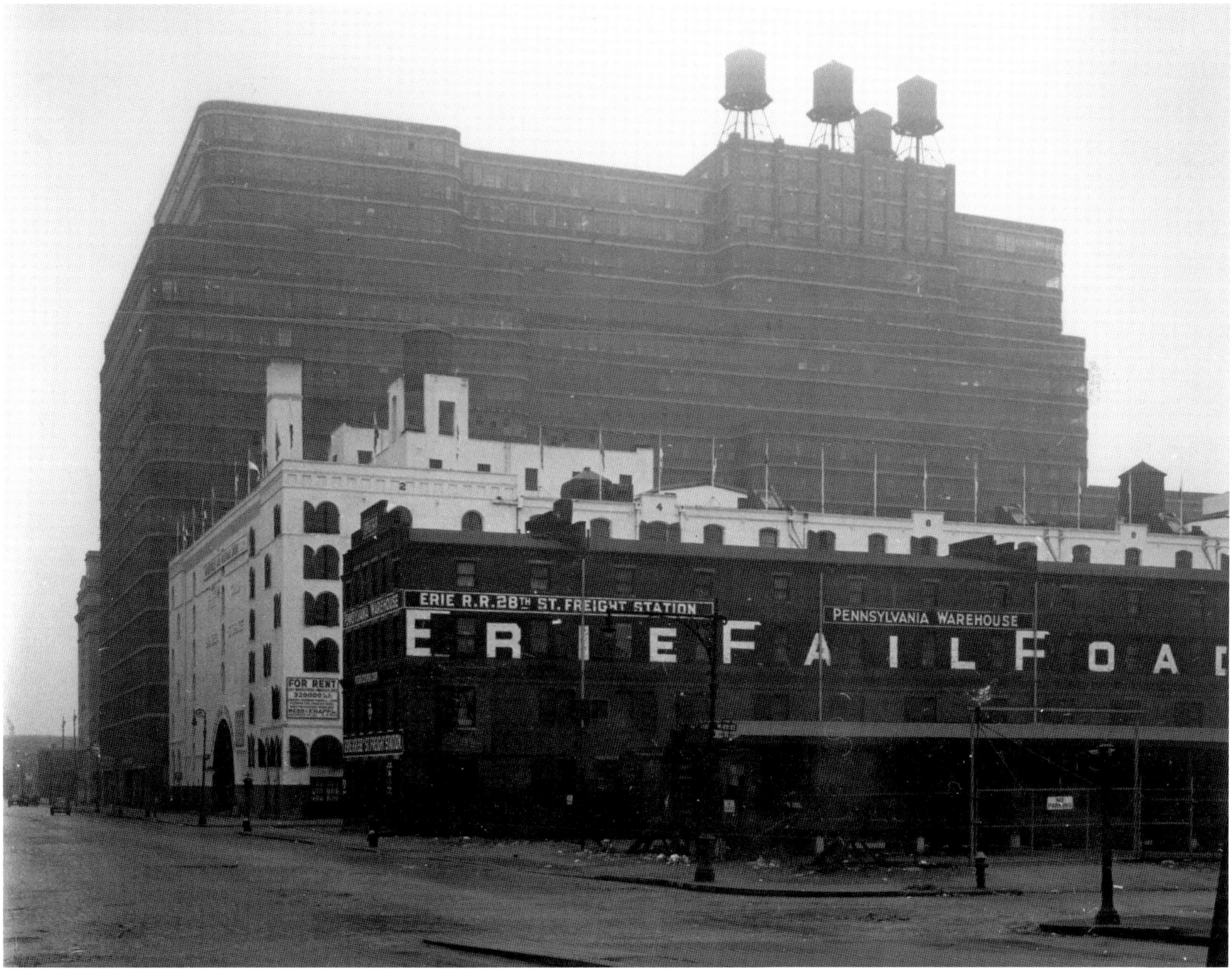
ERIE R.R. 28TH ST. FREIGHT STATION
PENNSYLVANIA WAREHOUSE
FOR RENT

64
New York Moment I, 1940
Gelatin silver print
7 ¼ x 9 ¾ inches
Courtesy the Estate of Rudy Burckhardt
and Tibor de Nagy Gallery, New York

65
Sidewalk XIV, 1939
Gelatin silver print
16 x 20 inches
Courtesy the Estate of Rudy Burckhardt
and Tibor de Nagy Gallery, New York

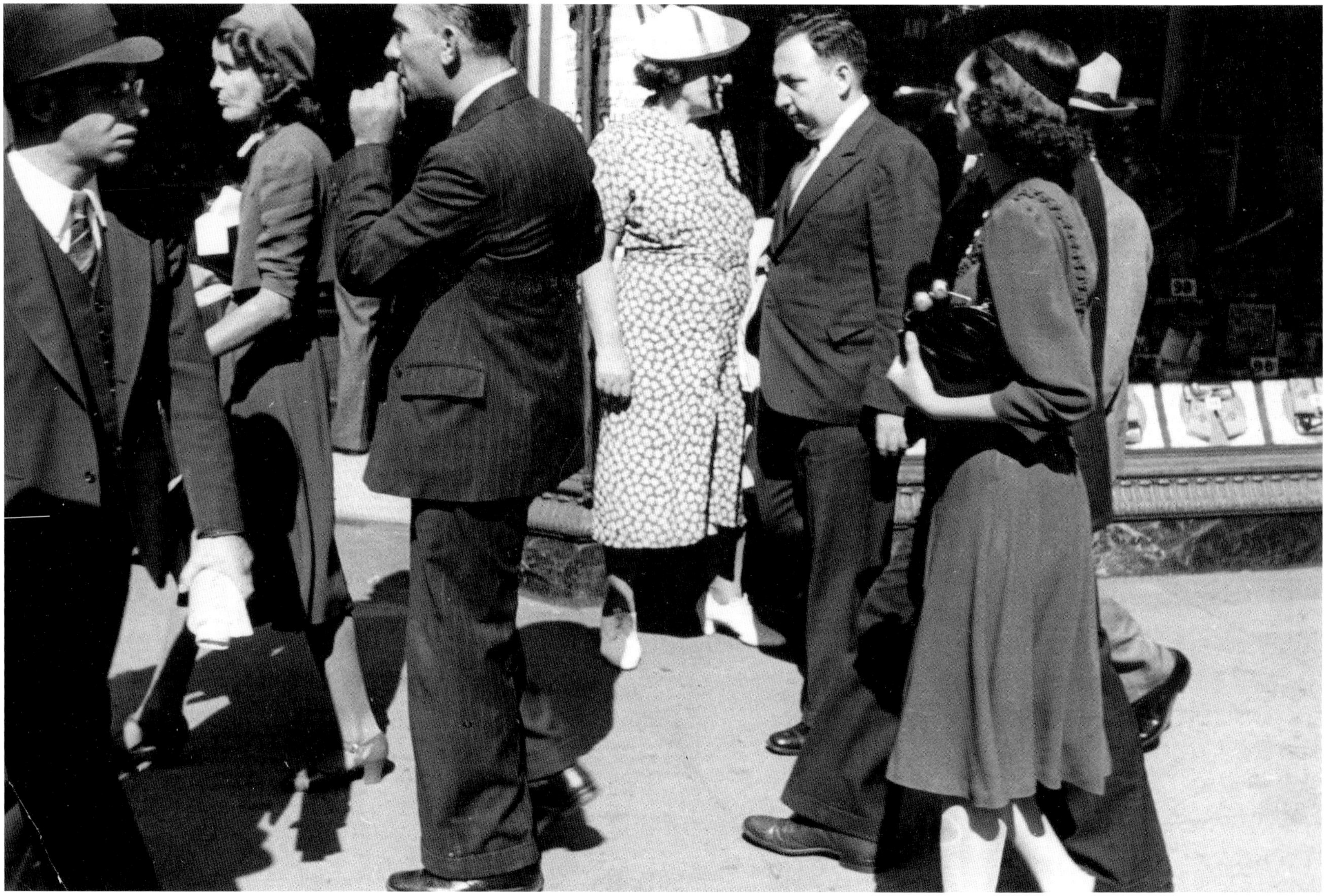

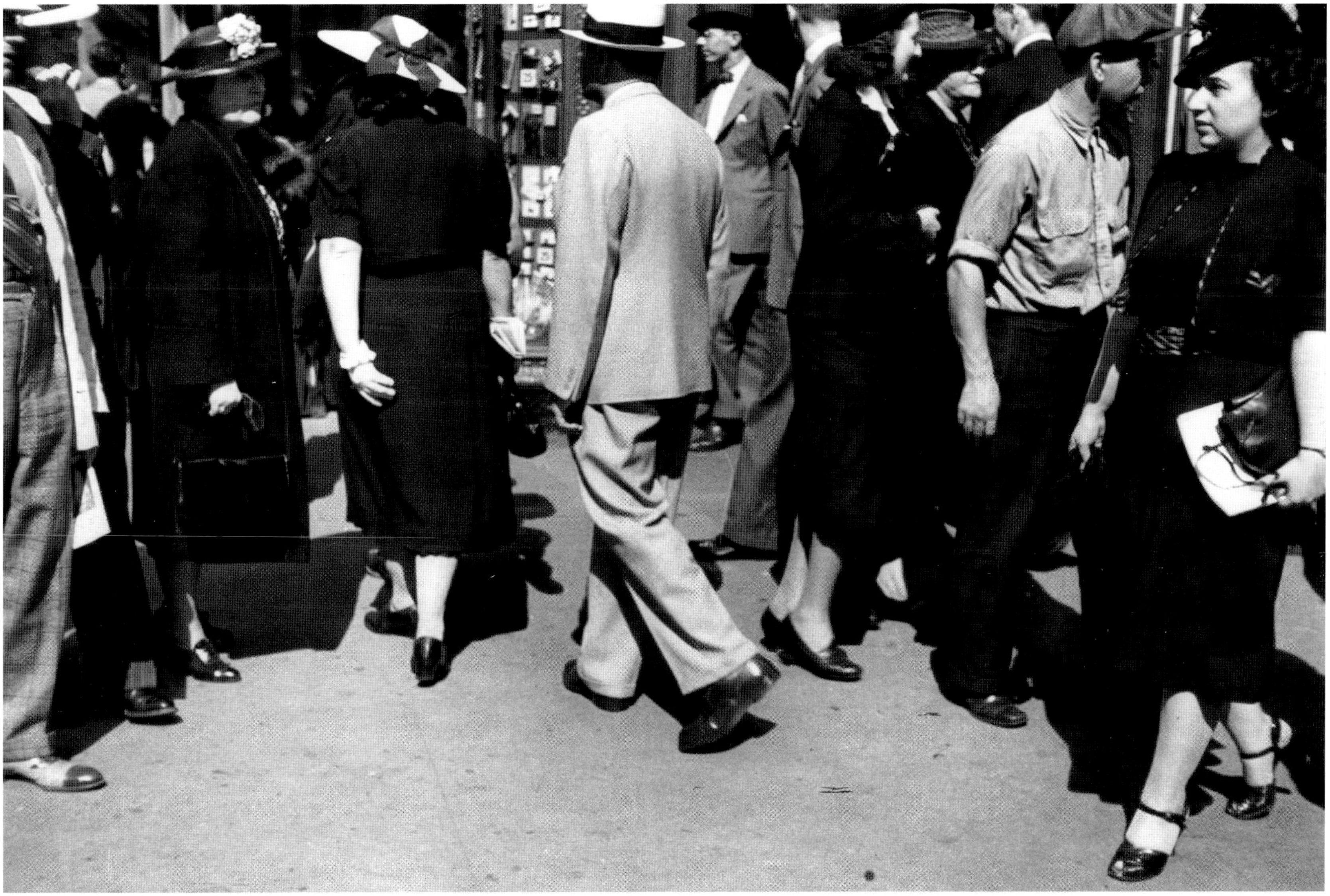

66
Astor Place, 1947
Gelatin silver print
10 x 10 inches
Collection of Matt Goldman, courtesy
Tibor de Nagy Gallery, New York

67
Flatiron Building, Summer, 1947
Gelatin silver print
9 x 6 ½ inches
Colby College Museum of Art,
Gift of the Alex Katz Foundation, 2006.034

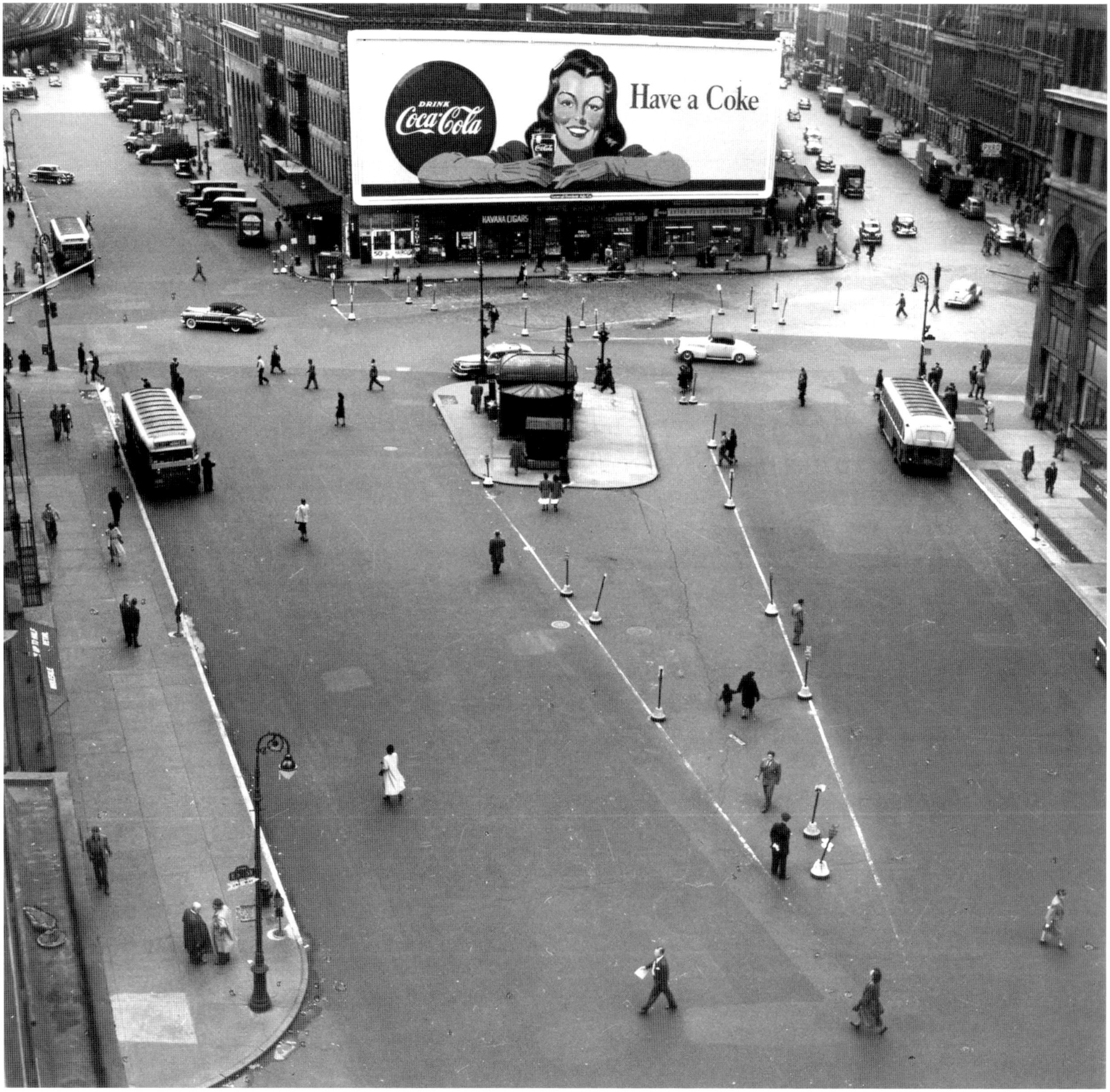

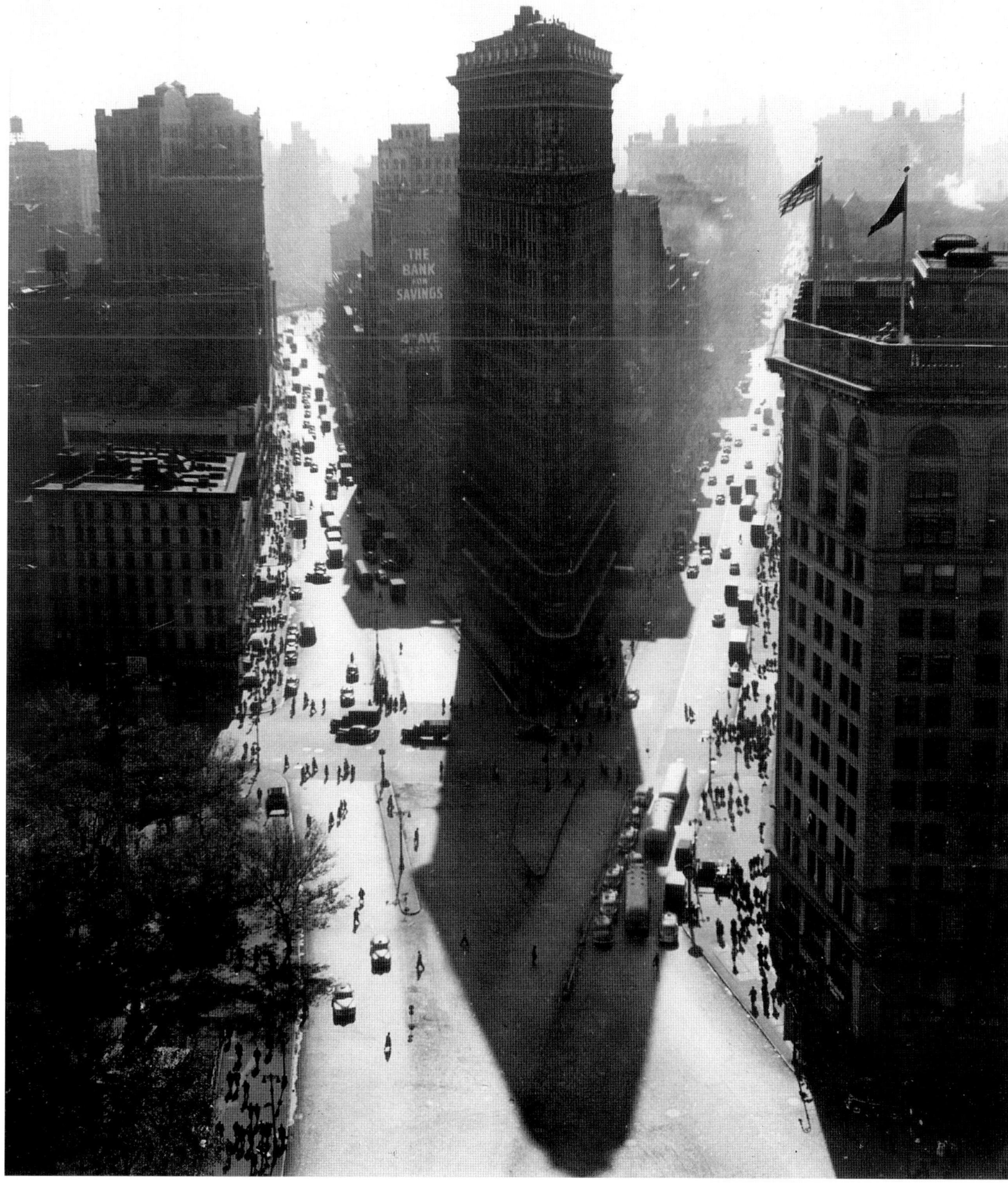
THE
BANK
SAVINGS

68
Empire State Building, c. 1947
Gelatin silver print
13 x 10 ¾ inches
Courtesy the Estate of Rudy Burckhardt
and Tibor de Nagy Gallery, New York

69
Times Building, 1947
Gelatin silver print
10 x 7 ½ inches
Courtesy the Estate of Rudy Burckhardt
and Tibor de Nagy Gallery, New York

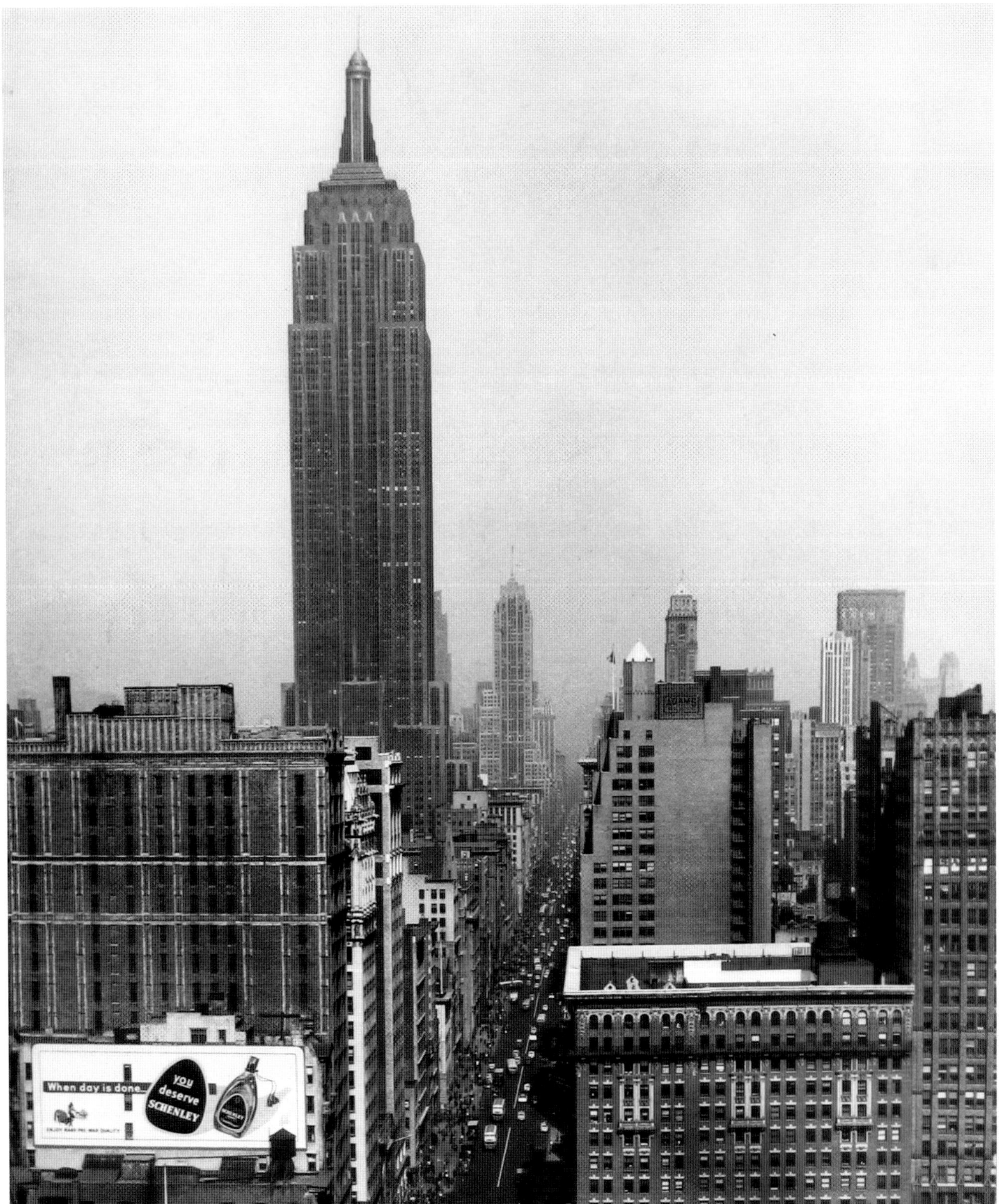

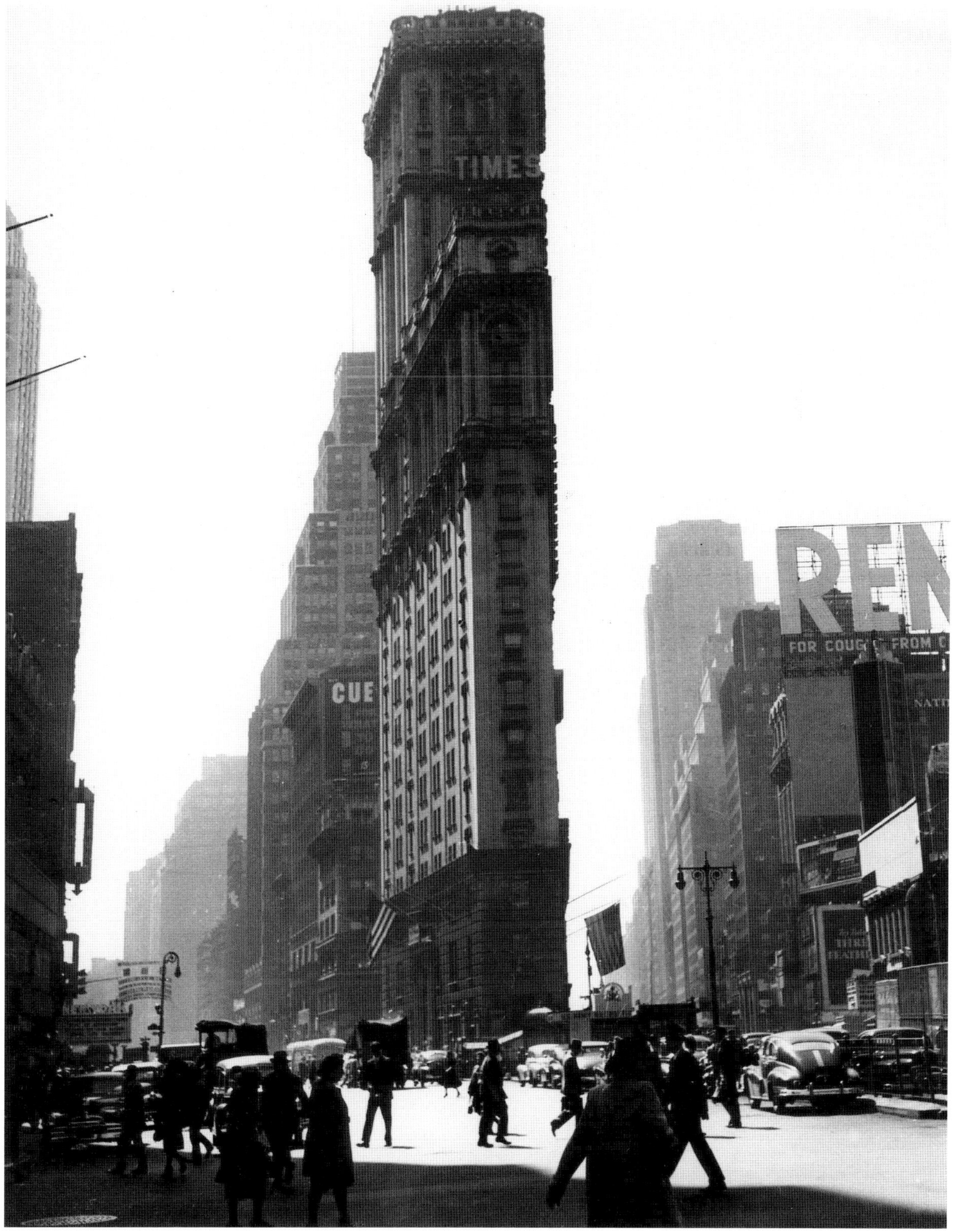
TIMES
CUE

70
Flatiron Building I, c. 1975
Gelatin silver print
12 x 8 ½ inches
Courtesy of the Alex Katz Foundation

71
Flatiron Building II, c. 1975
Gelatin silver print
14 x 11 inches
Courtesy of the Alex Katz Foundation

72
Flatiron Building, 1973
Gelatin silver print
13 ¾ x 9 ⅛ inches
Courtesy of the Alex Katz Foundation

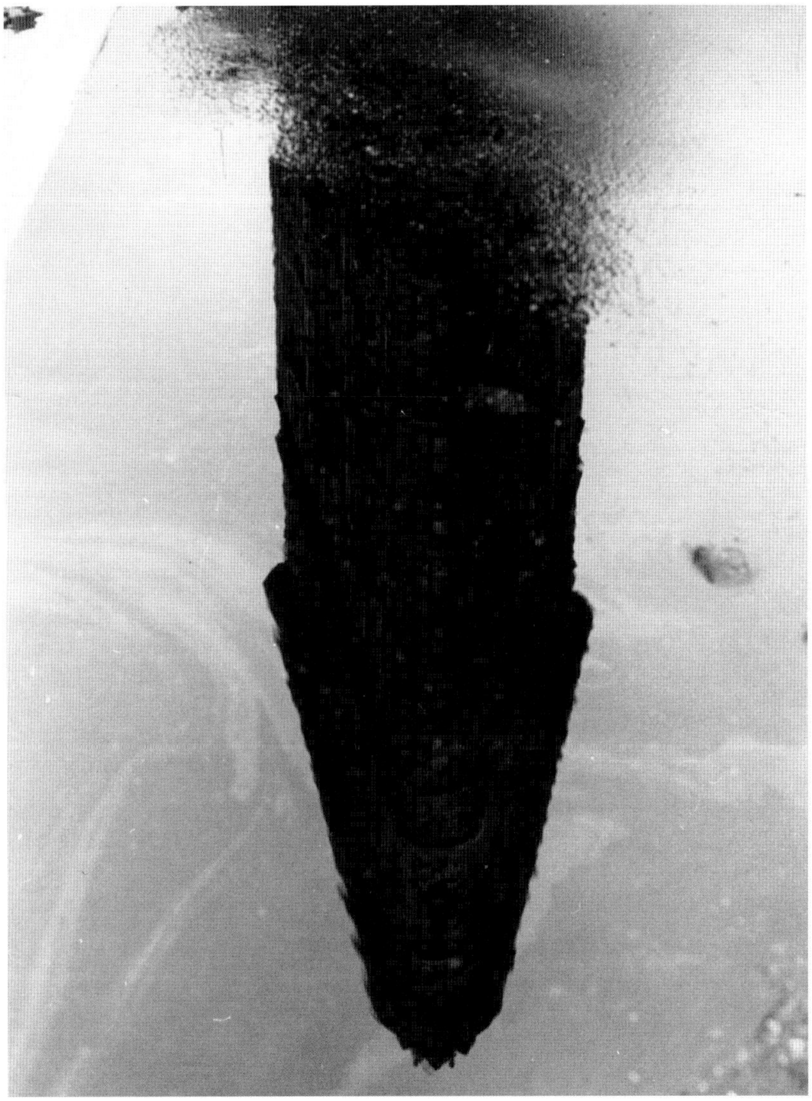

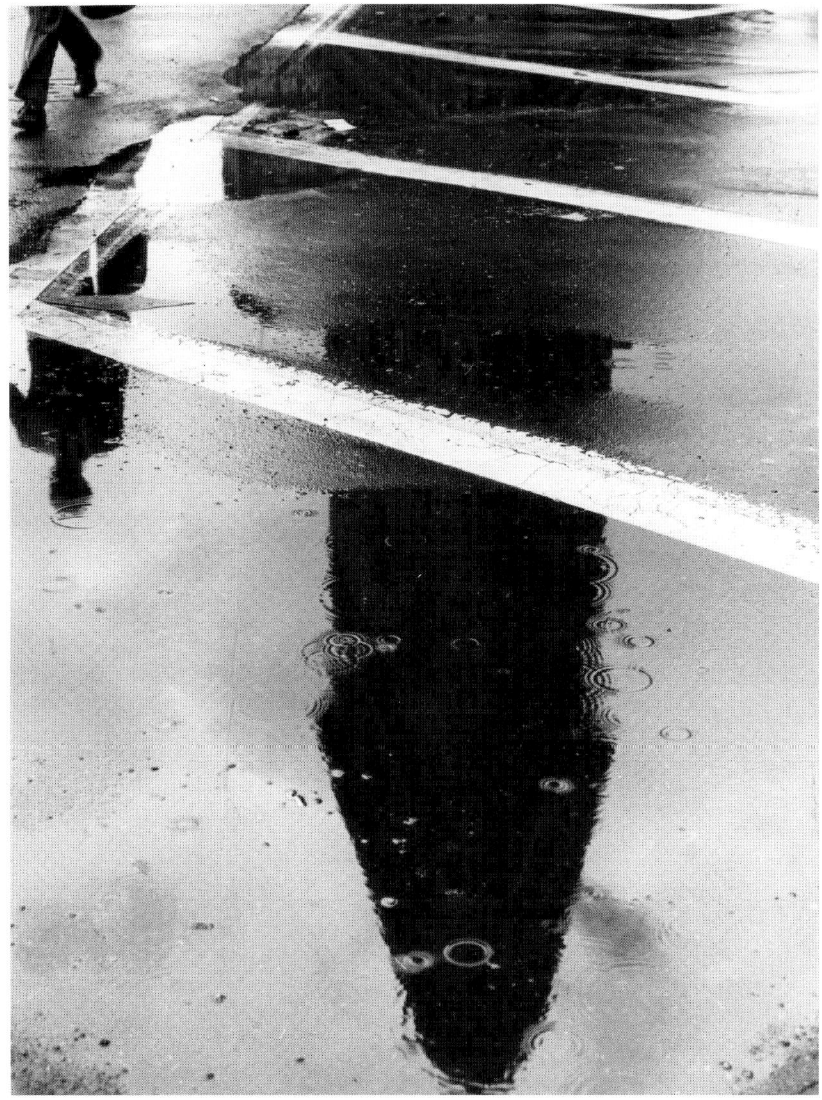

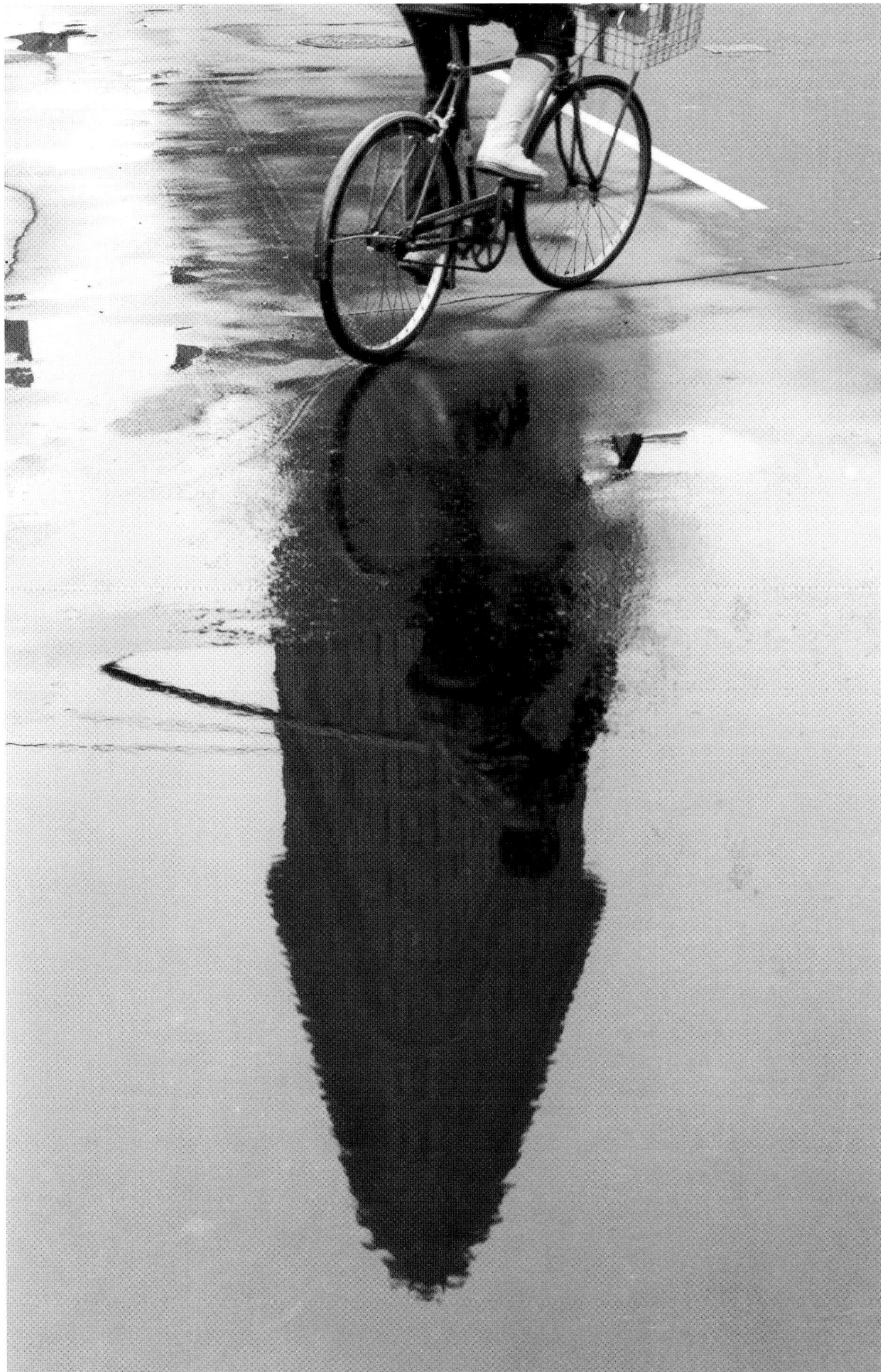

73
Subway Grate, c. 1975
Gelatin silver print
7 x 10 inches
Courtesy of the Alex Katz Foundation

74
Untitled, c. 1985
Gelatin silver print
7 5/8 x 10 inches
Courtesy of the Alex Katz Foundation

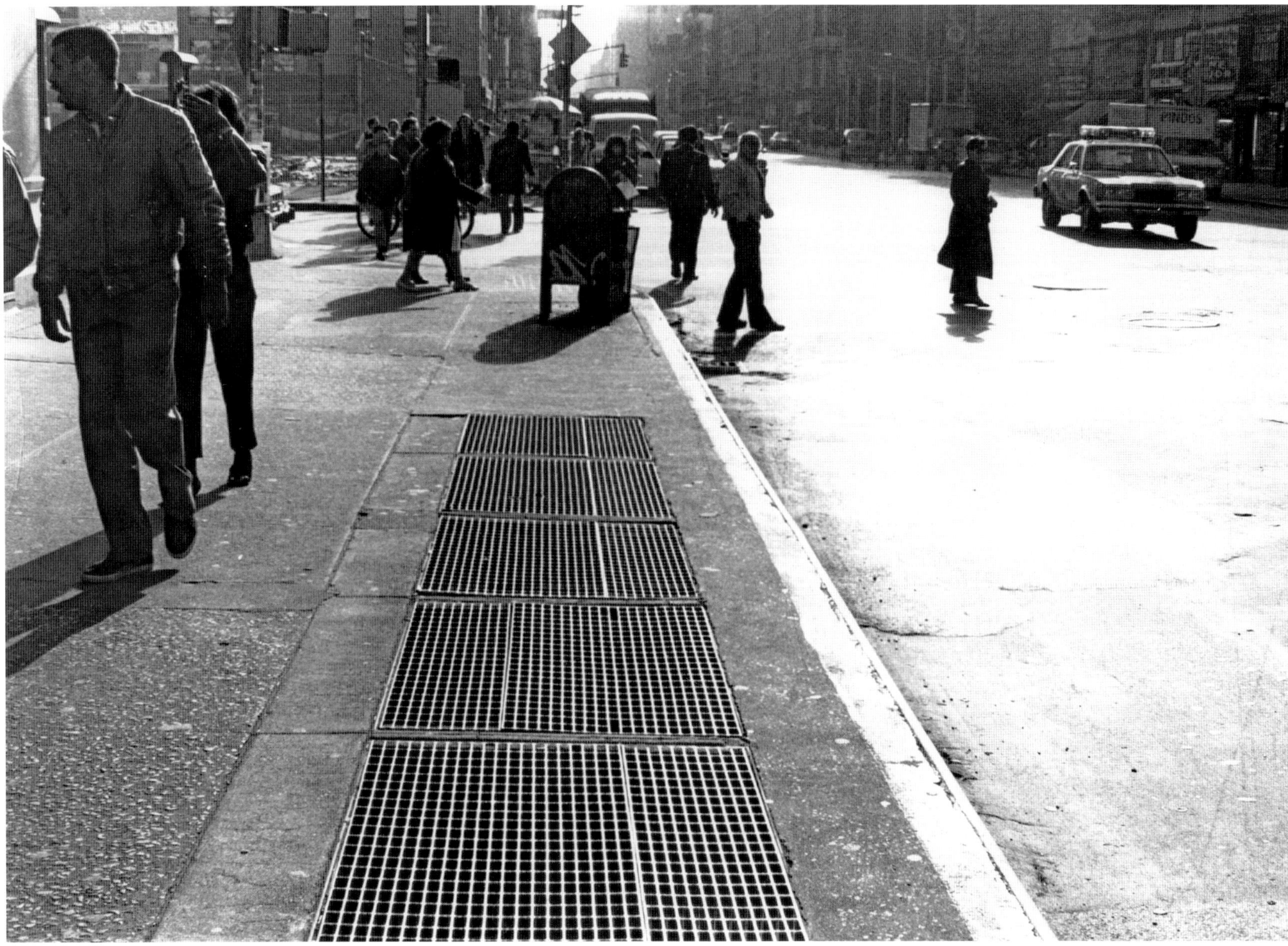

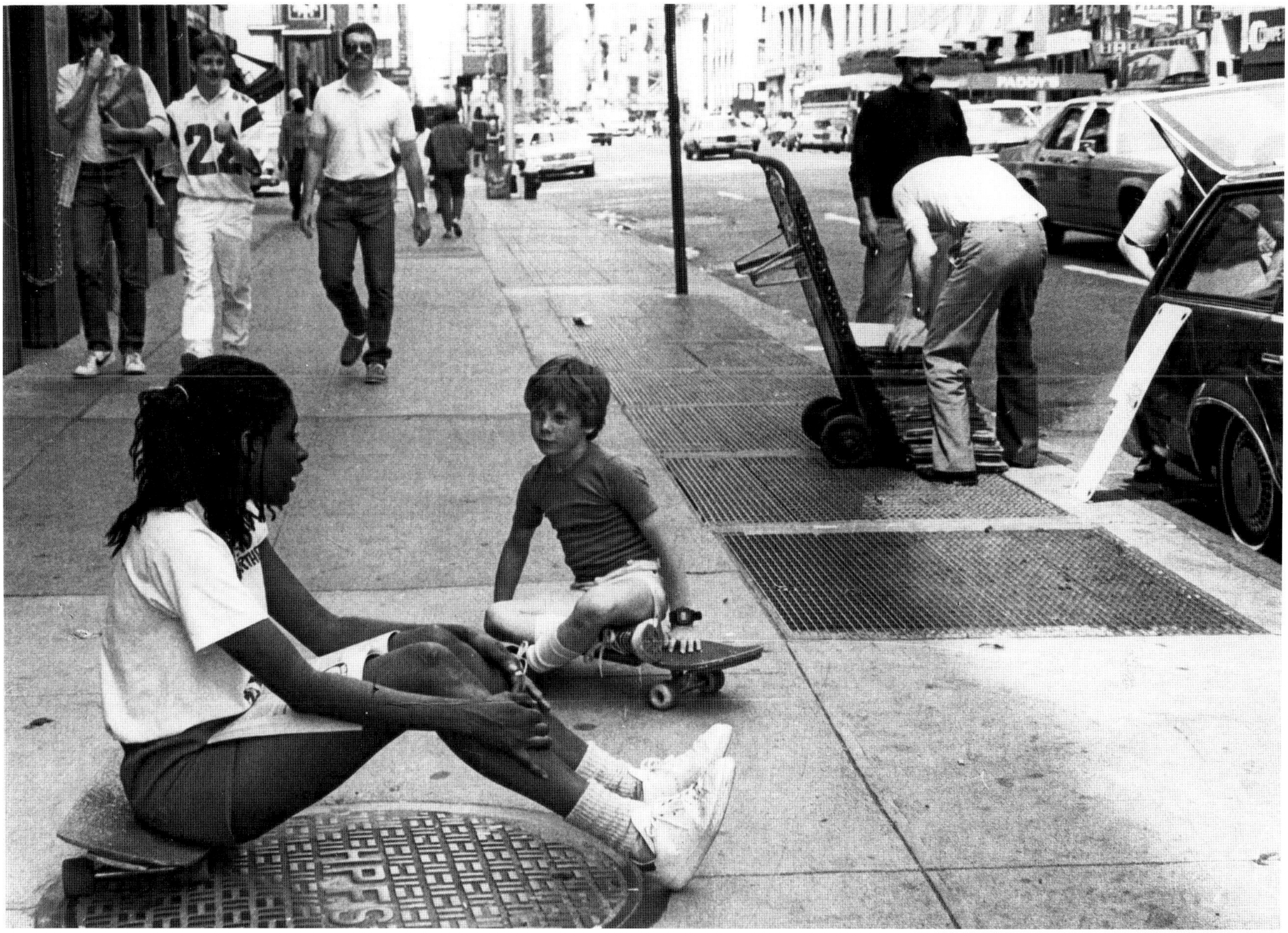
22

75
Untitled, c. 1975
Gelatin silver print
10 x 8 inches
Courtesy the Estate of Rudy Burckhardt
and Tibor de Nagy Gallery, New York

76
Untitled, c. 1985
Gelatin silver print
9 ⅞ x 7 ¾ inches
Courtesy of the Alex Katz Foundation

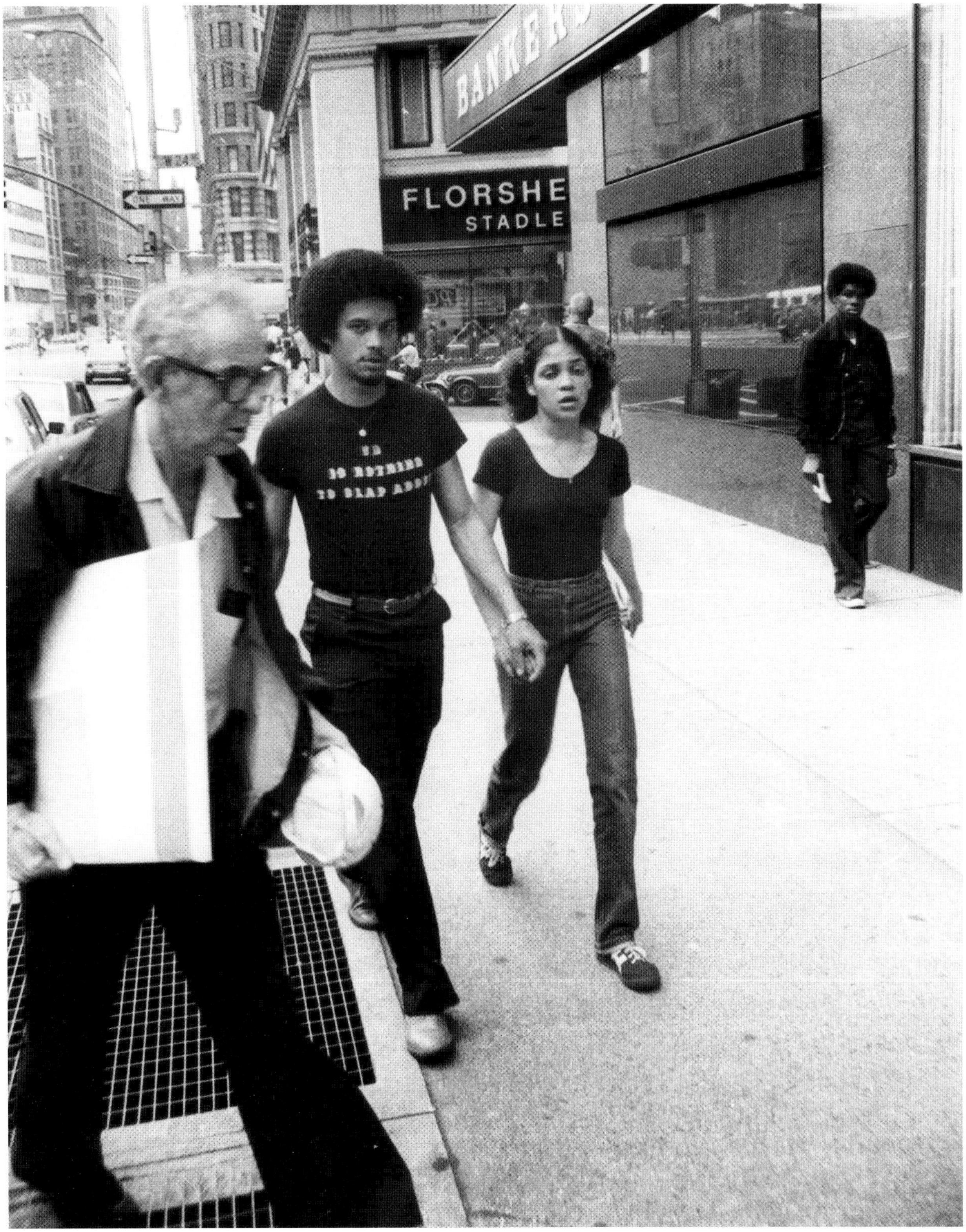

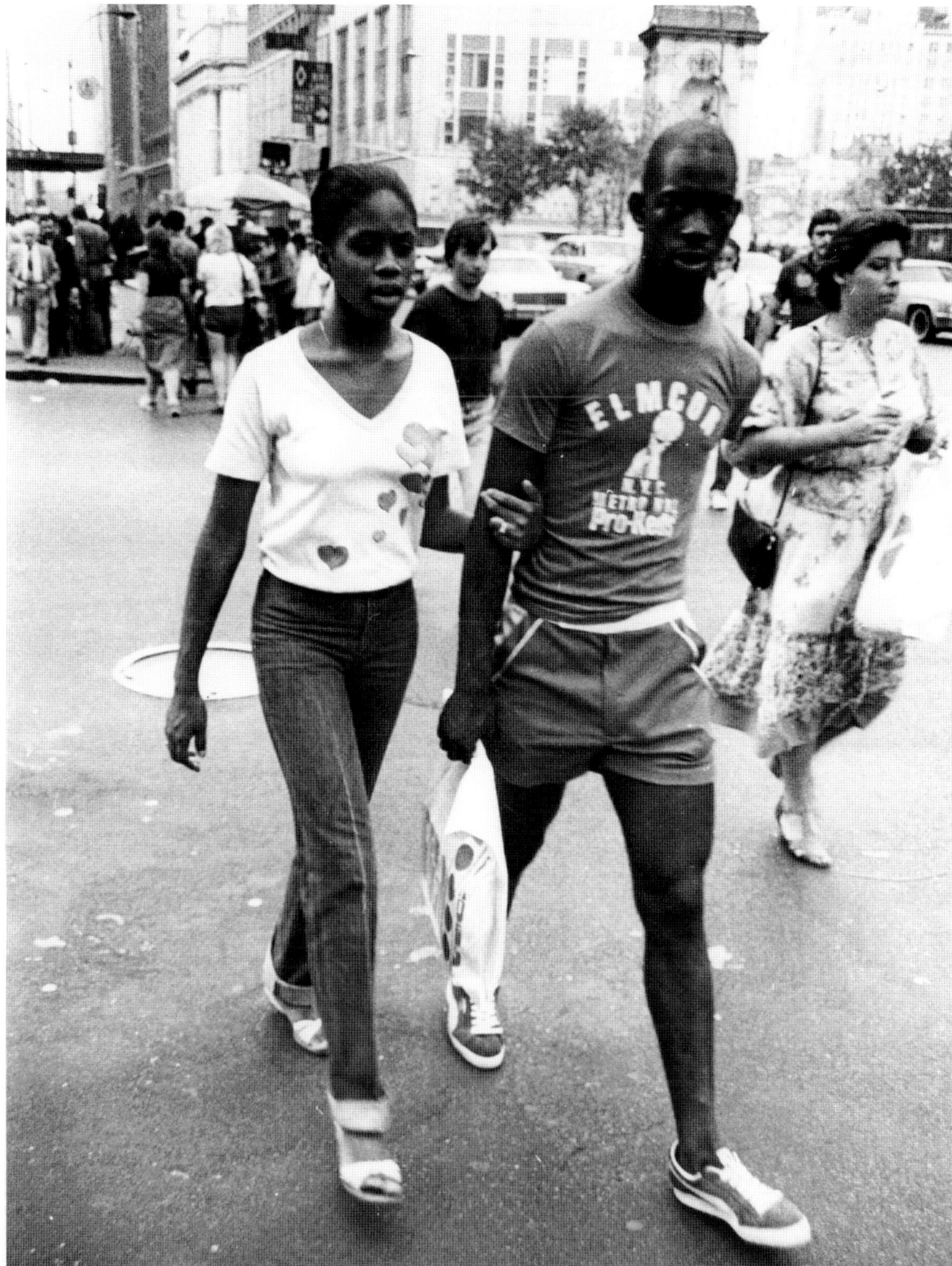

77
Untitled, c. 1978
Gelatin silver print
8 x 10 inches
Courtesy of the Alex Katz Foundation

78
V-Back, 1985
Gelatin silver print
7 ¾ x 10 inches
Courtesy of the Alex Katz Foundation

FOLLOWING PAGES

79
5:15 p.m. 53rd & 5th Avenue, 1983
Gelatin silver print
10 x 8 inches
Courtesy of the Alex Katz Foundation

80
53rd & 5th Avenue, 1983
Gelatin silver print
9 ¾ x 7 ½ inches
Courtesy the Estate of Rudy Burckhardt and Tibor de Nagy Gallery, New York

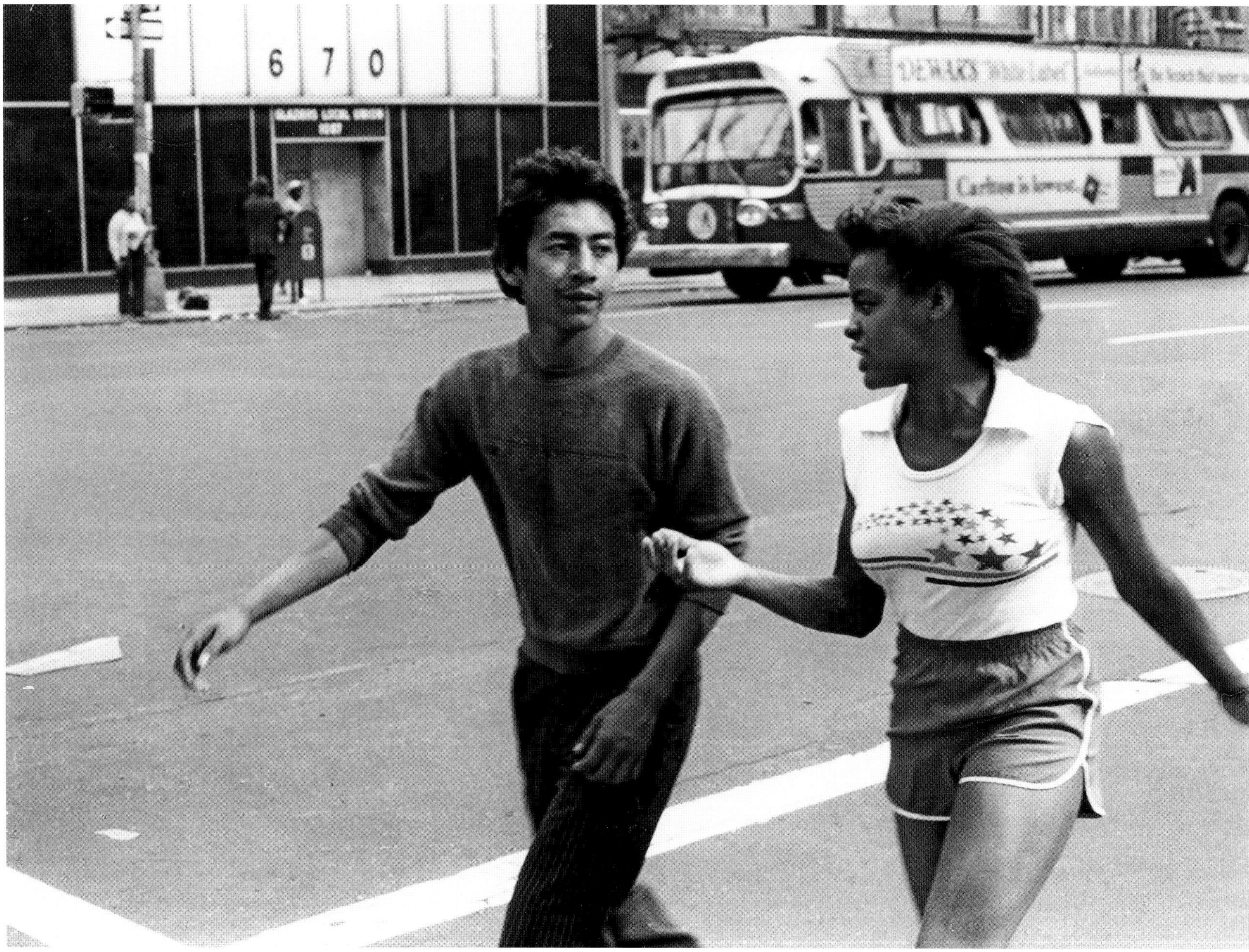

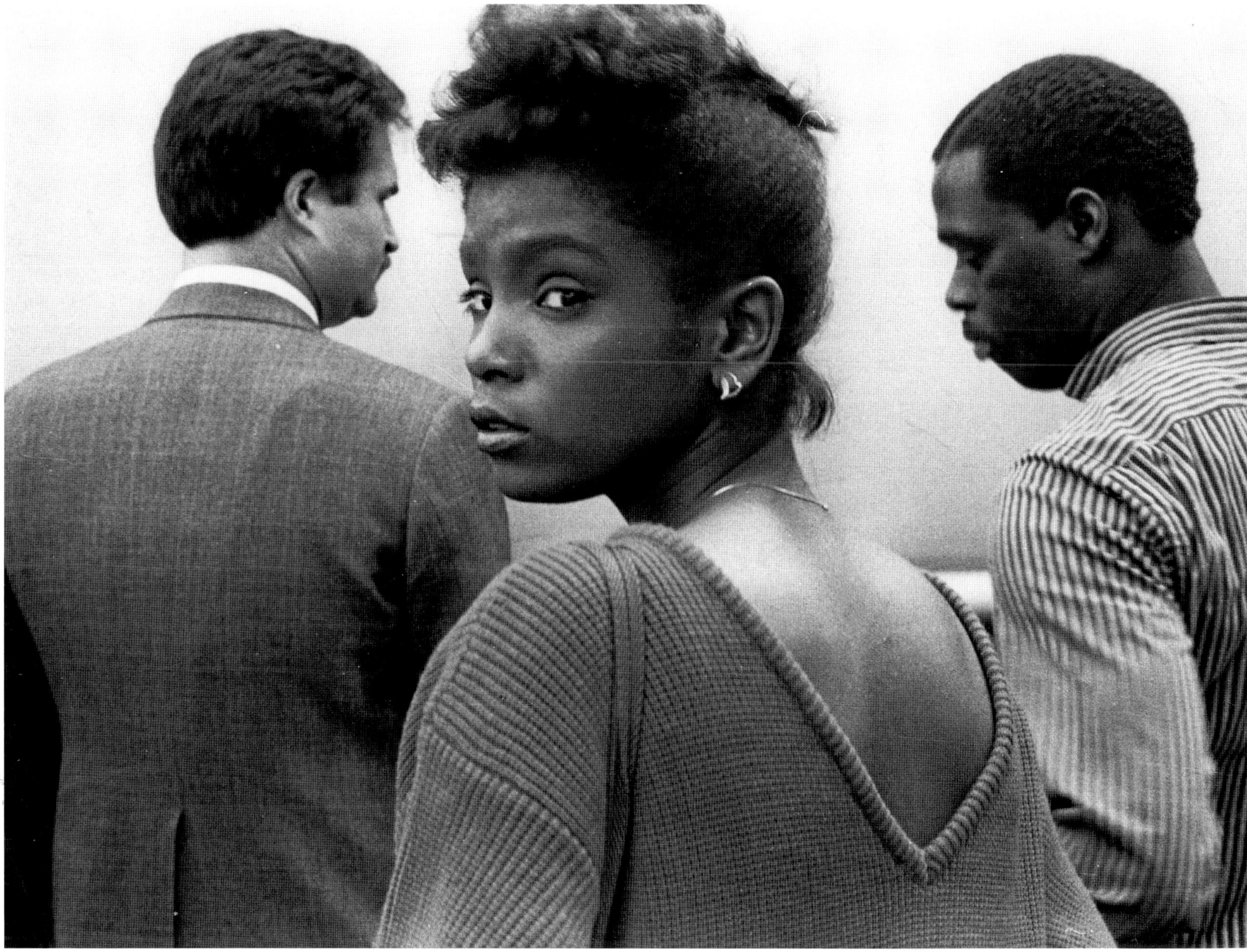

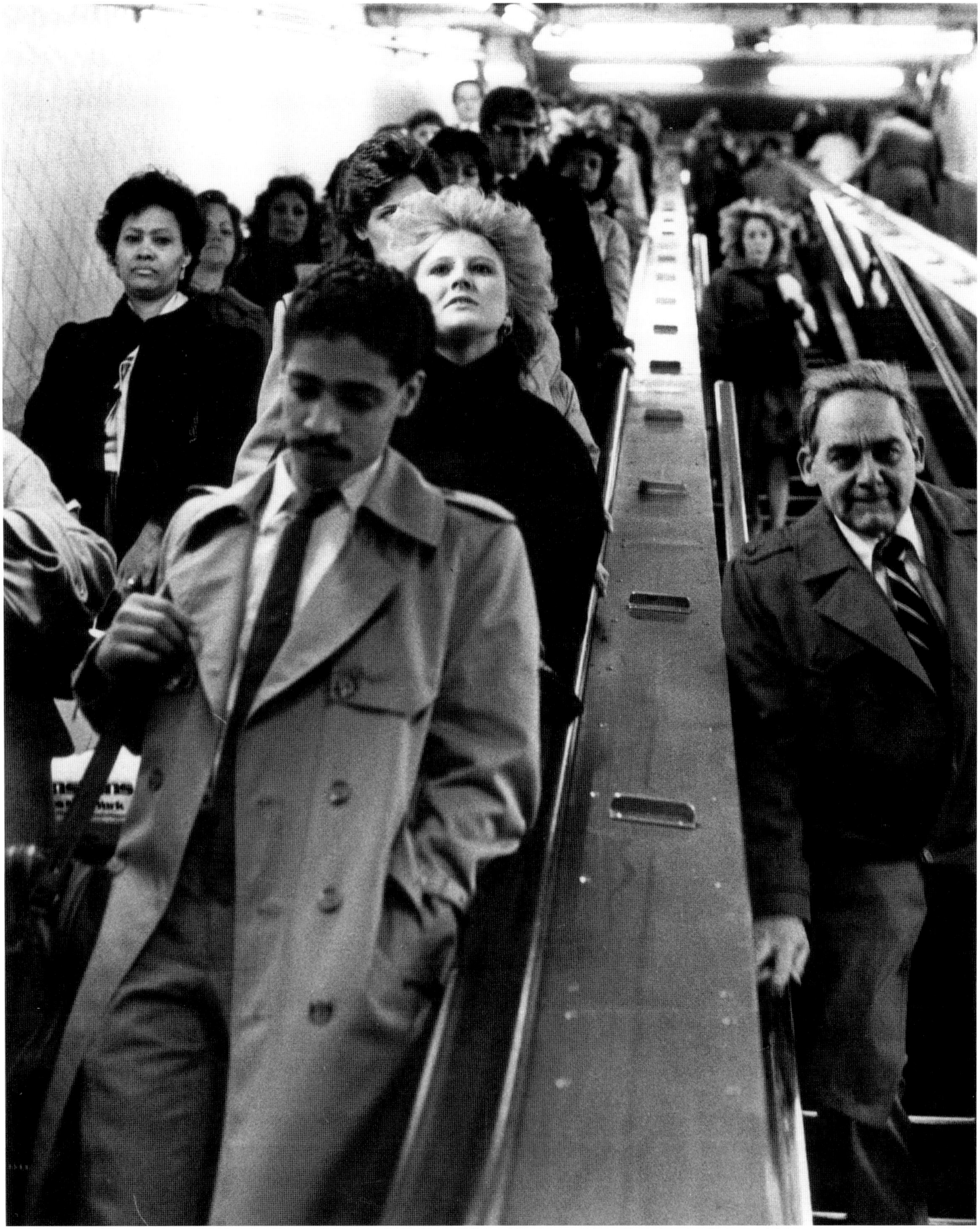

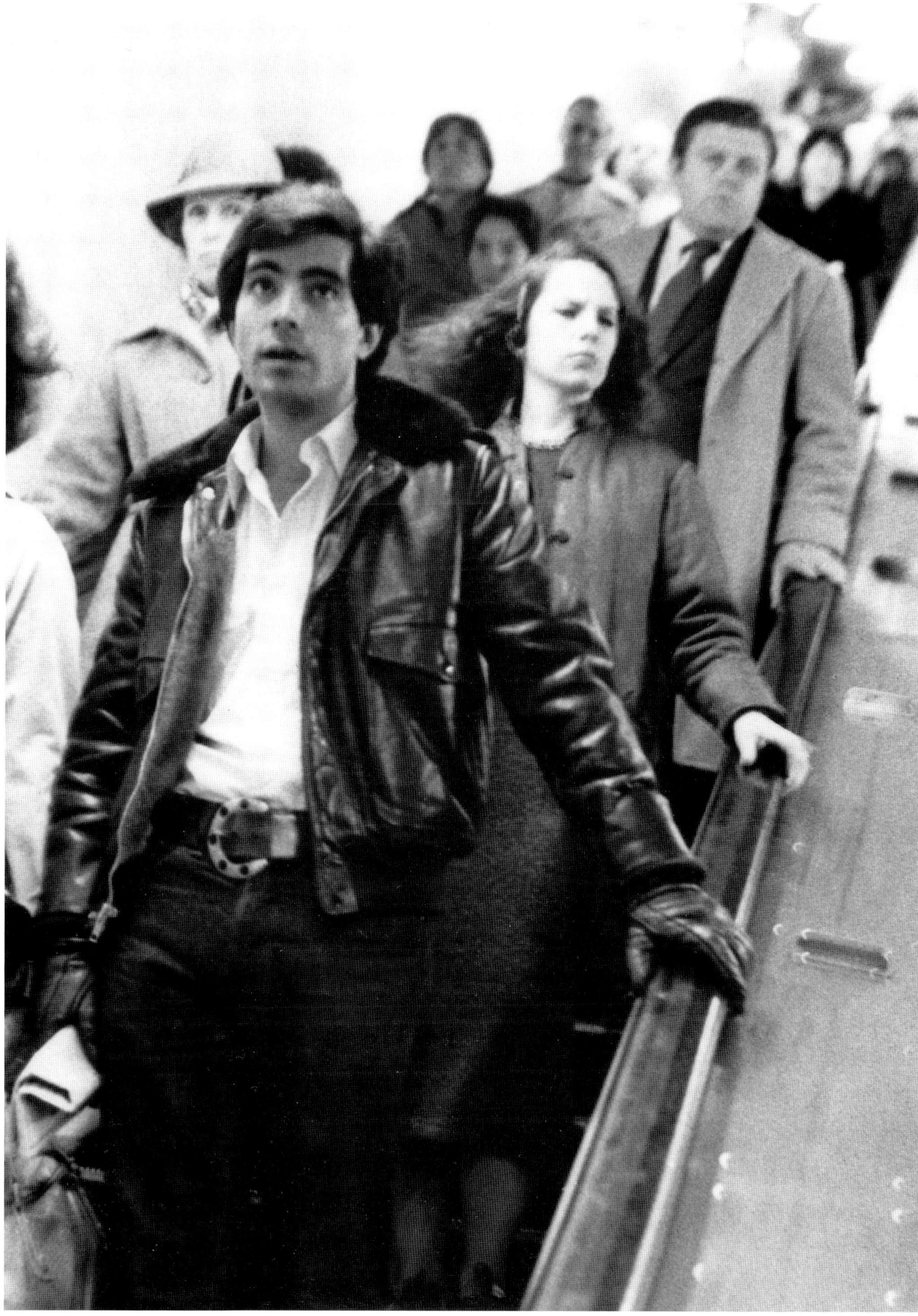

81
Subway I, 1985
Gelatin silver print
7 ¼ x 10 inches
Courtesy of the Alex Katz Foundation

82
Subway, c. 1985
Gelatin silver print
8 ½ x 11 inches
Courtesy the Estate of Rudy Burckhardt
and Tibor de Nagy Gallery, New York

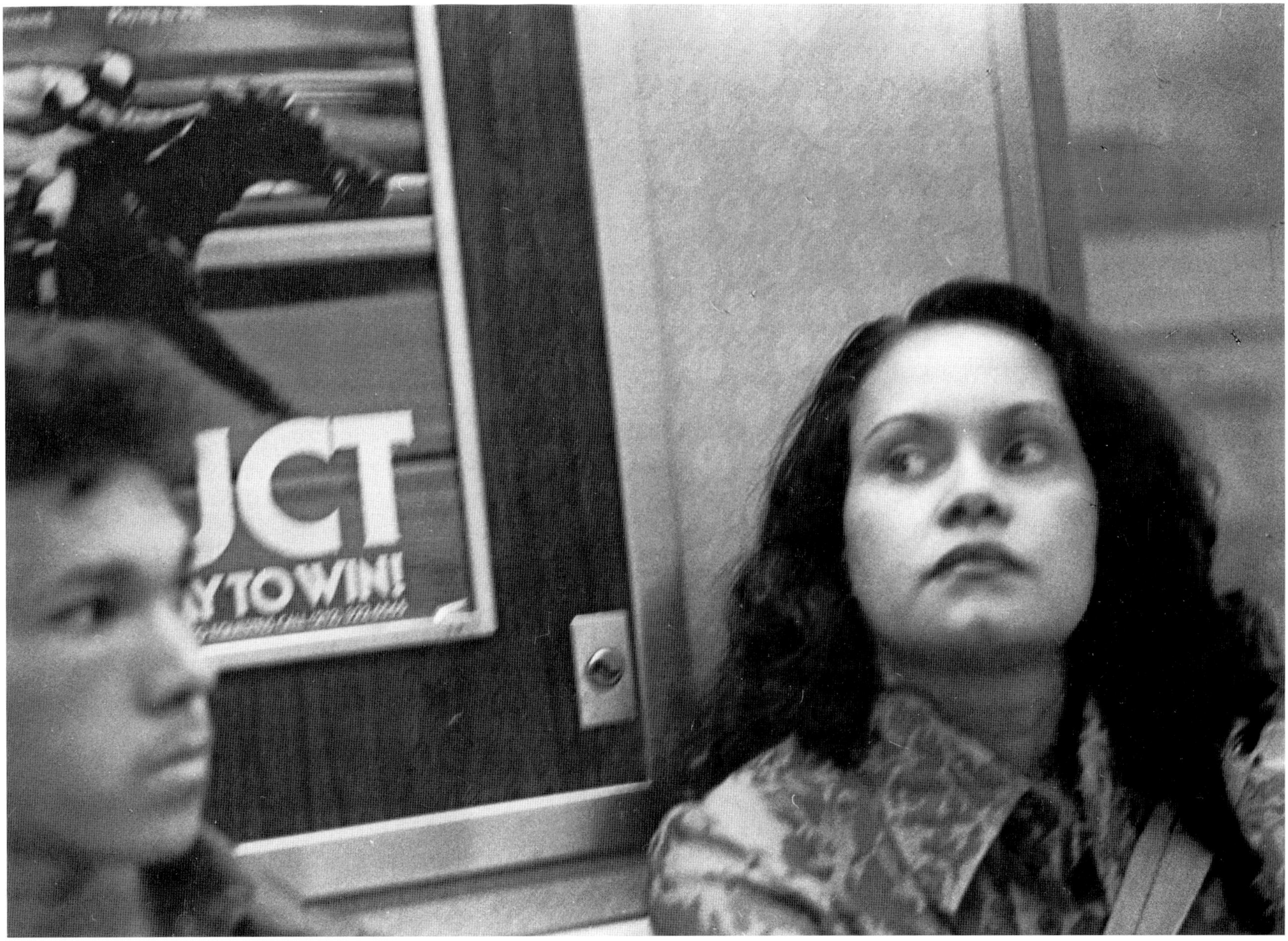

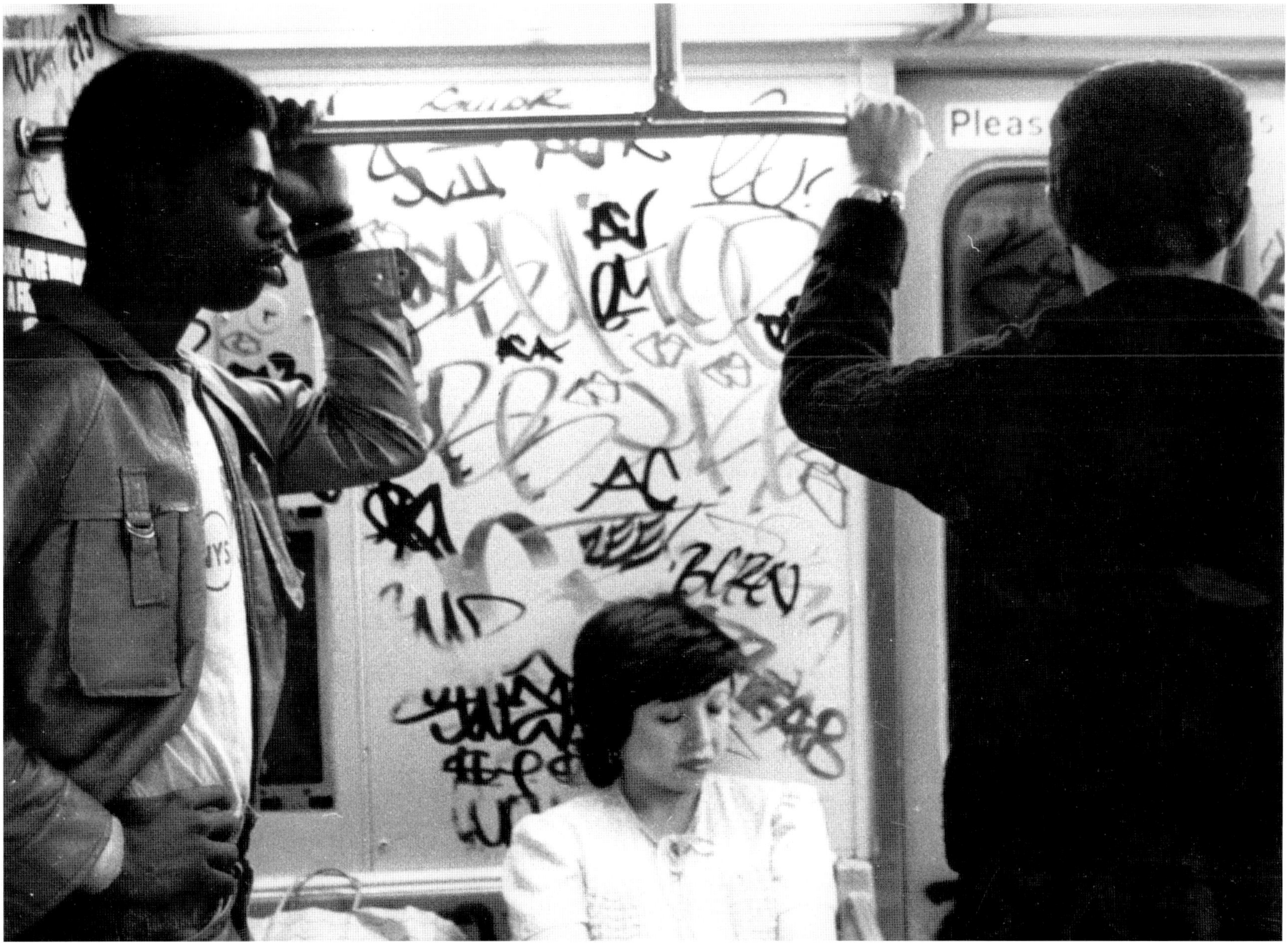
Pleas

83
Pants Shadow, 1976
Gelatin silver print
7 ¼ x 5 ¾ inches
Courtesy the Estate of Rudy Burckhardt
and Tibor de Nagy Gallery, New York

84
Untitled, c. 1970
Gelatin silver print
13 ½ x 9 ¼ inches
Courtesy the Estate of Rudy Burckhardt
and Tibor de Nagy Gallery, New York

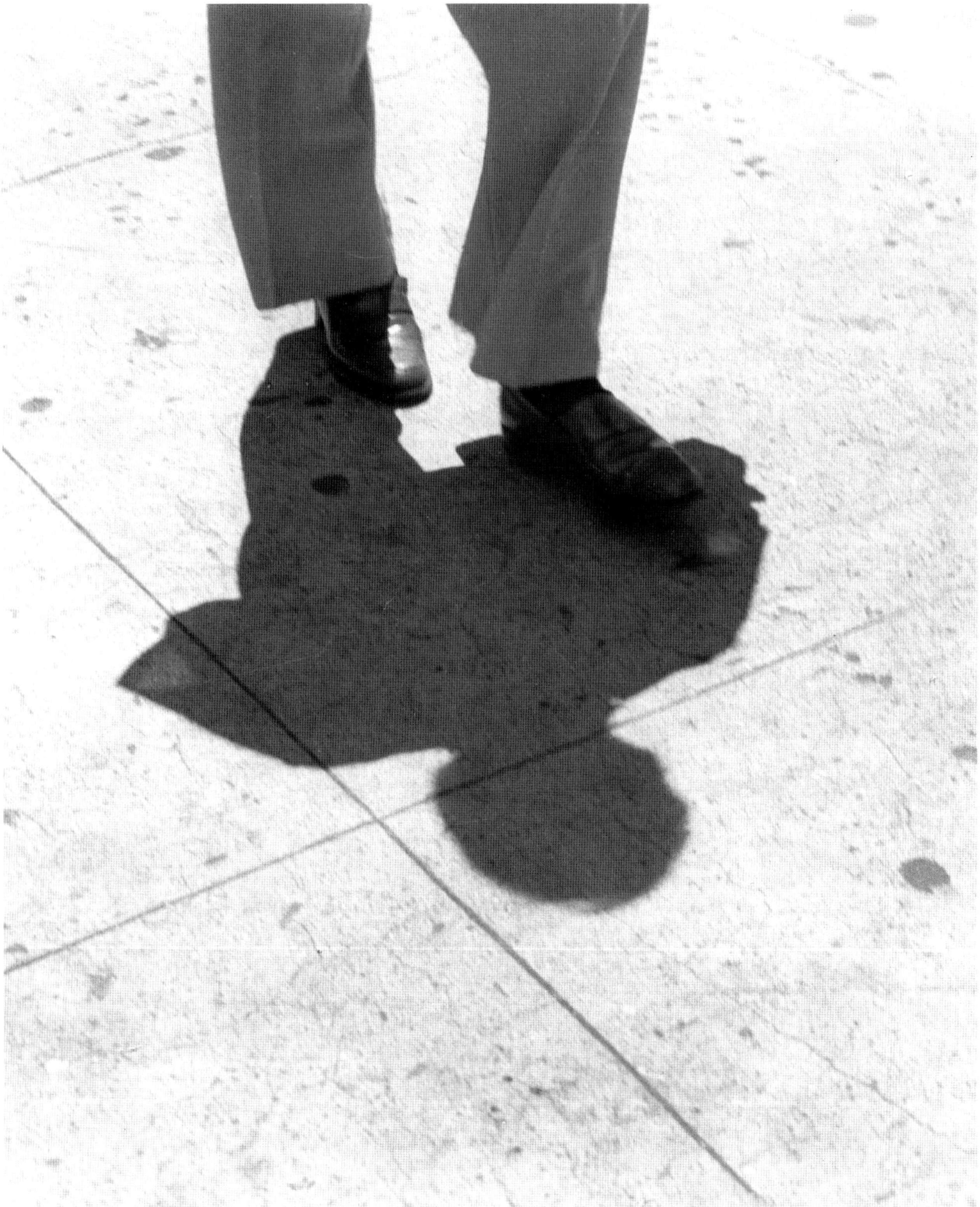

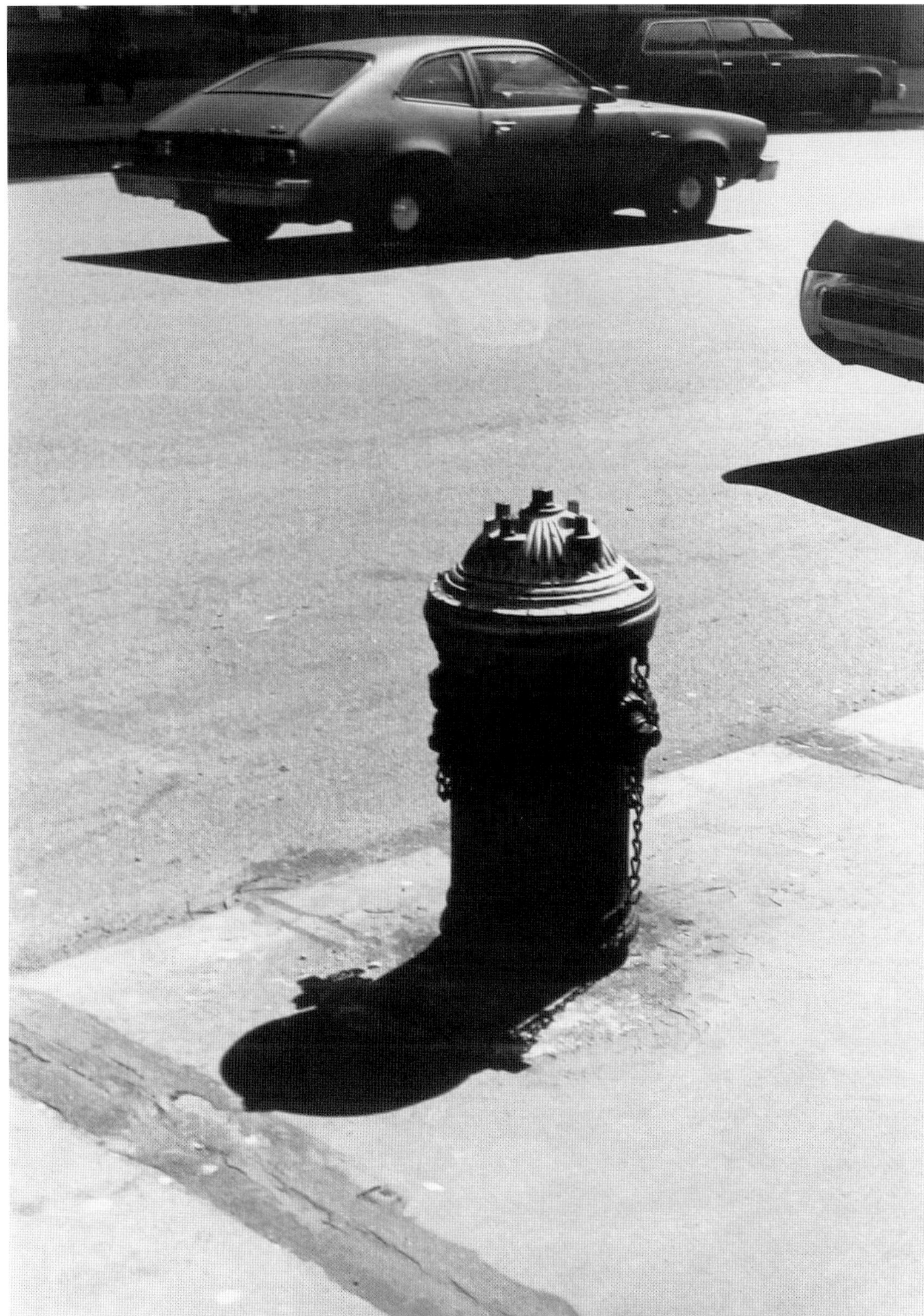

85
Lamp Shadow, 1968
Gelatin silver print
7 ⅝ x 10 inches
Courtesy of the
Alex Katz Foundation

86
Curb, c. 1974
Gelatin silver print
13 ½ x 16 ½ inches
Courtesy the Estate of Rudy
Burckhardt and Tibor de Nagy
Gallery, New York

FOLLOWING PAGES
87
Action, c. 1968
Gelatin silver print
10 x 7 ¾ inches
Courtesy the Estate of Rudy
Burckhardt and Tibor de Nagy
Gallery, New York

88
Sidewalk Manhole, 1995
Gelatin silver print
9 ⅝ x 7 inches
Courtesy of the
Alex Katz Foundation

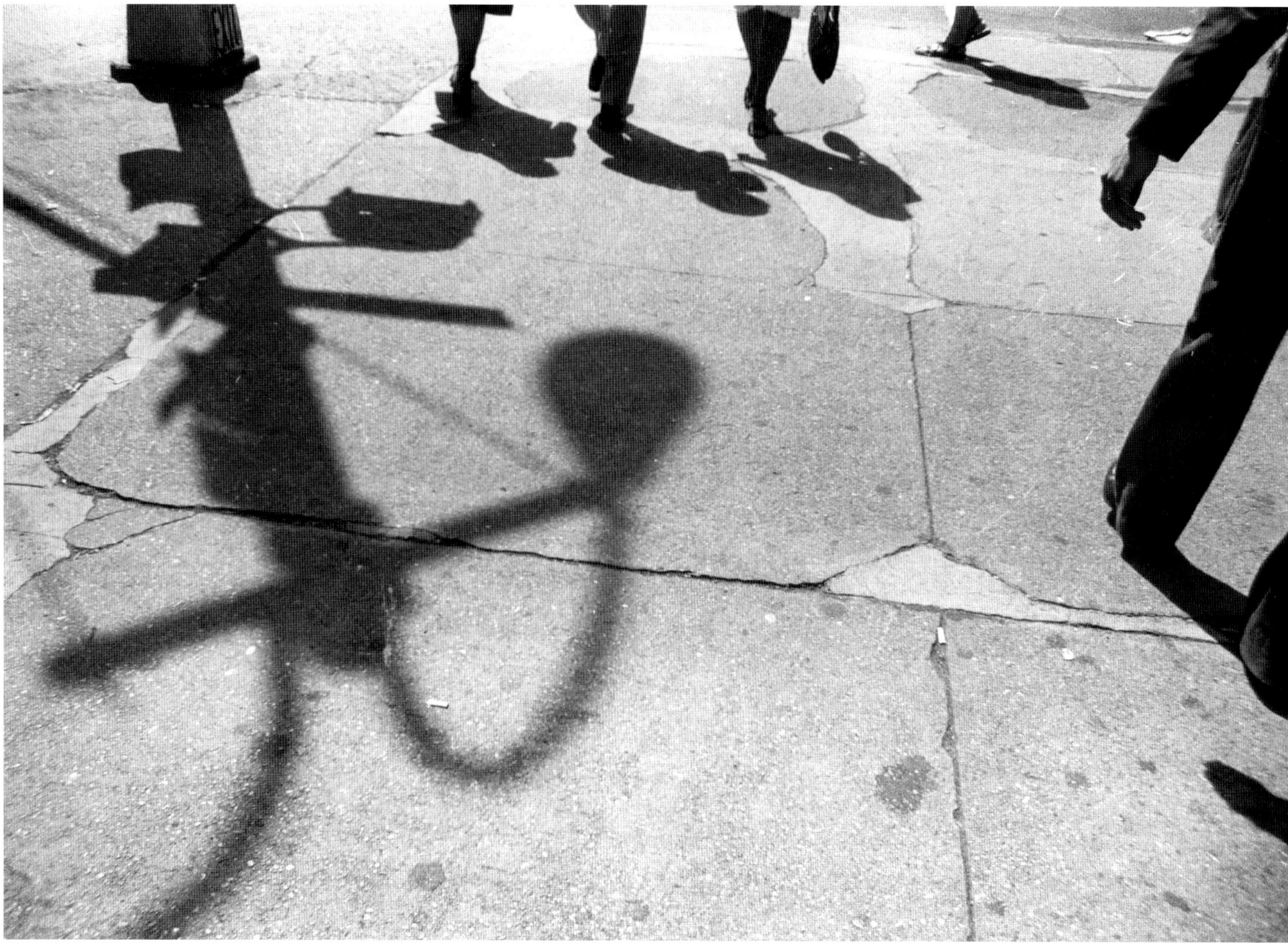

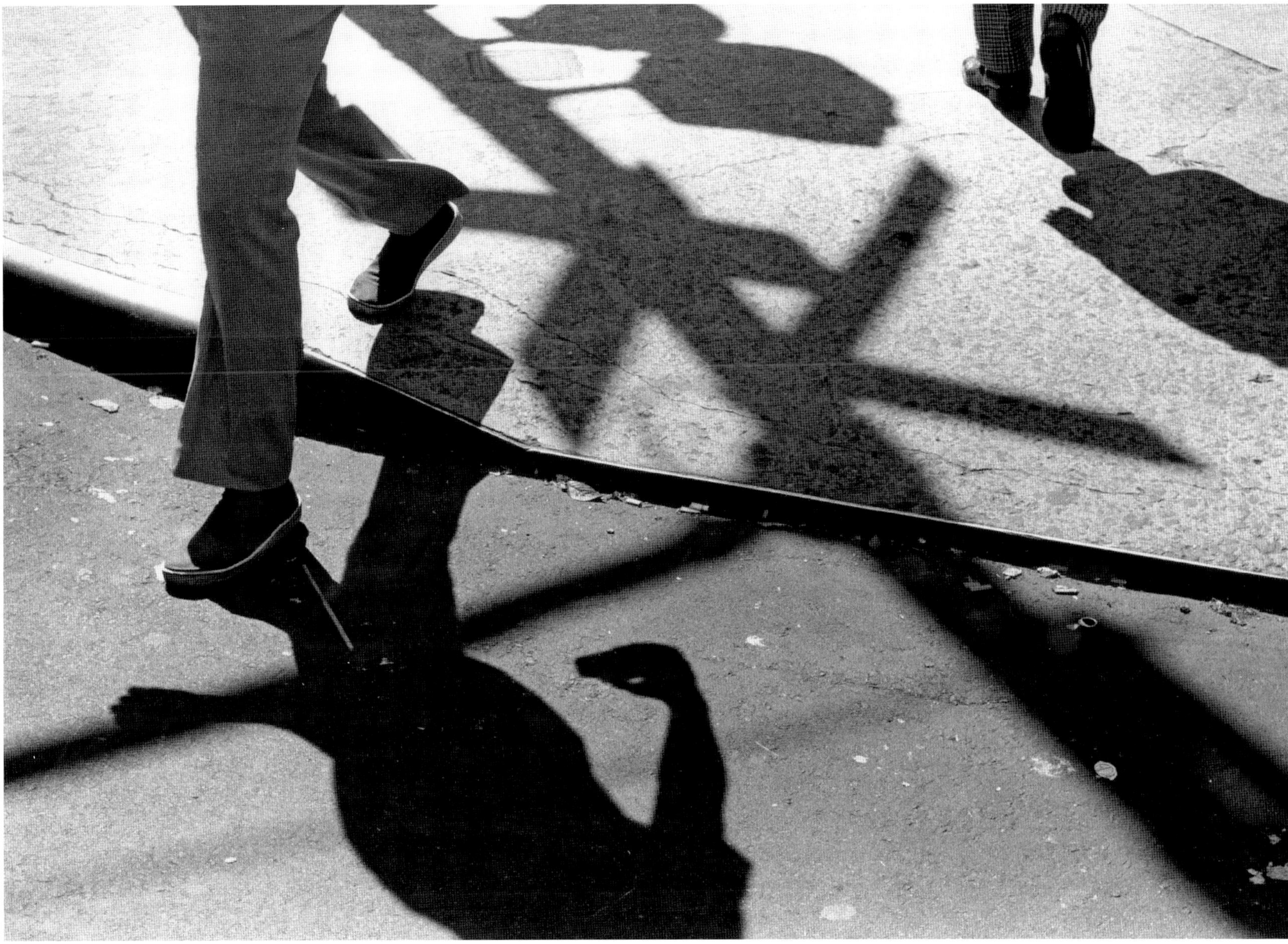

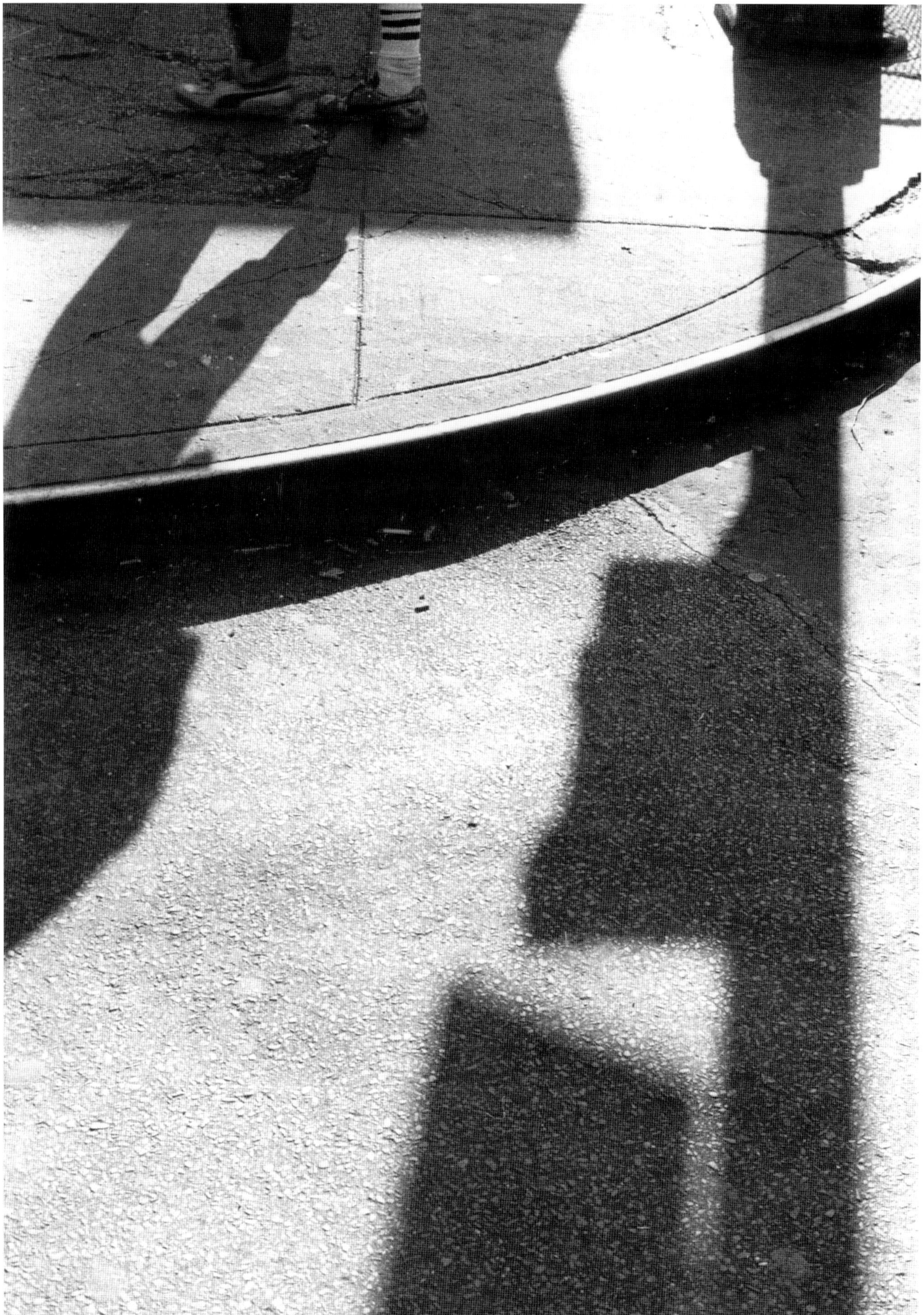

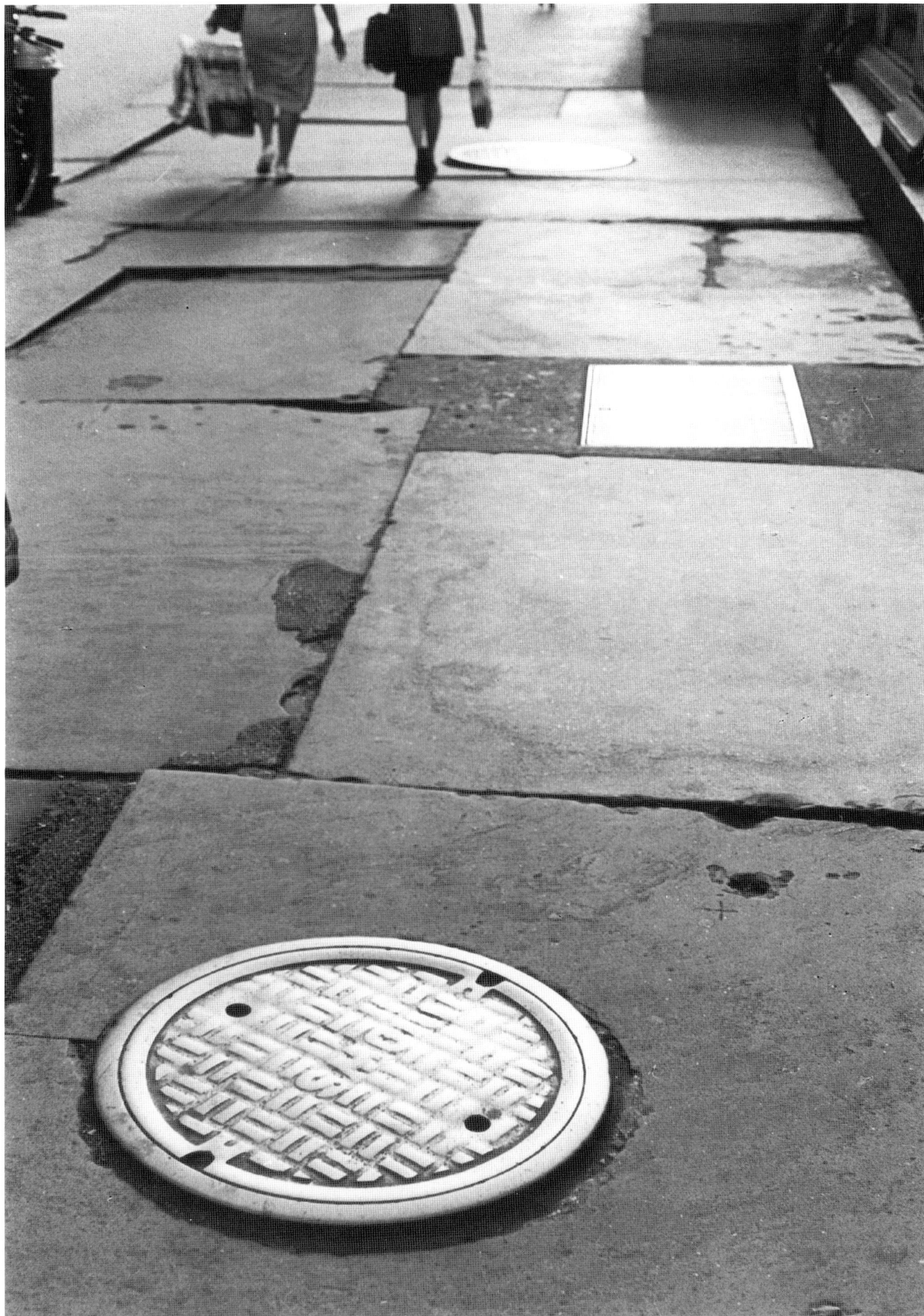

CHRONOLOGIES

YVONNE JACQUETTE

1934
Born in Pittsburgh, Pennsylvania.

1947–1952
Studies privately with Robert Roché in Connecticut, where family has moved.

1952
Enrolls at Rhode Island School of Design, completing three years.

1955
Moves to loft on West 25th Street in New York, skipping her final year at RISD. Works at various commercial art and textile design jobs.

1958–1959
Lives on West 67th Street and later in Brooklyn Heights.

1961
Meets Rudy Burckhardt at party and subsequently lives with him at 40 West 29th Street, then on West 14th Street.

1962
Included in her first group exhibition at the Kornblee Gallery, New York. From this date forward, Jacquette's work has been included in countless group exhibitions in museums and galleries, in solo gallery shows at Fischbach, Brooke Alexander, and DC Moore galleries in New York, and in solo museum exhibitions around the country.

1964
Marries Rudy Burckhardt; son Thomas is born.

1971
Makes first drawings from airplanes.

1975
Moves with Burckhardt to 50 West 29th Street loft, which she still occupies.

1976
Makes first night view of New York City in pastel. Receives Ingram Merrill Foundation Award for Painting.

1978–1980
Teaches at University of Pennsylvania, Graduate Division.

RUDY BURCKHARDT

1914
Born in Basel, Switzerland.

1934
Meets American dance critic and poet Edwin Denby in Basel.

1935
Moves to New York City to live with Denby.

1938
Begins to photograph New York City.

1947
Marries the painter and writer Edith Schloss.

1948–1949
Studies with Amédée Ozenfant.
First exhibition of photographs, at Photoleague Gallery, New York.

1949
Birth of son Jacob.

1950–1951
Studies painting in Naples and Rome.

1950–1964
Photographs artists for *ARTnews* magazine.

c. 1953
Exhibition of photographs, Limelight Gallery, New York.

1964
Marries painter Yvonne Jacquette; birth of son Thomas.

1972
Exhibition of photographs, Gotham Bookmart, New York.

1975
Exhibition of photographs, Brooke Alexander Gallery, New York.

1978
Exhibition of photographs, Brooke Alexander Gallery, New York.

1983
Exhibition of photographs, Marlborough Gallery, New York.

YVONNE JACQUETTE

1979
Exhibits first New York night paintings at Brooke Alexander Gallery, New York.

1981–1984
Teaches at Parsons.

1982
At Skowhegan with Rudy Burckhardt. Interest in Buddhism begins.

1985–1990
Teaches at University of Pennsylvania, Graduate Division.

1988
Elected an Associate of the National Academy.

1990
Receives American Academy of Arts & Letters' Painter's Award.

1991
Collaborates with Rudy Burckhardt on film *Night Fantasies.*

1991–2001
Teaches at Pennsylvania Academy of Fine Arts, Graduate Division.

1994
Elected an Academician of the National Academy. Resident artist at Skowhegan.

1997–1998
Awarded residency at World Trade Center through Lower Manhattan Cultural Council's World Views program. Awarded Guggenheim Foundation Grant for Painting.

1998
Awarded Andrew Carnegie Prize for Painting, National Academy Museum.

1999
Rudy Burckhardt dies.

2002–2003
Solo exhibition, *Aerial Muse: The Art of Yvonne Jacquette,* organized by Stanford University, traveling to Colby College, Utah Museum of Fine Arts, and the Hudson River Museum.

2003
Inducted into the American Academy of Arts & Letters.

RUDY BURCKHARDT

1987
Retrospective of films, Museum of Modern Art, New York.
Exhibition of photographs, Brooke Alexander Gallery, New York.

1991
Receives Brendan Gill Award from the Municipal Arts Society, New York.

1995
Exhibition of photographs, Tibor de Nagy Gallery, New York.

1996
Exhibition of photographs, Swiss Consulate, New York.

1998
Retrospective exhibition of photographs, paintings, and films at Institute of Modern Art, Valencia, Spain.

1999
Dies in Searsmont, Maine.

CONTRIBUTORS' BIOGRAPHIES

BILL BERKSON

Poet and art critic Bill Berkson was born in New York in 1939 and became active in the literary and art worlds more than a half century ago. He is the author of several books of poetry, including *Saturday Night: Poems 1960–61, Shining Leaves, Recent Visitors, Enigma Variations* (with drawings by Philip Guston), *Blue Is the Hero, Lush Life, Serenade, Fugue State, Gloria* (with etchings by Alex Katz), *Hymns of St. Bridget* (with Frank O'Hara), and *Our Friends Will Pass Among You Silently.* Other recent publications include a selection of his criticism, *The Sweet Singer of Modernism & Other Art Writings, What's Your Idea of a Good Time: Letters & Interviews 1977–1985* (with Bernadette Mayer), and *Sudden Address: Selected Lectures 1981–2006.* His work has been included in many literary journals and anthologies. He is also a Corresponding Editor for *Art in America* and has been a regular contributor to *Artforum, Modern Painters, Art on Paper, American Craft* and other magazines. From 1971–78, he was editor-publisher of Big Sky magazine and books. He has received awards and grants for poetry from the Poets Foundation, the Fund of Poetry, the National Endowment for the Arts, Yaddo, the Briarcombe Foundation, and Marin Arts Council, and in 1990 was given an Artspace Award for Art Criticism. He has also curated exhibitions of individual artists such as George Herriman and Ronald Bladen and of contemporary painting, and served as an adjunct curator for *Facing Eden: 100 Years of California Landscape Art* at the Fine Arts Museums of San Francisco. He has taught at the San Francisco Art Institute since 1984. He was Distinguished Paul Mellon Fellow at Skowhegan School of Painting and Sculpture for 2006.

ANDREA HENDERSON FAHNESTOCK

Andrea Henderson Fahnestock is Curator of Paintings and Sculpture at the Museum of the City of New York. Since 2001 she has curated seven exhibitions, cocurated three with the Prints and Photographs department, and organized ten installations, ranging from 18th- and 19th-century portraits to 20th-century cityscape paintings, from the Museum's permanent collection. Exhibitions include *Hirschfeld's New York* (2001); *"Highlights of Manhattan:" The Drawings of E. H. Suydam* (2002); *The Paintings and Watercolors of Louis Comfort Tiffany* (2004); *Still New York: Watercolors by Frederick Brosen* (2005); and *New York Creative: Portraits by Everett Raymond Kinstler* (2006). Recent publications include *The Day Our World Changed: Children's Art of 9/11* (coeditor, Abrams, 2002), *Five Decades of New York Streets: The Paintings of William Clutz* (2003), and *Picturing New York: The Paintings of Peter Ruta* (MCNY, 2004). Before joining the Museum of the City of New York, she cocurated an exhibition on the 19th-century landscape and marine painter William Stanley Haseltine for the Fine Arts Museums of San Francisco and coauthored the accompanying catalogue, *Expressions of Place: The Art of William Stanley Haseltine* (Hudson Hills Press, 1992), the only monographic study of the artist. She has contributed articles on Haseltine to several publications, including the *American Art Review* and *Life Lines: American Master Drawings from the Munson-Williams-Proctor Institute.* Previously, she was an editor at *Artforum,* contributed to the National Gallery of Art's catalogue of *American Naïve Paintings* (Cambridge University Press, 1993), and worked for the Commission for Art Recovery, a foundation dedicated to the discovery and restitution of art looted during WWII.

VINCENT KATZ

Vincent Katz is an art critic, editor, and curator. He curated an exhibition on Black Mountain College for the Reina Sofia museum in Madrid, whose catalog, *Black Mountain College: Experiment in Art,* was published by MIT Press in 2002. He curated the first museum retrospective of the photographs, films, and paintings of Rudy Burckhardt in 1998 at the Institute of Modern Art in Valencia, Spain. In 2000, he cocurated with Lynn Gumpert *Rudy Burckhardt and Friends: New York Artists of the 1950s and 60s* for the Grey Art Gallery at New York University, which paired Burckhardt's photographic portraits of artists with works by those artists. Katz writes frequently on contemporary art and has published essays or articles on the work of Francesco Clemente, Jim Dine, Robert Rauschenberg, Kiki Smith, Philip Taaffe, and Cy Twombly. Vincent Katz and Vivien Bittencourt's documentary, *Kiki Smith: Squatting The Palace,* played for two weeks at Film Forum in New York in January, 2007, and was screened at the 25th Montreal International Festival of Films on Art, 2007, as well as at film festivals in Milan, Naples, and Florence. Their documentary, *Man in the Woods: The Art of Rudy Burckhardt,* featuring interviews with Burckhardt, Yvonne Jacquette, Robert Storr, and Brian Wallis, was screened at the 22nd Montreal International Festival of Films on Art, 2004, and was awarded the "Best of Festival" prize in the Arts category at the Berkeley Film and Video Festival, 2004. Katz is the author of nine books of poetry, including *New York Hello!* (1990, with photographs by Rudy Burckhardt) and *Boulevard Transportation* (1997, with photographs by Rudy Burckhardt). Katz won the 2005 National Translation Award, given by the American Literary Translators Association, for his book of translations from Latin, *The Complete Elegies of Sextus Propertius* (Princeton University Press, 2004). He was awarded a Rome Prize Fellowship in Literature at the American Academy in Rome for 2001–2002 and was a Guest of the Director at the American Academy in Berlin in spring, 2006.

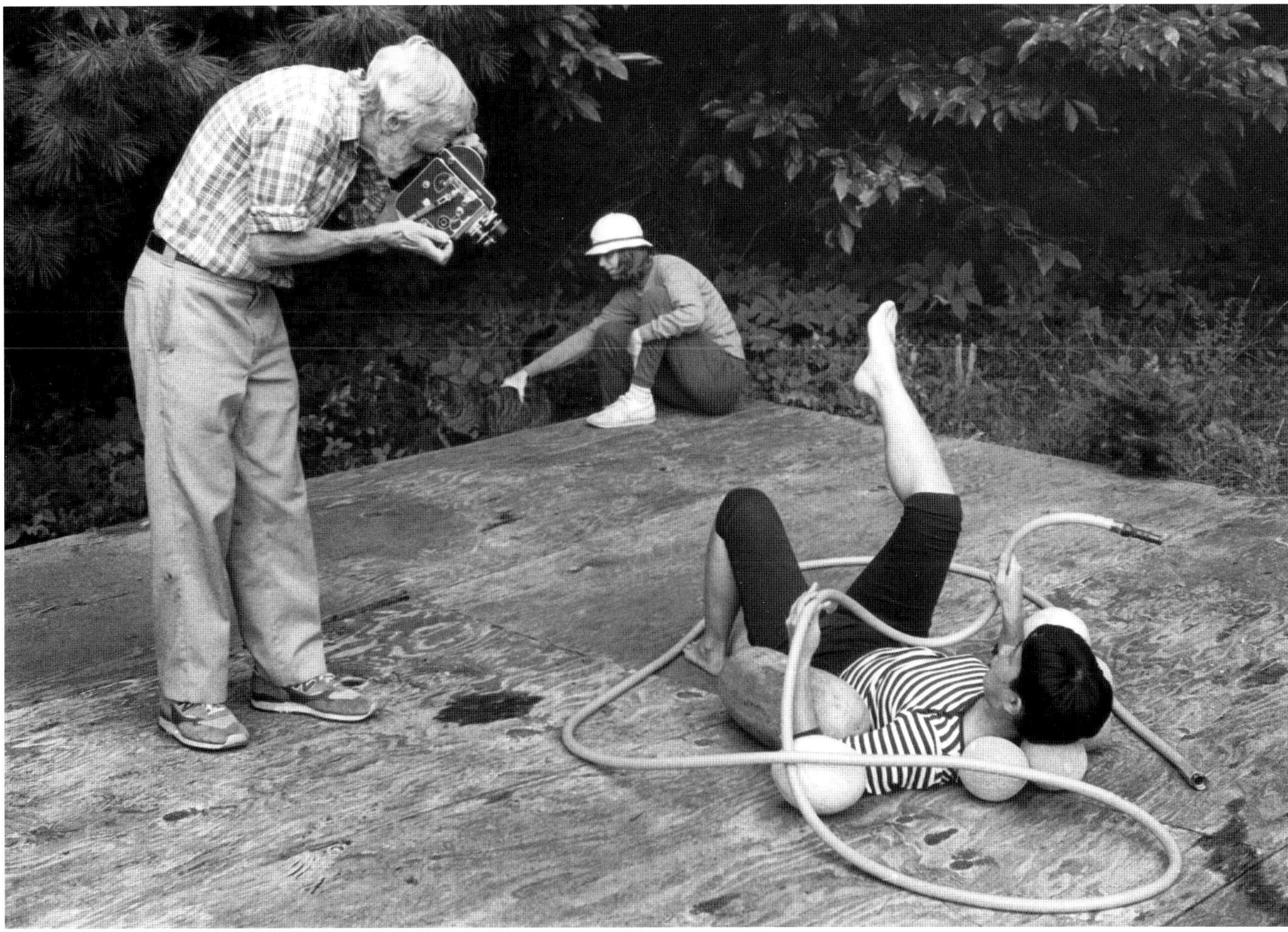

Rudy Burckhardt filming the dancer Yoshiko Chuma, with Yvonne Jacquette (and cat) in the background, Searsmont, Maine, c. 1985
Photograph by Jacob Burckhardt

CREDITS

PHOTOGRAPHY CREDITS ARE GIVEN IN THE CAPTIONS BELOW ALL REPRODUCTIONS, WITH THE EXCEPTION OF THE FOLLOWING:

Kevin Ryan, New York, courtesy DC Moore Gallery
Plates 4, 14, 17–23, 25, 27–32.

Ali Elai, Camerarts, New York
Plates 11, 16, 24, 26, 33, and figure 20 on page 86.

Chan Chao, Takoma Park, Maryland
Plate 8.

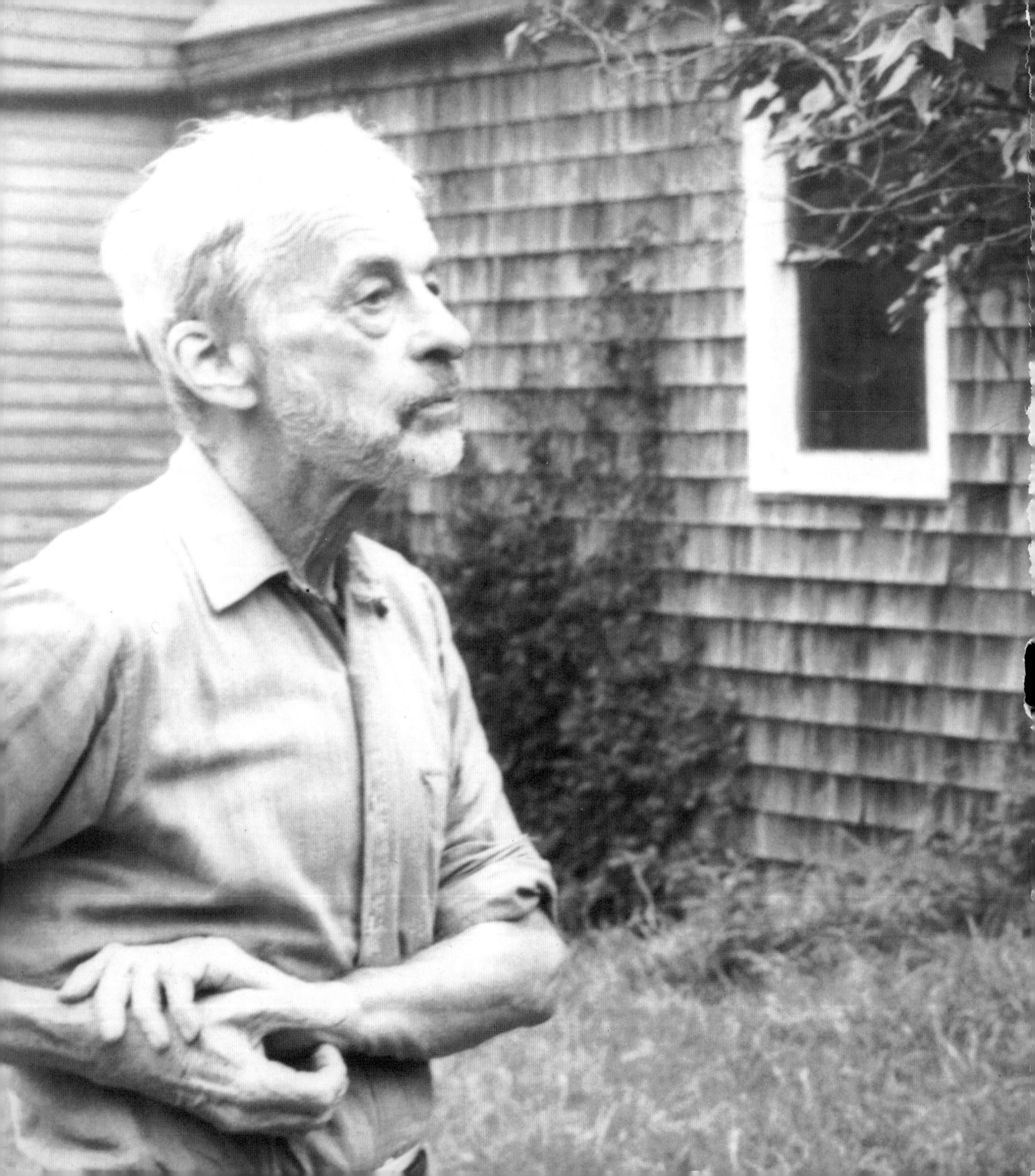